ETHNIC CONFLICTS AND CIVIL SOCIETY

Ethnic Conflicts and Civil Society

Proposals for a New Era in Eastern Europe

Edited by
ANDREAS KLINKE
ORTWIN RENN
JEAN-PAUL LEHNERS

Ashgate

Aldershot • Brookfield USA • Singapore • Sydney

© Andreas Klinke, Ortwin Renn and Jean-Paul Lehners 1997

All rights reserved. No part of this publication may be reproduced, stored in a retrieval system, or transmitted in any form or by any means, electronic, mechanical, photocopying, recording or otherwise without the prior permission of the publisher.

Published by
Ashgate Publishing Ltd
Gower House
Croft Road
Aldershot
Hants GU11 3HR
England

Ashgate Publishing Company
Old Post Road
Brookfield
Vermont 05036
USA

British Library Cataloguing in Publication Data
Ethnic conflicts and civil society : proposals for a new
  era in Eastern Europe
    1. Europe, Eastern - Ethnic relations 2. Europe, Eastern -
    Politics and government - 1989- 3. Europe, Eastern - Social
    conditions - 1989- 4. Former Soviet republics - Ethnic
    relations 5. Former Soviet republics - Politics and
    government 6. Former Soviet republics - Social conditions
    I. Klinke, Andreas II. Renn, Ortwin III. Lehners, Jean-Paul
    957'.0854

Library of Congress Cataloging-in-Publication Data
Ethnic conflicts and civil society : proposals for a new era in
  Eastern Europe / edited by Andreas Klinke, Ortwin Renn, Jean-Paul
  Lehners.
    p. cm.
  ISBN 1-84014-455-6 (hard). -- ISBN 1-84014-462-9 (pbk.)
  1. Europe, Eastern--Ethnic relations. 2. Former Yugoslav
republics--Ethnic relations. 3. Europe, Eastern--Politics and
government--1989- 4. Ethnic relations. 5. Conflict management.
I. Klinke, Andreas. II. Renn, Ortwin. III. Lehners, Jean-Paul.
DJK51.E893   1997
305.8'00947--dc21
                                                    98-6524
                                                       CIP

ISBN 1 84014 455 6 (HBK)
ISBN 1 84014 462 9 (PBK)

Printed and bound by Athenaeum Press, Ltd.,
Gateshead, Tyne & Wear.

Contents

List of Editors and Contributors   VII
Abbreviations   IX
Preface   XI

I INTRODUCTION

1 Ethnic Conflicts and Cooperation Among and Within States   3
   Andreas Klinke, Ortwin Renn and Jean-Paul Lehners

II THEORETICAL APPROACHES

2 Conflicts Between Different Nationalities:
   Chances for and Limits to Their Settlement   35
   Ursel Schlichting

3 Reducing Ethnic Conflicts: Contemporary
   Approaches to Conflict Resolution in Western Europe   53
   Albert F. Reiterer

III CASE STUDIES: DOMESTIC EXPERIENCES OF ETHNIC CONFLICTS

4 Temptations of Transition and Identity Crisis in Post-
   Communist Countries: The Example of Former Yugoslavia   83
   Nadia Skenderovic Cuk

5 Autonomy as One of the Means of
   Minorities' Protection: The Case of Slovenia   99
   Silvo Devetak

VI   Ethnic Conflicts and Civil Society

6   Ethnic Conflicts in Croatia?   115
     Drago Roksandic

7   Ethnic Politics in Ukraine   127
     Zenovia A. Sochor

8   The Relationship Between the Majority and the Minority
     in a Composed Region: The Case of Vojvodina   151
     Mirijana Morokvasic

9   The Media: Social Constructions in
     Inter-Ethnic Communication in Romania   177
     Carmen Dumitriu-Seuleanu

IV   **CASE STUDIES:**
     DEMOCRATIC EXPERIENCES OF
     SUCCESSFUL CONFLICT MANAGEMENT

10   Ethnic Coexistence and Cooperation in Switzerland   203
     Kurt R. Spillmann

11   Conflict and Integration: The Main Principles of
     Social Cohesion in the United States   221
     Ortwin Renn

V   **SYNOPSIS**

12   Ethnic Cooperation and Coexistence:
     International Mediation, International Governance,
     and Civil Society for Ethnically Plural States   251
     Andreas Klinke and Ortwin Renn

List of Editors and Contributors

Editors

Andreas Klinke
M.A., Political Scientist and Sociologist at the Center of Technology Assessment in Baden-Wuerttemberg, Stuttgart (Germany). Associate Researcher at the "German Scientific Advisory Council on Global Change".

Ortwin Renn
Dr., Professor of Environmental Sociology at the University of Stuttgart. Member of the board of directors at the Center of Technology Assessment in Baden-Wuerttemberg, Stuttgart (Germany). Member of the "German Scientific Advisory Council on Global Change".

Jean-Paul Lehners
Dr., Professor of History at the "Centre Universitaire de Luxembourg". He is working on the subjects: historical demography and the history of the family, interdisciplinary studies, and world-systems analysis.

Contributors

Silvo Devetak
Dr., Professor of International Law at the University of Maribor (Slovenia).

Carmen Dumitriu-Seuleanu
Director of the European Center for Studies on Ethnic Issues and Social Communication (ECSEISC) in Bucharest (Romania).

Mirijana Morokvasic
Dr., Senior Researcher at the "Centre National de la Recherche Scientifique" in Nanterre (France).

Albert F. Reiterer
Dr., Lecturer at the University of Vienna (Austria), department of Sociology and Ethnic Studies and freelance social scientist.

Drago Roksandic
Dr., Lecturer at the University of Zagreb (Croatia), department of History.

Ursel Schlichting
M.A., Senior Researcher at the University of Hamburg (Germany), department for Peace Research and Security Politics (IFSH).

Nadia Skenderovic Cuk
Dr., Senior Researcher at the Open University in Subotica (Serbia), European Civic Center for Conflict Resolution.

Zenovia A. Sochor
Dr., Associate Professor at the Clark University in Worcester (USA), department of Government.

Kurt R. Spillmann
Prof. Dr., Director of the Center for Security Studies and Conflict Research at the Swiss Federal Institute.

Abbreviations

ASA	American Sociological Society
CIS	Commonwealth of Independent States
CSCE	Conference on Security and Cooperation in Europe
DVZM	Hungarian Democratic Union of Vojvodina
EC	European Community
FR	Federal Republic
FRY	Federal Republic Yugoslavia
KGB	Komitet Gossudarstwennoi Besopasnosti
NATO	North Atlantic Treaty Organization
NGO	Non Governmental Organization
OAU	Organization of African Unity
OSCE	Organization for Security and Cooperation in Europe
PLO	Palestine Liberation Organization
RSFSR	Russian State of the Former Soviet Republic
SFR	Socialist Federal Republic
SPS	Serbian Socialist Party
SRS	Radical Serbian Party
SSR	Socialist Soviet Republic
UN	United Nations
UNESCO	United Nations Educational, Scientific and Cultural Organization
UNO	United Nations Organization
USSR	Union of Soviet Socialist Republics

Preface

Towards a Civil Society. Prerequisites of Peaceful Cooperation

During the time of heavy fighting in the former republics of Yugoslavia, the City of Luxembourg became a lively place of discussion, debate, and discourse among representatives of those groups whose leaders were obsessed with the idea of ethnic "cleansing" and violent struggles over land and political power. Over a two-day period twelve analysts and observers from troubled Eastern and Central European Countries as well as from Western Europe and the United States came together to address one of the most pressing issues in contemporary politics: How can ethnic and political cooperation be accomplished in ethnically and politically heterogeneous countries after the collapse of the communist regimes which left a dangerous void for nationalist and even chauvinist movements? In other words, what are the personal and institutional prerequisites for achieving a civil society capable of resolving conflicts in a peaceful and constructive manner? All the invited scholars from academia, the arts, international research institutes, and various international agencies agreed on one fundamental principle: For policies to be effective and legitimate, we need to empower people on the local and regional level to build traditions and institutional means for resolving conflicts and coping with ethnic, social, and political tensions. There is no technocratic solution nor a centralized top-down approach that would be able to provide long-lasting and stable conditions for peaceful cooperation. For a period of transition, however, international control and centralized efforts to keep order were seen as an inevitable, but in the long term insufficient, step in the difficult process of building a nation based on mutual respect and civil rights.

The workshop was organized by three institutions: Clark University, represented by Prof. Walter Schatzberg; the Centre Universitaire in Luxembourg, represented by Prof. Jean-Paul Lehners; and the Center of Technology Assessment in Stuttgart Germany, represented by Prof. Ortwin Renn and Andreas Klinke. Ortwin Renn and Jean-Paul

Lehners structured and moderated all sessions and discussions. The deliberations were organized in the form of a round table seating the twelve participants and the two moderators. The last panel discussion was open to the public. Among others, diplomats from various embassies and officials from the Ministry of Foreign Affairs in Luxembourg attended this last session. The major objectives of the workshop were:

- to promote a better understanding of the contemporary "ethnic" conflicts and their social, cultural, and political causes;
- to determine the historical, structural, and political developments that have led to or intensified these conflicts;
- to analyze and develop "positive role models" for coping with such conflicts;
- to provide constructive proposals for future conflict resolution mechanisms; and
- to identify the crucial elements for building trust-generating institutions on the basis of the civil society model.

The conference was limited to addressing issues of ethnic conflicts in Eastern and Central Europe with a special focus on the former republics of Yugoslavia. In addition, the participants had agreed to design their contributions in line with basic ideas of the Civil Society, as expressed, for example, in the famous works of A. Etzioni. Furthermore, from the many positive role models available, only two were considered: Switzerland and the United States. These two countries also face ethnic problems and often intense conflicts but, in spite of a few exceptions, have developed institutional means to cope with these conflicts in a predominantly peaceful manner.

Most of the recent literature on ethnic conflicts, particularly with respect to Central and Eastern Europe, has focused either on historical accounts of hate-relationships between different ethnic groups and their cover-up during the communist era or on studies of political regimes that are incapable or ineffective in dealing with ethnic conflicts. The main idea of the conference was to go beyond the analysis of causes and manifestations of such conflicts and offer constructive ideas for the Post-Civil-War period after the violence. None of the participants shared the illusion that a small conference in Luxembourg could change the world or could trigger repercussions onto the political power elite in the respective countries. However, all expressed hope that in due course such constructive ideas would be needed in some future time when people were tired of hate and violence and the political elite would be in a position to invite or even welcome joint institution building. "Something needs to be in place", one of the contributors told the audience, "when insanity collapses and people look for models of cooperation".

As much as the conference was inspired by the joint desire to articulate constructive suggestions to overcome ethnic violence and conflict, there was also the experience of grief, pain, and mourning; in particular among those who represented the different ethnic fractions in Bosnia and beyond. Some of the participants had lost all their belongings during the Civil War, were expelled from their homes and had been exposed to hostility and violence themselves. A few had even lost some of their relatives through actions of violence. There was always the Damocles Sword of emotional turbulence hanging over the deliberations of the representatives when they faced each other at the round table in Luxembourg. It never fell, however. Over the three-day period opportunities for mutual accusations and "verbal revenge" were usually not seized. The participants made all efforts to avoid offensive language and personal attacks. They did not hesitate, however, to name alleged or real culprits during the debate. There was a common consensus among all directly affected participants that the people of each ethnic groups had been exploited by power-hungry political leaders who had perfected their populist skills to play with the emotions of a confused and disappointed public. This line of argument was not unanimously shared by outside observers from the United States and Western Europe, but it helped the participants to acknowledge each other as victims of the violence rather than as villains. Furthermore, it forged a tie of common fate around them which fueled interest in each other. In addition to the intensive official sessions during the day, these participants used almost all night to continue their discussion and get involved in each other's life story. The result has been the creation of some unusual personal friendships.

The workshop was divided in three major sections. Section 1 dealt with the analysis of reasons and causes for ethnic conflicts. Section 2 included reports from troubled countries, partly from the perspectives of the victims, partly from the view of outside observers. Part 3 consisted of two potential role models for ethnic cooperation: the Cantonal system of Switzerland and the "melting pot" model of the United States. In a last panel discussion, all participants summed up their impressions and made suggestions for future efforts leading to a more civilized form of conflict resolution. There was an agreement at the end that troubled nations need new models of putting the ideals of civil society into practice. As a first step, this idea has to enter the mindsets of all people living in these troubled countries; a second or parallel step the idea needs to be the guiding principle for building new social institutions. Without institutional stability, so the common accord, peaceful cooperation will not survive in countries that lack traditions for the intrinsic values of civil societies.

After the workshop, the participants composed their papers based on the discussions and the commonly agreed directions. Since many of the workshop participants were dispersed all over the world, it was a major effort to collect papers and ask all authors to make the final revisions. Not all participants of the conference decided to deliver a full manuscript. The main theses, that were put forth during the workshop, however, are represented in this volume. In addition to the papers, the editors composed a scholarly introduction to the theme and wrote a synopsis at the end. This conclusion reflects the last panel discussion as well as the main lessons derived from the ideas and arguments expressed in each paper.

This book would have not been possible without the support and effort of many people. We are especially grateful to all the contributors who participated in this unique attempt to submit their own thoughts to a common framework of constructive proposals towards a civil society. We want to express our appreciation for the tremendous and tedious work done by the translator of one contribution written originally in French, Norbert Zudrell, and the language editor, Ed McNamara, who had the difficult task of revising all papers by non-native English speakers in accordance with the standards of proper English language style. We are also grateful to Mrs. Gmelin-Zudrell who helped organize the conference and took care of the needs and problems of all participants. The project was financed by the three organizing institutions, the Luxembourg Study Program of Clark University, the Centre Universitaire of Luxembourg, and the Center of Technology

Assessment in Stuttgart. We are very grateful for the generous financial support by these three sponsors. Without their support, we would have not been able to pursue the elaborate procedure culminating in this book. Last but not least we would like to thank Mrs. Zimmermann and Raphael Bayer for giving the manuscript the final look in form of layout and graphical appearance, and also Elke Schneider, Hans Kastenholz and Florian Lattewitz for reviewing our chapters.

Stuttgart and Luxembourg 1997

Ortwin Renn
Andreas Klinke
Jean-Paul Lehners

PART I

INTRODUCTION

1 Ethnic Conflicts and Cooperation Among and Within States

ANDREAS KLINKE, ORTWIN RENN
AND JEAN-PAUL LEHNERS

1 Problem Approach and Questions

After the Second World War the number of armed conflicts and wars in the world has continually increased and this tendency has aggravated since the end of the 1980s. Empirical research on violent conflicts and wars in the world reveal that internal wars in societies or civil wars within states had occured more frequently since the Second World War as compared to intergovernmental or international wars.[1] The internal wars are essentially concerned with the enforcement, the maintenance, or the coup of the prevailing political power and/or social revolutions, the struggle for fundamental reforms or restoration and/or separation or autonomy conflicts of ethnic or religious minorities (Gantzel/Siegelberg 1990: 236, footnote 23). Thus a distinction can be made between two basic types of internal strife: fights for independence against colonial powers and separation or autonomy wars.

Gantzel and Siegelberg (1990: 229) noted that armed conflicts did not take place any more within or between modern capitalistic societies after the Second World War. Multiple socio-economic interdependences have civilized, in the sense of pacification, the relations among the industrialized states in the Western World. For the second half of the twentieth century North America and Western Europe have been areas without internal armed conflicts and international wars among each other. This part of the world is characterized by a structure of at least "negative" peace[2] in an otherwise anarchic world. Conversely, the current situation in the non-western world is characterized by armed conflicts in a large number of societies in Eastern Europe, the former

Soviet Union and the so-called "Third World". The collapse of the communist system and the appearance of newly created countries have again created questions about ethnic conflict and cooperation in the process of nation-(re)building (comp., e.g., Wimmer 1995). Two notable examples are the Caucasian republics and former Yugoslavia, where wars broke out on account of ethnic-structured conflicts between quasi national majorities and ethnic minorities struggling for nation-state independence, contending claims to territories and borders or at least regional autonomy (comp., e.g., Wollefs 1994: 126). Although it is a matter of internal rather than interstate wars, ethnic armed conflicts often reach an international dimension. The case of former Yugoslavia accentuates the international political explosiveness of violent ethnic conflicts after the decline of central authorities and at the same time demonstrates the dissension and the helplessness of the international community. More than ever, the previous interventions of the international community as military and/or humanitarian peace keepers and/or enforcement seem to remain ineffective.[3] Successful prospects for settling the conflict merely seem to be diplomatic endeavors with the possibility to achieve consensual results among all opponents in the form of conflict mediation.

Dealing with issues of ethnic conflict and cooperation in domestic politics and among nations arises two main questions. The first asks, what seem to be the most appropriate structural requirements for domestic politics in nation-states for settling ethnic conflicts and ensuring ethnic coexistence? The second asks, what can be done in the international system when ethnic conflicts become armed conflicts and attain international dimensions?[4] From the perspective of peace and conflict studies Wollefs (1994: 126) emphasizes questions about the essence and character of ethnic conflict, their causes, coherent impacts, and the driving mechanisms of escalation in order to find conflict resolving concepts.

This book contains theoretical contributions as well as specific case studies which focus on answering the following questions: Which democratic models of nation-states ensure institutionalized structures for settling potentially violent ethnic conflicts and guarantee a fair and peaceful ethnic coexistence? Which legal capacities, apart from overriding the traditional barriers of sovereignty through military peace keeping or enforcement, did international organizations, especially the

UN or the Conference on Security and Cooperation in Europe (CSCE), attempt in transnational and internal ethnic conflicts? What should the structure of the international system look like in order to decrease violent conflicts? Which actors' behavior in the international system promote cooperation and conflict settlement in a peaceful manner?

The authors' contributions provide conceptual and theoretical approaches to ethnic conflicts and cooperation as well as case studies with specific practical experiences from Eastern Europe and the Commonwealth of Independent States (CIS) and from models of Western democracies. The theoretical papers discuss both conflict anatomy, causes and their settlement, and democratic theory. The empirical case studies range from ethnic conflict potential in Ukraine, Romania, and former Yugoslavia to the description of democratic models with successful ethnic conflict settlement and coexistence in Switzerland and the United States.

The underlying concepts analytically differentiate between the level of the international system and the level of the nation-states as subsystems. That is necessary because as fundamental premise it is assumed that in the global system international actors[5] do not accept a higher legitimate authority with monopoly of power in the sense of "world government". International actors collectively coordinate and organize themselves voluntarily and peacefully in the form of "international governance"[6] which has been understood as a functional equivalent to "international government". By contrast, legal orders with central authority exist in nation-states which execute the monopoly of violence by imposing and enforcing sanctions on social actors. At the international level it is possible to identify nation-states and international organizations as international actors participating in collective action and being present at international institutions.[7] However, ethnic groups or communities are not recognized as international actors on that score because they are not endowed with any legitimized power or sovereignty. In the analysis of regional, interstate or transnational conflicts, non-state actors such as ethnic and/or political groups without internationally recognized nationhood must be considered as conflicting opponents.[8] Only the national level ethnic groups or communities have naturally to be taken into account as socially relevant actors in political processes. This means that for every single case, the politically relevant actors and/or the conflict opponents have to be identified because an obviously conceptional problem solution for conflict settling or suggesting a democratic model for transition societies requires an exact analysis. This connection raises an important question in the contemporary debate about sovereignty: How can international interventions in national sovereignty be justified and legitimated? In accordance with international law, international actors are virtually not allowed to infringe on nation-state sovereignty and influence internal affairs. Hassner (1993: 62) perceives an international accordance about accepted and legitimated intervention prevailing in three categories of cases: "(I)n cases in which aggression is committed against an internationally recognized state (The Iraqi invasion of Kuwait); in cases in which states massacre their own citizens, whether for ideological or ethnic reasons (Cambodia); and in cases in which a breakdown in law and order leads to anarchy and massive suffering (Somalia)". All three categories hold true in the case of former Yugoslavia.

Before discussing the international and nation-state dimension of ethnic conflict and cooperation and their respective conflict settling mechanisms, an approach to the term "ethnicity" will first be attempted.

2 Ethnicity and Ethnic Group

The subsequent description of the term ethnicity will explicate only an approximate and relatively reduced understanding because several contributions in this book are concerned more specifically with this social phenomenon that appears to be a universalistic category which is fundamentally distinctive for human nationalization and socialization.[9] A general definition of ethnicity describes it as the subjective affiliation to an ethnic group having cultural commons, for instance language and tradition. Members of the group jointly share historical and actual experiences and ideas of common descent which create the basis of a particular awareness of identity and solidarity (Comp., e.g., Heckmann 1992: 30). Ethnicity gains implications through political, social or economic conditions and circumstances which transform cultural affinities into politically and socially acting groups (Seger 1989: 231). Regarding the contemporary world, Eriksen (1992: 219) noted ethnicity and ethnic conflict as a paradoxical phenomenon.

Rather than vanishing or losing its significance in modern societies, ethnicities has become an ever more important principle for political organization, and a focus for individual identity. (...) (That) indicate(s) that ethnicity has both a strong emotional appeal and equally strong politically mobilizing potential.

According to Wollefs (1994: 127), the following ethnic categories can be summarized: a common name of the ethnic group; cultural elements such as a common language and religion; the myth of origin; an ethnic-historical memory; and a sense of solidarity and attachment to a specific territory. The mutual perception of differentiation, which is able to generate a manifest conflict between incompatible positions, is relevant for conflict situations between ethnic groups and their reasons for political and social conflict acting. "As anthropological research has shown, it is not the actual cultural differences between groups that create ethnicity, but rather the insistence of group members, or outsiders, on stressing such differences and making them relevant in interaction" (Eriksen 1992: 220). Concluding the short portrayal of the definition of ethnicity Brass' assumption can be pointed out "that ethnic identity is itself a variable, rather than a fixed or 'given' disposition" (1991: 13) which is important for analyzing ethnic conflicts in societies and among them.

3   National and International Dimensions of Ethnic Conflicts

Several phenomena demonstrate the dimensions of ethnic conflicts within states and in international politics.[10] Unstable multi-national states face the problem of intra-ethnic conflicts threatening to spill over into intergovernmental relations. "For instability in certain states may tempt outside powers to intervene in these conflicts to pursue their own self-interest, so triggering a spiral of conflict escalation that can lead to a more general war" (Ryan 1990: XV). Problems also emerge from the spread of ethnic groups over more than one state or when ethnic groups are divided among a number of states and do not reach a majority in any one.

(T)he most frequent scenario is where a dominant group in one state is separated from co-nationals, who make up a minority group in one or more other states. Such a situation can often give rise to irredentism, which is the desire to redraw the existing political boundaries in order to 'redeem' these 'lost' co-nationals. (Ryan 1990: XVI)

Ethnic conflicts linking with nation collapse and nation-(re)building are usually very violent and involve a risk of horizontal escalation. If nationalities are spread over several states and minorities in one state form the majority in a neighbor state, the extension of the conflict is obvious. This applies especially to secessions which can be successful when minorities are encouraged by external support of at least one outside power (Schlotter/Ropers/Meyer 1994: 70). Gurr and Harff (1994: 119) argued that the external support depends "on the sympathies of international actors and on the legitimacy accorded to the group's demand". There is also a danger that neighboring states want to misappropriate areas from the legacy of a declining state (Schlotter et al. 1994: 70). Additionally, problems of international implications in multi-ethnic states exist when the state is oppressing or even attempting to exterminate one or more of its ethnic minority groups through "ethnic cleansing" (comp. Moynihan 1993: 144) or genocide. States persecute individuals or groups of ethnic minorities and ignore human rights because they demand internal autonomy or secession to establish a new state. "Less dramatically, the oppression of ethnic groups can manifest itself in discrimination in employment, housing, access to education and disenfranchisement" (Ryan 1990: XVIII).

Gurr and Harff (1994: 118) also perceived the current international dimensions of ethnic conflicts in a rather comprehensive context of international politics:

> (T)he primary identity of people coincides with the territorial state... The increasing fluidity of international borders is evident not only in the increase in ethnic strife and separatist movements but also in the ever-increasing pool of expatriate labor. Foreign capital penetration and global environmental concerns further diminish the importance of national borders. As borders become less significant, functional interest groups and communal groups may become the main focus of the study of international relations.

Aside from the international significance of ethnic conflicts already mentioned, Suhrke and Garner Noble (1977: 15) proposed a thesis concerning the strength of cross-boundary ethnic links: "If a group that is divided by state boundaries has a common language, religion, and culture, for instance, it can be said to be united by stronger ethnic ties than if it shares fewer symbols of ethnic identity." Correspondingly, the likelihood for any kind of military support is higher with strong ethnic links than by weak ties.

The dimensional implications of ethnic conflicts can not be reduced to affairs or consequences of domestic politics because in a changing global system manifold international factors affect the issues, the cleavages, and the potential rivalries between the rival groups of ethnic conflicts. The dimensions outlined above can virtually be subsumed under three general factors (Gurr/Harff 1994: 7pp.).

The first of these is the tension between the state system and the people. In present human societies, two competing developments can be identified. On one extreme side, there is a revival of xenophobia in long-established nations like, e.g., Germany, France, and Great Britain where enhanced ethnic identity escalates in anti-foreign violent clashes. Just as extreme yet more violent are endeavors for ethnic purity and ethnic cleansing in formerly heterogeneous federal states, illustrated by the behavior of the Serbian nationalists in former Yugoslavia. On the other side are "oppressive leaders who defend existing boundaries at all costs, despite historically justified claims by national people, such as Eritreans in Ethiopia and Kurds in Iraq" (Gurr/Harff 1994: 9).

The second consideration is the impact of the end of the Cold War. The East-West-conflict between the communist bloc and the Western world had generated a relatively stable bipolar world which has been transformed into an ethnically fragmented multipolar world after the decline of the Soviet system. Then, more instability and uncertainty coin the world view and complicate a "new world order".

Third is the changing nature of international responses to ethnic conflict. During the Cold War the United Nations and regional organizations had adopted an ambiguous attitude concerning interference in internal conflicts. The UN played the role of significant peacekeeper when the superpowers came to an agreement about the course of action. This occured in conflicts, e.g., in the Congo, Cyprus, the Middle East, and Cashmere. In other cases the UN, as well as the superpowers, were usually indifferent to ethnopolitical conflicts and dictatorship in the "Third World" like, e.g., in Equatorial Guinea and in Uganda. However, regional organizations like the Organization of

African Unity (OAU) were also unable to intervene in such domestic conflicts because its charter was limited to mediating conflicts among African states and not within them. In addition they had few resources to be allocated to such conflicts. After the Cold War, in the early 1990s, the OAU redefined its charter concerning noninterference to include the authority to monitor elections, make assessments of emerging conflict situations, and send envoys to such emerging crises. Since 1991 the UN has expanded its role as international peacekeeper with the encouragement of the American government and other states. In Cambodia, for instance, the UN carried out the greatest and most expensive peacekeeping operation since its foundation. In line with the UN the USA mobilized the reluctant European allies to intervene militarily in Iraq and to enforce peace in Somalia "in a renewed spirit of collective responsibility" (Gurr/Harff 1994: 13). In Europe the supranational EC, just as the military organization NATO, has been divided and paralyzed over the question of whether and how they should interfere in the escalating ethnic conflicts in Eastern Europe, especially in former Yugoslavia.

Finally, a brief excursion to an author whose applied term of civilization shows decisive features which largely define the term ethnicity. In the article "The Clash of Civilizations?", Huntington (1993: 22) suggested the hypothesis that "(t)he great divisions among humankind and the dominating source of conflict will be cultural" and not ideological or economical and "(c)onflict between civilizations will be the latest phase in the evolution of conflict in the modern world". He differentiated between eight major civilizations[11] in the world defined by history, language, culture, tradition, and religion. These factors substantially determine ethnicity and ethnic groups in our understanding. It could therefore be assumed that civilization is a higher term of ethnic identity comprising a number of similar people and nations which have fundamentally ethnic sources and a basically common ethnic affiliation. With Huntington's conflict lines of civilization, all conflicts in world politics would be reduced to ethnic causes. Additionally, the importance of ethnic conflicts within a civilization would be prone to neglect. But as has been already mentioned, conflicts are often labeled as ethnic conflicts although economic or political factors form the main reasons of the conflict.

4   Ethnic Conflict and Cooperation in an Anarchical World

Dealing with ethnic conflict in this context, a concept of conflict theory in (international) politics will be applied which refers to a sociological understanding of the term conflict (comp. Dahrendorf 1972: chapter 2). It is based upon the assumption that the irreconcilability between goals, interests, or values of different actors is the cause of the conflict. The irreconcilability between actors is called positional difference. Accordingly, the necessary condition of a conflict is the existence of positional differences between two or more actors in (international) politics. A significant question for conflict definition is whether conflict causes, conflict behavior or conflict settling/management should be considered as the central requirement. In this connection an objective and a subjective variation can be distinguished. The decisive requirement for a conflict in the subjective variation relates to conflict behavior and conflict settling or management. Here, the objective variation takes as a starting point the determination of a conflict exclusively on account of positional differences among actors, i.e., conflicts are determined irrespective of conflict behavior and conflict management. This important distinction is taken into consideration as a differentiation between latent and manifest conflicts. Latent conflicts are situations in which actors have opposing natures but there is no obvious conflict behavior or action. Therefore conflict settlement is not possible. Manifest conflicts are situations where actors are featured by positional differences with visible conflict behavior or action making conflict settlement possible. Thus, positional differences are initially conscious and then action determining.

According to Czempiel (1981: 15pp.) who, following Easton (1965), applied the contemporarily most fruitful definition of politics as authoritative allocation of values through the political system; conflicts in (international) politics will be defined as positional differences about the allocation of values in three fields: security, welfare, and power. Values can be physical security, influence or participation in power, material and immaterial chances of development, freedom, welfare etc. Not only does every positional difference constitute a conflict, but simply the irreconcilability of positional differences give reasons for a conflict. These conflicts are all-pervasive elements of human societies and consequently components of international relations. Such an understanding views the international system as a system of conflicts with conflicts simply characterizing the content of politics. Due to the omnipresence of positional differences in the international system, differing situations cannot only be distinguished by the existence of incompatible positions but by the actors' conflict behavior and by the form of conflict management. Seen from this perspective the relatively simple thesis arises that positional differences can have differential impacts concerning the form of conflict behavior and conflict settling.

Within the framework of contemporary theoretical conceptualizations of conflicts in international relations, four forms of conflict settling or conflict management can be differentiated according to Efinger, Rittberger and Zürn (1988: 54pp.): unregulated conflict management, regulated conflict management, conflict termination, and conflict resolution. In situations of unregulated conflict management the actors involved behave in accordance with their individually rational calculations of interest and power, strive for achieving their goals, and prevail over the interests of others. Armed conflicts or wars are forms of unregulated conflict management just as, for example, are economic sanctions. This conflict situation does not exclude compromise or cooperation but it merely takes place ad hoc. The institutionalization of patterns of behavior cannot be achieved. In situations of regulated conflict management the irreconcilability of the different goals or the means of obtaining the goals certainly remains, but the conflict opponents maintain commonly agreed rules and norms for the mutual relations with their furthermore incompatible positions. In the case of conflict termination no one or only one conflict party can completely achieve his goals, i.e., the goals or their means remains totally or partially incompatible, though the conflict actors recognize the manner of conflict management through the commonly agreed decision making mechanisms and they do not aspire to abolish the incompatible positions. Conflict termination needs maintenance via norms and rules. Conflict resolution is a process where all conflict actors reach their goals and the irreconcilable nature of their positions concerning the allocation of a value vanishes, hence the existence of rules and norms for regulating conflict behavior is unnecessary.

Efinger et al. (1988: 57) conclude the four forms of conflict management or settlement mentioned above into two categories. The first contains two forms of regulated conflict management namely conflict regulation and conflict termination. Whereas by conflict termination the controversial values are once and sustainably allocated for a relatively long-term period, conflict regulation does not once distribute the contentious conflict object but instead the allocation has to be renewed steadily. The second category contains the other two forms of conflict management without norms and rules. Norms and Rules do not exist in unregulated conflicts. After a conflict resolution norms and rules are unnecessary because positional differences do not exist any longer. Conflict resolution entails a sustainable distribution of formerly controversial values while unregulated conflict management can continually change the allocation of the controversial values.

Concluding this theoretical discussion, ethnic conflicts, as defined in this book, can be understood as incompatible positional differences about the allocation of ethnic goals, interests, and values. It can be taken for granted that the sources of the so-called ethnic conflicts can be reduced not only to ethnicity or ethnic identity, but that the distribution of controversial values contain political, economic, and social, as well as ethnic, goals and interests. After the dissolution of the Soviet Empire and the communist ideology "realistic" power interests and demands for territory and border of the newly emerged nations were often labeled as ethnic conflicts. Therefore "within and between newly independent nations, conflict is more likely than cooperation" (Hassner 1993: 50). The multiple contents of such conflicts should not be neglected because incompatible political, economic and social positions and claims can be derived from the ethnic origins and vice versa.

> (T)he Eastern concept of nationhood is an ethnic one (based on common culture defined in terms of race, language, tradition or religion), rather than a constitutional one (based on state, territory, citizenship and political principles) as in the West. (...) (P)olitical evolution in the East has been arrested, and ethnic identity has been repressed by decades of ideological and external domination. This explains the aspiration many have to create ethnically homogenous political entities. (Hassner 1993: 50)

The four forms of conflict management make it possible to ascertain whether the outlined cases of internal conflicts and interstate conflicts are unregulated or regulated situations and which model of conflict settling is most appropriate for conflict termination or even conflict resolution.

The "realistic" theorem that has to be acknowledged when considering the international system is that an anarchic structure depicts the world as independent states which behave egoistically and deny a common higher authority.[12] From the traditional perspective of international relations nation-states are sovereign actors in an anarchical, decentralized self-help system where the interactions are characterized by the hierarchy of politics. The nation-states compete for shares of power and attempt to maximize their security which is based on the assumption of the security dilemma. The security dilemma[13] describes the constellation between states as a situation of competition where they can never be safe from attacks of other states because a central monopoly of power is lacking in world politics. Not having to submit to superior states, power will be accumulated more and more in order to be able to face the other power. That causes increased uncertainty by the others who attempt to compensate their own position by strengthening their military capabilities or their alliances. This vicious circle of demands for security and power accumulation emerges and is expressed in the concept of an arms race. The security dilemma can be applied for newly created states and their internal uncertain situations in Eastern Europe and in the CIS after the Cold War.

> The barriers to cooperation inherent in international politics provide clues to the problems that arise as central authority collapses in multi-ethnic empires. The security dilemma affects relations among these groups, just as it affects relations among states. Indeed, because these groups have the added problem of building new state structures from the wreckage of old empires, they are doubly vulnerable. (Posen 1993: 29)

When the hegemonic power had declined in the Soviet Empire and the central authority disappeared, a structure of decomposition and anarchy in the new states and among them remained. The emerging ethnic groups calculate their power relative to each other and try to anticipate their relative power in the future. Such calculations are very difficult and contain a number of unknown factors. "However, the complexity of these situations makes it possible for many competing groups to believe that their prospects in a war would be better earlier, rather than later" (Posen 1993: 34).

Senghaas (1992: 124) describes the security dilemma of ethnic conflicts as follows: The self-centeredness of ethnic groups increases in the course of an escalating conflict as a result of the identity forming polarization against other ethnic groups. The boundary to other ethnic groups will be overdrawn, the conflict becomes "autistic", and the conflict escalation develops a momentum of its own. The ethnic actors are driven into a situation where they are not sensitive to their environment, especially concerning the costs of a conflict. Nobody knows with certainty what the other has in mind and everyone obviously takes the worst case as a starting point. Security will only be guaranteed by self-assertion and self-assertion will be understood as a function of mobilizing power resources such as the military one.

The absence of a central authority, uncertainty, striving for relative power, and the lack of commonly institutionalized conflict settling mechanisms determine the relations among the ethnic groups within the societies and between the states. These factors do not foster peaceful ethnic cooperation or even coexistence. The ethnic-structured groups attempt to prevail power interests against each other and dissociate themselves and their ethnic identity by separating from other ethnic groups even in armed conflicts or war.

Nevertheless, cooperation among competing and selfish actors is absolutely conceivable and in many cases also practically feasible, even among antagonistic ethnic groups (as can be subsequently seen in some cases in this book). First of all, the progressive interest of cognition has to be emphasized according to which "cooperation under anarchy"[14] is possible. So anarchy in this context means that "the term refers to a lack of common government in world politics, not to a denial that an international society - albeit a fragmented one - exists" (Axelrod/Keohane 1985: 226). The game theory stresses the central significance that cooperation can evolve in a collective of egoistic actors without any central authority.[15]

> Cooperation is not equivalent to harmony. Harmony requires complete identity of interests, but cooperation can only take place in situations that contain a mixture of conflicting and complementary interests. In such situations, cooperation occurs when actors adjust their behavior to the actual or anticipated preferences of others. (Axelrod/Keohane 1985: 226)

Hence it follows that the nation-states or the ethnic groups will be seen as rational actors who are striving to increase their benefits and realize their own interests with respect to ethnic identity. As a result of egoistic motives, but also on account of forces of circumstances, the actors are interested in effective institutionalized cooperation in some conflict situations which would canalize and standardize conflict management in order to find a peaceful solution for their conflictual relations. The institutionalization of international or interstate cooperation occurs when actors coordinate and organize themselves voluntarily and peacefully in a form conducive to international governance. Within a state, whether a former or newly emerged one, cooperation among ethnic groups can achieve a peaceful separation like, e.g., the former Czechoslovakia. Or the antagonistic groups can agree to establish a (con)federal structure in a multi-ethnic nation with relatively autonomous federal states where minority rights and ethnic identity can be guaranteed by political institutions by virtue of a commonly negotiated constitution. Despite relatively promising prospects for cooperation of egoistically acting ethnic groups it has to be realized that orientations toward competitive and hostile actions are out of the question if the actors understand the damage and loss of the others as their own benefit or advantage in the sense of a zero sum game.[16] According to the knowledge of international relations theory, especially peace and conflict studies, the relative importance of issue-area[17] typologies to conflict management should be stressed. Issue-area typologies are based on the assumption that the issue-area structure prejudges the method of conflict management (Efinger et al. 1988: 87).

The following theses[18] are significant in order to be able to approach an assessment of the prospects for successful conflict management of ethnic conflicts because it is assumed that ethnic conflicts consist of several different conflict objects and issue-areas in almost every case. First of these is the functionalistic thesis that "low politics" are more appropriate in establishing cooperation structures than "high politics".[19] Secondly, it is the thesis of policy-analysis that material issues of welfare are cooperatively managed, unlike immaterial issues, e.g., security. Thirdly, the closer political issue-areas concern territory the lower is the willingness of the states to accept a collective (international) decision making. The fourth thesis derives from the game theory that zero sum games do not allow common gains. Therefore cooperation is particularly difficult in such issue-areas, which mainly concern security, because non-reciprocated cooperation can threaten one's existence.

Efinger et al. (1988: 92pp.) outlined a conflict issue typology categorizing types of conflict and assessing their cooperation or regime[20] conduciveness. They analyzed types of conflict and their regimes in the East-West-Relations. This conflict typology and the "issue-related hypotheses" resulting from the typology will be at least partially applied because it makes assessing the chances for cooperation and possibly coexistence in different ethnic conflict situations easier. First of all, Efinger et al. (1988) assumed that power can be quite divisible; contrary to Czempiel (1981: 213) who understood power as indivisible. Power can be divided by vertical separation of powers in federal states or confederation of states as well as within power organizations. Despite the differing perspective Efinger et al. (1988) integrated "power" in their hypotheses as indivisible in contrast with "gains" which are characterized as divisible. With reference to three distinctive theoretical conflict typologies, they summarize their conflict typology in four important hypotheses (Efinger et al. 1988: 97):

(i) The types of conflict can be distinguished between conflicts of interests about absolutely assessed goods, conflicts of means, conflicts of interests about relatively assessed goods, and conflicts of values. The hypothesis is that according to the above-mentioned sequence the cooperation conduciveness (or regime-conduciveness) of the respective type of conflict decreases.[21]

(ii) The objects of conflict will be differentiated according to whether they are divisible or indivisible, and at the same time the objects of conflict are classified as the categories "power" (indivisible) and "gains" (divisible). The hypothesis is that the object of conflict "gains" is conducive for cooperation (or regime-conducive) whereas the conflict object "power" is not cooperation-conducive (or regime-conducive).[22]

(iii) The issue-areas will be distinguished by the substance of the controversial value. The hypothesis is, the closer the issue-area to the core of territorial sovereignty (like, e.g., security, borders, and spheres of influence) the less the conduciveness of cooperation (or regime-conduciveness).

(iv) A further distinction of issue-areas relates to the substance of the controversial value. The hypothesis is that the issue-area "power" is considerably less cooperation-conducive (or regime-conducive) as the issue-area "economy".

Types of Conflict and Cooperation-(Regime) Conduciveness

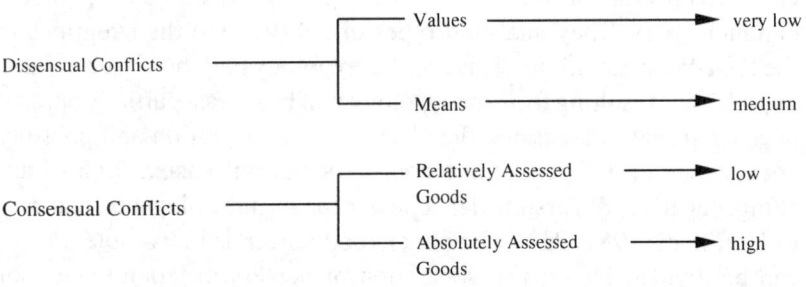

Source: Efinger et al. (1988: 96)

As has already been mentioned above, ethnic conflicts can often consist of various aspects from political, social, and economic issue-areas and imply different kinds of conflict objects like, e.g., power, territory, or borders just as religion and culture. The contentious objects of ethnic conflicts can concern the whole range of the typology from the most difficult cooperation-conduciveness of values to the high cooperation-conduciveness of absolutely assessed goods. Therefore, it is very important to be able to filter out, at least partially, the core elements and the main reasons for an ethnic conflict. In other words, if we can identify the substantial issue-area(s) or the main conflict object(s), it is more likely to predict the cooperation-conduciveness more definitely, and thus, an adequate conflict settling strategy can be selected which enhances the prospects of peacefully overcoming the anarchic structure of ethnic conflict situations.

The more theoretical approach to ethnic conflicts in international politics so far corresponds with Ryan's concluding suggestion of two categories which come rather close to the intention of our book:

> The first is the suggestion that an effective system of minority protection should be created based not on states but an international organization. Such a regime would do two things. It would guarantee the rights of ethnic groups and also remove the grievances that might give rise to violent conflicts. The second suggestion is that more thought should be given to improving the techniques of conflict resolution so that a more constructive response can be made to violent ethnic conflicts when they occur. (Ryan 1990: 45)

5 Domestic Structures of Ethnic Conflict and Cooperation

For an equal and lasting peaceful cohabitation of different ethnic minorities in a modern democratic multi-ethnic nation, several factors have to be ensured. These include minority rights, self-determination of ethnic groups (comp., e.g., Moynihan 1993: chap. 2), relatively autonomous positions, access to power for ethnic minorities within (con)federal structures, and fair and non-discriminating equal treatment against majorities; factors which should be incorporated into a constitution in order to ensure that ethnic minorities have no motives for rebellion or attempt to strive for their own national independence. The reasons for political mobilization of ethnic groups "include unequal treatment by dominant groups, competition with other groups for access to power in new states, the contagion effect of ethnopolitical activism elsewhere, and patterns of state power and policy that channel communal energies into either protest or rebellion" (Gurr 1993: 123) because "(r)arely has ethnic self-determination been achieved through negotiations or ratified by plebiscites" (Gurr/Harff 1994: 118).

Following Meyer (1994: 109), the term minority will be used in accordance with the practice of the CSCE and international law. Minorities are those groups within a state who possess citizenship but differ from the majority in ethnic, religious, or linguistic features, and do not hold dominant roles in the state. These groups want to preserve their common distinct characteristics and strive for legal access to power and real equality with the majority.[23]

Today approximately 180 states exist, of which fewer than 20 are ethnically homogenous; meaning that ethnic minorities account for less than 5% of the population (Welsh 1993: 65). Welsh (1993: 67) observed that "voters in ethnically riven societies are more tightly tied to ethnically based parties than are voters in societies in which the principal basis of party preference is socioeconomic class". Undoubtedly, the ethnic conflict depends on the structure and the ethnic composition in a state which varies from state to state. Nevertheless, "(a) common syndrome is the case of the minority that is frozen out of power (or share of power) over time" or is not provided with a status of politically autonomous self-determination so that "politicians from these minority groups perceive themselves as the victims of a 'tyranny of the majority'" (Welsh 1993: 67). Therefore, it can be deduced that "for the management of ethnic conflict ... no salient group should be prohibited from a share of effective power" and "(p)olitical institutions should be designed to ensure that minorities are proportionately represented in parliaments and bureaucracies and that their interests - political, cultural and economic - are heeded" (Welsh 1993: 76).

If ethnic groups feel economically disadvantaged, culturally infiltrated by foreigners, and politically incapacitated or without rights, they use ethno-nationalistic mobilization as a means of maintaining their own identity and enforcing their own interests. Senghaas (1992: 118) has distinguished between three causal constellations of ethnic conflicts in Eastern Europe and the former Soviet Union. The first constellation concerns the protection of ownership; ethnic groups feel economically exploited because an outflow of resources takes place from relatively well developed regions into less developed regions. The second point is the resistance against foreign infiltration; the perception of foreign domination in important spheres of politics and the immigration of workers will be perceived as serious attacks to their own identity because of the threat of local ethnic majorities becoming minorities. Third is the protection against assimilation; minorities attempt to resist the oppression of assimilation of the majority.

To summarize some of the domestic causes of ethnic conflicts in nation-states it may be said that a few relatively simple factors are the prerequisites of potentially violent ethnic tensions. Because the vast majority of states in the world are ethnically heterogeneous, the conflicts are based on a mixture of ethnic groups and communities who are competing with each other for political power and status. Ethnic conflicts entail a situation in which at least one ethnic group feels aggrieved or discriminated due to the existing political allocation of power among the different groups. If these perceived grievances cannot be mitigated or remedied by legal and political means which improve the situation and the status of the discriminated groups and their access to power, then a violent conflict will likely follow (comp. also Nevers 1993: 32).

The connection between ethnicity and nationalism seems to be obvious even though nationalism and the nation-state are not necessarily based on ethnicity. Kellas (1991: 51) emphasized that "ethnicity is not a 'given', but a construct of the state itself". According to Kellas, ethnic nationalism is one characteristic form of nationalism.[24] The ethnic nationalism excludes people who do not share a common ethnic descent from membership of the nation. Nobody can gain this ethnic affiliation by adopting an ethnic identity. Elsewhere in the literature, ethnicity and nationalism were treated as ideologies which underline the cultural similarity of their adherents (Eriksen 1991: 264). The distinction between them is one of degree, not one of kind. The decisive questions are whether the nationalists form the majority in the state or whether they are involved in power-sharing or whether they are legitimated by the prevailing political authority.

> (T)he major difference between ethnicity and nationalism lies (...) in their relationship to the state. Unsuccessful nationalism (...) tend to become transformed into ethnicities whose members reside more or less uncomfortably under the aegis of a state which they do not identify with their own nationality or ethnic category. (...) Nationalism entails the ideological justification of a state, actual or potential. Judged on this criterion, ethnicity can sometimes be interpreted as a form of stagnant nationalism which may eventually, or periodically, become manifest as nationalism. (Eriksen 1991: 265)

There is undoubtedly no question that democratic structures can most likely cope peacefully with the issues of multi-ethnic societies by reducing latent ethnic tensions before they become manifest, and by managing and regulating manifest and potentially violent ethnic conflicts without resorting to force. Nevers (1993: 45) suggested for the relationship between democratization and ethnic conflict "that democratization has the potential to help mitigate ethnic tension by allowing for the establishment of an inclusive means of governance to address the needs of all ethnic groups in the state". Therefore, the question revolves on what the most appropriate type of democratic system for ensuring a stable and fair ethnic coexistence is for each society, depending on the ethnic composition and the underlying constellation.

Since the second half of the 1960s there has been a reassessment in political science of ethnic phenomena. The optimistic expectation that the progressive process of modernization would gradually integrate multi-ethnic societies into nations, as claimed by a great deal of "nation-building" literature (comp. exemplarily Deutsch 1972), increasingly gave way to more realistic assumptions about the viability and the political ability of ethnic mobilization. The place was taken by the concept of "state-building" which was increasingly focused on the restoration of political stability. Ethnicity, once considered an obstacle to nation-building, is now conceded to be a positive resource for the control of the political arena. For example, the stability of a state can be relieved, supported, or established by mutual paralysis along ethnic, religious, and social lines, by stirring up interethnic rivalries, or by ethnic or religious groups monopolizing key positions in the state (Scheffler 1990: 25pp.). Several models from political science can be stressed.

The political model of a cooperative concordance democracy is a social and political system which gives special emphasis to compromise regulations and proportional representation instead of competing majority rule for decision making. This system, like, for example, in the former Lebanon or in Switzerland has the possibility of restricting the consensus making procedures in their ethnic-structured societies to a union of the elites of ethnic groups, as will be seen in the Swiss case study from Spillmann in a later chapter. As a result, an overstraining of the political system by participatory claims can not only be prevented, but also positive democratic elements like tolerance, willingness to compromise, and minority protection will be developed. An almost identical model of consociational democracy was synchronously conceptualized for the example of the Netherlands (Lijphart 1977). It is a type of liberally constituted, pluralistic democracy in which deep social cleavages between social groups are not stabilized by competition and majority principles, but by cooperation of the elites. The social foundation in the society is not united by a basic consensus, but reflects religious, socio-economic, or ethnic conflict lines which form subcultures with their own structures of socialization and values. Political stability will be attained by pragmatic cooperation of the elites. The contribution of Reiterer in this book will subsequently give a more detailed consideration of consociational democracy in the context of democratic theory.

For an effective avoidance or mitigation of ethnic conflicts in a democratic system, power-sharing among different ethnic groups must be guaranteed. Following Lijphart (1969), an effective power-sharing system must provide a collective exertion of power by the relevant ethnic groups, group self-determination and autonomy, proportionality in representation, and a minority veto.

Beside concordance or consociational democracy, (con)federal systems can fulfill, for the most part, the claims of a plural society for a stable and peaceful multi-ethnic coexistence with minority rights, self-determined autonomy, and access to power for different ethnic groups. Variants of federalism stretch from an alliance to a centralized state in which, on the one side, centrifugal forces determine the structure of the state, and, on the other side, centripetal forces. The range contains a continuum of federalist types from a confederacy which insists on independence and diversity as highest aims to a unitary federation or a centralized state which conceives integration and equality of living conditions as their uppermost objectives (comp. the graph of Schultze 1983: 93). Referring to a sociological definition of federalism, societies with territorially subdivided ethnic, religious, economic, and historical differentiations independent from their political organization were designated as federal.[25] For Livingston's sociological understanding, the essential part of federalism is not founded on constitutional or institutional structures, but on the society itself (Livingston 1956: 2). According to Livingston every society is featured by a certain degree of social variety. The fact that a society is composed of members with different economic, religious, cultural, political, ethnic, and other characteristics is still not the only deciding factor for its federal quality. A substantial differentiation criterion of federal society in contrast to other social systems is its territorial segmentation.

> If they are grouped territorially, i.e. geographically, then the result may be a society that is federal. If they are not grouped territorially, then the society cannot be said to be federal. In either case coherence in the society may depend on the devolution upon these groups of the exercise of functions appropriate to the diversities that they represent. (Livingston 1956: 2)

The federal system which represents a compromise between opposite demands for recognition of diversity, on the one hand, and integration, on the other hand, has created so-called "instrumentalities" on the political level which provide this adjustment beside the constitution. According to Livingston, it includes the manner in which the constitution and its institutions function as well as such things as habits, attitudes, acceptances, concepts, and theories. So it includes, for instance, the rules of the American Senate and the make-up of the

Canadian cabinet (Livingston 1956: 6pp.). Because a federal government has to react to special requirements in a society, there consequently exists different types of "instrumentalities" which reflect the diversity of the society and protect it at the same time.[26]

For example, the United States of America and Canada are considered to be plural societies and ethnic melting pots in which federal or confederal systems with institutionalized conflict solving mechanisms successfully guarantee minority rights, autonomy and power-sharing for ethnic groups and their demands. "The status of the various Indian nations/tribes within the United States is changing from that of wards of the federal government to that of a federacy" (Elazar 1991: 304). The distinct federal structure of the USA is constitutionally based on the principle of "concurrent government", i.e., on the separation of exercise fulfillment and financing of the federal government, the federal states, and the communities. The constitution determines the distribution of exercises between federal government and federal states so that the federal responsibilities are particularly listed and all other competencies are generally assigned to the federal states. The power is divided between the executive, a bicameral legislature, and judiciary within the general government. It is further divided between the federal government, the federal states, and local arenas of government. "This compound division of power has given rise to a non-centralized matrix of governing bodies with sufficient redundancy of structure and function to ensure efficient operation" (Elazar 1991: 310). The American society has created a common culture among people whose objective interests are often fundamentally opposed. In other words, an American culture functions in such a way as to deny conflict and to build a sense of cohesion or oneness (comp. Sollors 1986).

Notes

1. For the period of 1945 to 1976 István Kende (1982: 30) documented 102 internal wars as opposed to 18 international wars. Ferdowsi (1987: 16) lists other empirical research about wars with differing periods and their underlying quantitative and qualitative features. Although the results are partially inconsistent, the fact that substantially more internal than intergovernmental wars occurred in the modern age remains significant. Comp. also Gantzel, Schwinghammer and Siegelberg (1992), Billing (1992: 40-51) and Gantzel and Schwinghammer (1995).

2. Comp. Galtung (1975: 9 and 32). Peace has two fundamental aspects which are inseparably connected with the term of violence. Generally, peace has been understood as the absence of violence. Galtung distinguished the term of peace in "negative" and the extending "positive" or "just" peace. The absence of personal violence defines "negative" peace, i.e. physically direct violence or, in other words, the lack of war as organizationally military use of force. The lack of direct violence and the absence of indirect or structural violence defines the "positive" peace. Whereas direct violence can be attributed to concrete actors, structural violence is inherent in societal systems and subsystems as unequal balances of power and hierarchies of power, and therefore, asymmetrical chances of survival. Galtung described "positive" peace as social justice. See also Boulding (1978) concerning the term of peace. He differentiated between "unstable" and "stable" peace. The first one describes a current situation without direct military conflicts, but the threat and preparation for war pervasively exist in the patterns of interaction. The latter means the use of direct violence is ostracized in the interactions of the societies and between themselves.

3. For the current discussion about problems of outside interventions in internal conflicts comp., for example, Cooper and Berdal (1993); Brock and Elliesen (1994); Debiel and Nuscheler (1996); and Weiss (1996).

4. "Although ethnic politics transpire mainly within individual states, they are often affected by external forces and increasingly spill over international borders. Ethnic solidarities become internationally significant by irredentist pressures, by the activities of diaspora, by strategic targeting, by international organizations, and by transnational economic, political, and criminal networks" (Esman 1995: 111).

5. Here, the theoretical concept of Neo-Institutionalism is applied as opposed to Neorealism; according to which the relevant actors in the international system are nation-states and non-state actors, especially international organizations. Comp. e.g. Keck (1991).

6. The term "international governance" stands for the formation of institutionalized and sustainable structures of cooperation among states in the international system, i.e., institutions of collective conflict management in which nations voluntarily cooperate in accordance with predetermined norms and rules. See Rittberger (1989: 183). On the nation-state level forms of self-controlling and self-coordinating between societal actors exist as well. Within societies the following forms of self-coordination can be distinguished: Lindblom (1980) distinguished between the state authority, the exchange of goods in markets among self-interesting actors, and the function of control by consciousness. Ostrom (1990) conceptualized the problem of "Common-Pool Resources" which concerns the

7   The application of the term international institution refers to Neo-Institutionalism where institutions are structural features of cooperation subsuming international regimes, organizations, and conventions. Comp. Keohane (1989: 3) and Keck (1991: 638). The underlying definition of institution relates to the social sciences and comprises formal organizations as well as stable patterns of behavior. See Zürn (1992: 140). Thus, such institutions have the common characteristic of being capable of realizing goal-orientated actions and they are marked by sustainable and stable patterns of behavior being founded on a set of rules. According to Keohane it can be assumed that the generally neo-institutionalistic definition of "institution as 'persistent and connected sets of rules (formal and informal) that prescribe behavioral roles, constrain activity and shape expectations'" (Keohane 1989: 3) and, in a specific manner, "institutions ... as related complexes of rules and norms, identifiable in space and time. (...) (I)nstitutions differentiate among actors according to the roles that they are expected to perform, and institutions can be identified by asking whether patterns of behavior are indeed differentiated by role. (...) In international relations, some of these institutions are formal organizations, with prescribed hierarchies and the capacity for purposive action. Others, such as the international regimes for money and trade, are complexes of rules and organizations, the core elements of which have been negotiated and explicitly agreed upon by states." (Keohane 1989: 163) Distinguishing the three forms of international institutions, only international organizations have actor's quality. However, international regimes and conventions can not claim any actor's quality in international relations. "Organizations are physical entities possessing offices, personnel, equipment, budgets, and so forth." (Young 1986: 108) Formal organizations are potential actors in international relations possessing juridical entities or having social identity of one's own. "Formal international organizations are purposive institutions with explicit rules, specific assignments of roles to individuals and groups, and the capacity for action. Unlike international regimes, international organizations can engage in goal-directed activities such as raising and spending money, promulgating policies, and making discretionary choices." (Keohane 1989: 175)

8   For example, in the regional conflict in the Middle East the PLO as a non-state actor is struggling for territorial autonomy and independence. Another example is the ethnic conflict in the former Yugoslavia where different ethnic-structured actors were at war with one another.

9   Comp., for example, for fundamental and comprehensive treatises on ethnic group, ethnic community, ethnic identity, and ethnic nationalism Brass (1985 and 1991: part I), Smith (1993), and especially Horowitz (1975) for ethnic identity. Brass (1985) dealt with ethnic identity formation within the state structures in his volume. In his book from 1991 he took a definition of ethnic group and identity with "objective cultural markers" as a basis for his analysis. Smith stressed the historical and cultural factors in the revival of ethnic nationalism in his analysis.

10 For these dimensions of ethnic conflicts in international politics comp., for example, Esman (1990 and 1995). Comp. also Carment (1993: 137) who does not deal with international phenomena of ethnic conflicts, but who "offers some

preliminary conclusions about the policy and theoretical implications of the international dimension of ethnic conflict".

[11] Huntington's (1993: 25) major civilizations are the Western, the Confucian, the Japanese, the Islamic, the Hindu, the Slavic-Orthodox, the Latin-American, and the African civilization.

[12] This idea of an anarchical international system was conceived by Bull (1977).

[13] See Herz (1974: 39) for a detailed description of the security dilemma.

[14] Comp. Oye (1986) who attempted to answer questions as to what circumstances favor cooperation under anarchy, what features encourage cooperation, what features of situations preclude cooperation and what strategies can further the emergence of cooperation.

[15] The pioneering acknowledgment that cooperation can be achieved in international politics without authority has essentially to be ascribed to Axelrod (1984). He illustrated by computer simulations that under specific conditions, it does not have to lead to armed conflicts against each other if rationally acting egoists pursue self-interests; cooperation can happen. Axelrod analyzed the issues of cooperation as the model of the prisoners' dilemma, because many of the best developed models of political, social, and economic processes build on the prisoners' dilemma. It is decisive for the results of the game that the actors iteratively interact with each other for an unforeseeable period, i.e. the actors do not know the moment of game termination.

[16] See Scharpf (1991: 626 and 1988). His model of negotiations system refers to economic action theory which precludes interactions of ethnic conflicts. Scharpf (1991: 631, footnote 5) stressed that when such conflicts occur with mutually precluding interests, the Leviathan can not be substituted by negotiations systems or even majority democracy.

[17] The definition of issue will be used as "a matter involving and/or requiring the authoritative allocation of values by collective action" (Coate 1982: 46) and supplement the aspect of position incompatibility. Thus, in accordance with Efinger et al. (1988: 52. footnote 33) the term issue-area can be understood as interactions which consist of one issue or as several indissolubly perceiving issues, the conflict, and its actors deriving from.

[18] See Efinger et al. (1988: 91) for a detailed compilation of these theses about the relationship between issue-area and conflict management.

[19] See Mitrany (1976), since power and security were then understood as "high politics" and economy as "low politics".

[20] According to regime theory "(r)egimes can be defined as sets of implicit principles, norms, rules and decision-making procedures around which actors' expectations converge in a given area of international relations" (Krasner 1983: 2). This definition was specified and supplemented by Wolf and Zürn (1986: 6) who have added four constitutive criterions: those concerning issue area structure, effectivity, durability, and the changing behavior of actors involved.

[21] Here, Efinger et al. (1988) refers to Aubert (1972: 180) who differentiated between conflicts of interests and conflicts of values. A conflict of interests is based on a lacking situation. The actors want the same but not enough exists for everyone.

28 *Ethnic Conflicts and Civil Society*

        A conflict of value is based on a dissensus with regard to the normal status of an object. Efinger et al. apply the definition of Kriesberg (1982: 30pp.) to the conflict of means according to which a conflict of means exists when a dissensus arises about adopting the course aimed at achieving a common goal. Additionally, they (1988: 94pp.) defined absolutely assessed goods as goods which obtain their values irrespectively of how much of the same goods others or the other conflict party possess. On the other hand, a relatively assessed goods relate to a value that one conflict party possesses more of than the others (e.g. arms or status). Relatively assessed goods are significant because they are socially limited and conducive to social shortage by extensive using. Conflicts about such goods tend to the character of zero sum games.

[22]   Here, Efinger et al. quote Czempiel (1981).

[23]   Foreigners like foreign workers or refugees who live in the state for quite a while are not counted as minorities.

[24]   Kellas (1991: 51pp.) differentiated between ethnic, social, and official nationalism. Social nationalism defines its nation "by social ties and culture rather than by common descent. This type of nationalism stresses the shared sense of national identity, community and culture, but outsiders can join the nation if they identify with it and adopt its social characteristics." Official nationalism is "the nationalism of the state, encompassing all those legally entitled to be citizens, irrespective of their ethnicity, national identity and culture".

[25]   In addition, three further definitions of federalism can be distinguished: (a) the institutional-functionalistic definition: federalism is a political form of organization in which the perceiving of state assignments is divided up between regional substates and the entire state so that every state level can make definitive decisions in some fields; (b) the constitutional definition: political systems are federally organized when the decisive structural elements of the state legislative, executive, and judiciary exist on the national level as well as on the subnational level and when their existence is protected by a constitution and neither the national level nor the subnational level can be removed through intervention by the respective other level; (c) the social-philosophical definition: federalism is a model of order reaching beyond political organization which commits itself to the principle of subsidiarity and to the idea of cooperative society. It is based on extensive autonomy of small groups and decentral units. See Reissert (1989: 238).

[26]   The universal or essential instrumentalities are: a written constitution, a formal distribution of powers, constitutional interpretation in the legislature, dual citizenship, the federal executive and formal constitutional amendment. See Livingston (1956: 10).

Bibliography

AUBERT, Vilhelm 1972: Interessenkonflikt und Wertkonflikt: Zwei Typen des Konflikts und Konfliktlösung, in: Bühl, Walter L. (ed.) 1972: Konflikt und Konfliktstrategie. Ansätze zu einer soziologischen Konflikttheorie, München, pp. 178-205

AXELROD, Robert 1984: The Evolution of Cooperation, New York

AXELROD, Robert / KEOHANE, Robert O. 1985: Achieving Cooperation under Anarchy: Strategies and Institutions, in: World Politics, Vol. 38, No. 1, pp. 226-254

BILLING, Peter 1992: Eskalation und Deeskalation internationaler Konflikte. Ein Konfliktmodell auf der Grundlage der empirischen Auswertung von 288 internationalen Konflikten seit 1945, Frankfurt a.M.

BOULDING, Kenneth E. 1978: Stable Peace, Austin/London

BRASS, Paul 1991: Ethnicity and Nationalism. Theory and Comparison, New Dehli

BRASS, Paul (ed.) 1985: Ethnic Groups and the State, Worcester

BROCK, Lothar / ELLIESEN, Tillmann 1994: Humanitäre Intervention. Zur Problematik militärischer Eingriffe in innerstaatliche Konflikte, in: Hein, Wolfgang (ed.) 1994: Umbruch in der Weltgesellschaft. Auf dem Wege zu einer "Neuen Weltordnung"?, Hamburg, pp. 383-420

BULL, Hedley 1977: The Anarchical Society. A Study of Order in World Politics, New York

CARMENT, David 1993: The International Dimensions of Ethnic Conflict: Concepts, Indicators and Theory, in: Journal of Peace Research, Vol. 30, No. 2, pp. 137-150

COATE, Roger A. 1982: Global Issue Regimes, New York

COOPER, Robert / BERDAL, Mats 1993: Outside Intervention in Ethnic Conflict, in: Survival, Vol. 35, No. 1, pp. 118-142

CZEMPIEL, Ernst-Otto 1981: Internationale Politik. Ein Konfliktmodell, Paderborn

DAHRENDORF, Ralf 1972: Konflikt und Freiheit. Auf dem Weg zur Dienstklassengesellschaft, München

DEBIEL, Tobias / NUSCHELER, Franz 1996: Vor einer neuen Politik der Einmischung? Imperative und Fallstricke des humanitären Interventionismus, in: Debiel, Tobias / Nuscheler, Franz (eds.) 1996: Der neue Interventionismus. Humanitäre Einmischung zwischen Anspruch und Wirklichkeit, Bonn, pp. 13-50

DEUTSCH, Karl W. 1972: Nationenbildung - Nationalstaat - Integration, Düsseldorf

EASTON, David 1965: A Framework for Political Analysis, Englewood Cliffs

EFINGER, Manfred / RITTBERGER, Volker / ZÜRN, Michael 1988: Internationale Regime in den Ost-West-Beziehungen. Ein Beitrag zur Erforschung der friedlichen Behandlung internationaler Konflikte, Frankfurt a.M.

ELAZAR, Daniel J. (ed.) 1991: Federal Systems of the World: A Handbook of Federal, Confederal and Autonomy Arrangements, London

ERIKSEN, Thomas H. 1991: Ethnicity versus Nationalism, in: Journal of Peace Research, Vol. 28, No. 3, pp. 263-278

ERIKSEN, Thomas H. 1992: Ethnicity and Nationalism: Definitions and Critical Reflections, in: Bulletin of Peace Proposals, Vol. 23, No. 2, pp. 219-224

ESMAN, Milton J. 1990: Ethnic Pluralism and International Relations, in: Canadian Review of Studies in Nationalism, Vol. XVII, No. 1-2, pp. 83-93

ESMAN, Milton J. 1995: Ethnic Actors in International Politics, in: Nationalism and Ethnic Politics, Vol. 1, No. 1, pp. 111-125

FERDOWSI, Mir A. 1987: Regionalkonflikte in der Dritten Welt. Dimensionen, Ursachen, Perspektiven, in: Ferdowsi, Mir A. / Opitz, Peter J. (eds.) 1987: Macht und Ohnmacht der Vereinten Nationen. Zur Rolle der Weltorganisation in Drittwelt-Konflikten, IFO-Studien zur Entwicklungsforschung No. 18, München/Köln/London, pp. 13-53

GALTUNG, Johan 1972: Strukturelle Gewalt. Beiträge zur Friedens- und Konfliktforschung, Hamburg

GANTZEL, Klaus Jürgen / SCHWINGHAMMER, Torsten 1995: Die Kriege nach dem Zweiten Weltkrieg 1945 bis 1992. Daten und Tendenzen, Münster

GANTZEL, Klaus Jürgen / SCHWINGHAMMER, Torsten / SIEGELBERG, Jens 1992: Kriege der Welt. Ein systematisches Register der kriegerischen Konflikte 1985 bis 1992, Bonn

GANTZEL, Klaus Jürgen / SIEGELBERG, Jens 1990: Krieg und Entwicklung. Überlegungen zur Theoretisierung von Kriegsursachen unter besonderer Berücksichtigung der Zeit seit 1945, in: Rittberger, Volker (ed.) 1990: Theorien der Internationalen Beziehungen. Bestandsaufnahme und Forschungsperspektiven, Sonderheft der Politischen Vierteljahresschrift, Vol. 21, Opladen, pp. 219-239

GURR, Ted Robert 1993: Minorities at Risk. A Global View of Ethnopolitical Conflicts, Washington

GURR, Ted Robert / HARFF, Barbara 1994: Ethnic Conflict in World Politics, Boulder/San Francisco/Oxford

HASSNER, Pierre 1993: Beyond Nationalism and Internationalism: Ethnicity and World Order, in: Survival, Vol. 35, No. 2, pp. 49-65

HECKMANN, Friedrich 1992: Ethnische Minderheiten, Volk und Nation. Soziologie interethnischer Beziehungen, Stuttgart

HERZ, John 1974: Staatenwelt und Weltpolitik. Aufsätze zur internationalen Politik im Nuklearzeitalter, Hamburg

HOROWITZ, Donald L. 1975: Ethnic Identity, in: Glazer, Nathan / Moynihan, Daniel P. (eds.) 1975: Ethnicity. Theory and Experience, Cambridge/London, pp. 111-140

HUNTINGTON, Samuel P. 1993: The Clash of Civilizations?, in: Foreign Affairs, Vol. 72, No. 3, pp. 22-49

KECK, Otto 1991: Der neue Institutionalismus in der Theorie der Internationalen Politik, in: Politische Vierteljahresschrift, Vol. 32, No. 4, pp. 635-653

KELLAS, James G. 1991: The Politics of Nationalism and Ethnicity, London

KENDE, István 1982: Kriege nach 1945. Eine empirische Untersuchung, Militärpolitik Dokumentation, Vol. 27, Frankfurt a.M.

KEOHANE, Robert O. 1989: International Institutions and State Power. Essays in International Relations Theory, Boulder

KRASNER, Stephen D. 1983: Structural causes and regime consequences: regimes as intervening variables, in: Krasner, Stephen D. (ed.) 1983: International Regimes, Ithaca/ London

KRIESBERG, Louis 1982: Social Conflicts, Englewood Cliffs

LIJPHART, Arend 1969: Consociational Democracy, in: World Politics, Vol. 21, No. 2, pp. 207-225

LIJPHART, Arend 1977: Democracy in Plural Societies. A Comparative Exploration, New Haven/London

LINDBLOM, Charles E. 1980: Jenseits von Markt und Staat. Eine Kritik der politischen und ökonomischen Systeme, Stuttgart

LIVINGSTON, William S. 1956: Federalism and Constitutional Change, Oxford

MEYER, Berthold 1994: Überfordern Minderheitenkonflikte die "neue" KSZE?, in: Meyer, Berthold / Moltmann, Bernhard (eds.) 1994: Konfliktsteuerung durch Vereinte Nationen und KSZE, Frankfurt a.M., pp. 108-124

MEYER, Berthold / MOLTMANN, Bernhard (eds.) 1994: Konfliktsteuerung durch Vereinte Nationen und KSZE, Frankfurt a.M.

MITRANY, David 1976: The Functional Theory of Politics, New York

MOYNIHAN, Daniel Patrick 1993: Pandaemonium. Ethnicity in International Politics, Oxford

NEVERS, Renée de 1993: Democratization and Ethnic Conflict, in: Survival, Vol. 35, No. 2, pp. 31-48

OSTROM, Elinor 1990: Governing the Commons. The Evolution of Institutions for Collective Action, Cambridge

OYE, Kenneth A. 1986: Explaining Cooperation under Anarchy: Hypothesis and Strategies, in: Oye, Kenneth A. (ed.) 1986: Cooperation under Anarchy, Princeton, pp. 1-24

POSEN, Barry R. 1993: The Security Dilemma and Ethnic Conflict, in: Survival, Vol. 35, No. 1, pp. 27-47

REISSERT, Bernd 1989: Föderalismus, in: Nohlen, Dieter / Schultze 0, Rainer-Olaf (eds.) 1989: Politikwissenschaft. Theorien, Methoden, Begriffe. Pipers Wörterbuch zur Politik (edited by Dieter Nohlen), Vol. 1, München, pp. 238-244

RITTBERGER, Volker 1989: Frieden durch Assoziation und Integration? Anmerkungen zum Stand der Forschung über internationale Organisationen und Regime, in: Moltmann, Bernhard / Senghaas-Knobloch, Eva (eds.) 1989: Konflikte in der Weltgesellschaft und Friedensstrategien, Baden-Baden, pp. 183-205

RONGE, Volker 1980: Theoriestrategische Einführung: Quasi-Politik, in: Ronge, Volker (ed.) 1980: Am Staat vorbei. Politik der Selbstregulierung von Kapital und Arbeit, Frankfurt a.M., pp. 11-29

RYAN, Stephen 1990: Ethnic Conflict and International Relations, Aldershot

SCHARPF, Fritz W. 1988: Verhandlungssysteme, Verteilungskonflikte und Pathologien der politischen Steuerung, in: Schmidt, Manfred G. (ed.) 1988: Staatstätigkeit. International und historisch vergleichende Analysen, Sonderheft der Politischen Vierteljahresschrift, Vol. 19, pp. 61-87

SCHARPF, Fritz W. 1991: Die Handlungsfähigkeit des Staates am Ende des zwanzigsten Jahrhunderts, in: Politische Vierteljahresschrift, Vol. 32, No. 4, pp. 621-634

SCHEFFLER, Thomas 1990: Ethnisch-religiöse Konflikte und gesellschaftliche Integration im Vorderen und Mittleren Orient (Ethnizität und Gesellschaft: Occasional Papers No. 1), Berlin

SOLLORS, Werner 1986: Beyond Ethnicity. Consent and Descent in American Culture, New York

SUHRKE, Astri / GARNER NOBLE, Lela 1977: Introduction, in: Suhrke, Astri / Garner Noble, Lela (eds.) 1977: Ethnic Conflicts in International Relations, New York et al., pp. 1-20

WEISS, Thomas G. 1996: Humanitäre Intervention. Lehren aus der Vergangenheit, Konsequenzen für die Zukunft, in: Debiel, Tobias / Nuscheler, Franz (eds.) 1996: Der neue Interventionismus. Humanitäre Einmischung zwischen Anspruch und Wirklichkeit, Bonn, pp. 53-75

WELSH, David 1993: Domestic Politics and Ethnic Conflict, in: Survival, Vol. 35, No. 1, pp. 63-80

WIMMER, Andreas 1995: Interethnische Konflikte. Ein Beitrag zur Integration aktueller Forschungsansätze, in: Kölner Zeitschrift für Soziologie und Sozialpsychologie, Vol. 47, No. 3, pp. 464-493

WOLF, Klaus Dieter / ZÜRN, Michael 1986: International Regimes und Theorien der internationalen Politik, Tübinger Arbeitspapiere zur Internationalen Politik und Friedensforschung, No. 3, Tübingen

WOLLEFS, Elisabeth 1994: Vom ethnischen Konflikt zum (Bürger-)Krieg. Vorschläge zur Analyse der Ursache(n) von ethnisch-strukturierten Kriegen, in: Meyer, Berthold / Moltmann, Bernhard (eds.) 1994: Konfliktsteuerung durch Vereinte Nationen und KSZE, Frankfurt a.M., pp. 125-152

ZÜRN, Michael 1992: Interessen und Institutionen in der internationalen Politik. Grundlegung und Anwendungen des situationsstrukturellen Ansatzes, Opladen

PART II

THEORETICAL APPROACHES

2 Conflicts Between Different Nationalities
Chances for and Limits to Their Settlement

URSEL SCHLICHTING

Within the last few years a great number of conflicts, especially in Southeastern Europe and the former Soviet Union, which are often described as "interethnic", "ethno-national" or "ethno-social" conflicts, have increasingly attracted public attention. They have reached different stages of escalation, some of them are still latent, others, such as the dispute over Nagorno-Karabakh or the Abkhaz-Georgian conflict, have expanded into persistent armed conflicts. The potential for similar conflicts within the territory of the former Soviet Union, where 130-140 different peoples and ethnic groups are to be found, is extremely high. Compared to the Cold War or to the second Gulf-War, for instance, they are a "new" type of conflict which are regionally limited and in which ethnic identity indeed seems to play a great role. But is ethnic identity the real reason and the only explanation for the outbreak of such conflicts or is it just one of many different factors? Conflicts between different nationalities have complex historical, religious, economic and social backgrounds. Different conflict parties have different interests and aims. What does this complexity finally mean for conflict settlement? Before trying to answer to this, the first question must be: What are the main reasons for, and characteristics of, conflicts between different nationalities?

1 Characteristics of Conflicts between Different Nationalities

Analysing this new type of conflict, authors usually distinguish between three forms: territorial, minority, and status (autonomy, independence) conflicts.[1]

1.1 Forms of Conflicts

a) Territorial and Border Disputes

Territorial and border disputes are usually the result of ethnic settlements which do not correspond with administration structures and arbitrarily drawn borders between, for example, republics (in the former Soviet Union or now in the Russian Federation) or other administrative districts within a republic such as Autonomous regions. However, on account of the extremely mixed settlement of different peoples or ethnic groups in parts of Eastern and Southeastern Europe and especially in the former Soviet Union, this correspondence can hardly be achieved. Despite the disintegration of the Soviet Union into 15 independent (nominal) "national" states in December 1991, the potential for conflicts has not decreased. This problem particularly arises in Central Asia and in the crisis areas of North- and Transcaucasus.

Apart from disputed borders another cause for territorial conflicts is the former central migration policy, especially the settlement of Russians in other Soviet Republics. So for instance in Ukraine the existence of a significant number of Russians in the eastern industrial areas and on the Crimean peninsula has already led to serious disputes about secessional ambitions or about uniting these areas with Russia. In total there are about 25 million Russian people living as minorities in the successor states of the Soviet Union.

Another cause for territorial conflicts is the displacement of entire peoples in the Stalin era, for instance Germans and the Crimean Tatars, who now claim their right to return to their former living areas where in the meantime other peoples have settled. The resettlement, for example, of about 250,000 Crimean Tatars on the Crimean peninsula additionally aggravates the conflict between the Ukrainian government and the Russian population. This constellation illustrates, how many questions in connection with territorial and border disputes are still unsolved: Which or whose rights have precedence? Which are the criteria to decide? Is there a historical legitimation for territorial claims? etc.

b) Minority Conflicts

These few examples already show how close territorial and border disputes are connected with minority problems.[2] As mentioned above, it is hardly possible to distribute the more than 130 peoples and ethnic groups living within the territory of the former Soviet Union to "homogeneous" administrative districts under ethnic criteria much less to organise them as independent "national states". Some of the peoples do not even possess a compact settlement area which can be considered the most important condition for nation building. Others would probably not have the economic means to survive. For these reasons each successor state, republic, administrative district or region in the former Soviet Union is confronted with minority problems.

Besides the complex settlement structure another reason for minority conflicts in the successor states of the former Soviet Union is the Soviet nationalities policy which – since Lenin – strove to overcome the national or ethnic differences. This attempt to fuse of all peoples into a unified "Soviet people" underestimated the continuation of ethnic or national identity.[3] Furthermore the eventful history especially of the Caucasus region, innumerable conquests, changing rule among others by Mongols, Persians, Russians, and the Ottoman Empire, prevented peoples from building large or strong national states. For this same reason this region is characterised by religious fragmentation.

The parties involved in minority conflicts usually consist of the majority (in this case ethnic or religious) of the population or the "leading nation" in a state, a republic or an administrative district on the one hand, and more or less numerous (ethnic or religious) minorities on the other. Such conflicts are even more dangerous if the concerned minority is the "leading nation" or majority in a neighbouring state, republic or administrative district or even in a state further away (e.g., Russians in Moldova). If such a so-called "national minority" expects or gets support from its "motherland", this can lead to international tension or even war.

The immediate cause of minority conflicts is usually the factual or supposed discrimination against minorities, which find expression in deficient possibilities of political participation, economic disadvantage, smaller chances for education and social advancement or the prohibition or obstruction to maintain or to practice its own culture, language or religion.[4] If a minority then sees the possibility of changing this status quo – in the Soviet Union for instance especially the process of perestroika gave minorities a chance to at least articulate their interests and to point out their discrimination – it will possibly strive for more autonomy. This can mean cultural autonomy, but it can also mean – either from the beginning of a conflict or in a further stage of an escalating conflict – the request for a greater number of economic, social and political rights and competencies. Finally this process can escalate to the demand for national independence or – in the case of "national minorities" – for uniting with a neighbouring country (for instance Nagorno-Karabakh with Armenia or South-Ossetia/Georgia with North-Ossetia, which means secession from Georgia and affiliation with the Russian Federation). If minorities choose this way to solve their problems, if they strive for greater regional autonomy, conflicts become obvious. Such conflicts often lead to quicken escalation and to radicalisation of demands. Striving for national independence or affiliation with another state can finally lead to violent secession conflicts and civil (or even international) war.

c) Status and Secession Conflicts

As seen above, status and secession conflicts on the one hand are the result of a minority's attempt to solve the problem of factual or supposed discrimination by means of an (enlarged) status of autonomy or even national independence either from the beginning of the conflict or as result of its escalation.

On the other hand, status and secession conflicts can be the consequence of inadequate or deficient federal structures, especially in multinational states like the Soviet Union or in the Russian Federation, where an actual example is given by the Chechen conflict. The claims for sovereignty on the part of the 15 (former) republics of the Soviet Union, designated as "sovereign states" in the Soviet constitution (Art. 76), were incompatible with the sovereignty of the Soviet Union. "Democratic Centralism", the most important element of the organisational structures of the Communist Party as well as the organisational principle of the Soviet state (Art. 3, Soviet constitution), did not only abolish the horizontal separation of legislative power, executive power and jurisdiction. It also undermined vertical decentralisation in the form of federalism. The resolution of the Estonian Supreme Soviet in November 1988 to change the Estonian constitution such that legal norms of the Union could only come into force in Estonia after their approval by the Estonian parliament led to a permanent constitutional conflict. It was the impulse for all other Soviet republics to demand their "sovereignty" in the sense of factual economic and political competencies. It was also the beginning of the decay of the Soviet Union: the declaration of independence of Lithuania in March 1990 was followed by similar declarations by all 14 other republics of the Soviet Union during 1990. "Sovereignty" was explained either as extension of competencies within a union that would have to be reformed (an interpretation of "sovereignty" that was incompatible with Western comprehension of international law) or as national independence.

This type of conflict quickly carried on to subordinated administrative levels: the Union republics themselves were confronted with demands for enlarged autonomy or even independence from the part of their own autonomous republics, oblasts and other administrative districts. However, the republics' governments themselves were not prepared to concede those rights to their own minorities which they required from the Union. In some cases they even tried to suppress such demands by violence. Conflicts of this type were to be found for instance in Russia (Chechnya and others), in Georgia (Abkhazia; South-Ossetia) and in Moldova (Dniestr region); in some sense the Nagorno-Karabakh conflict also belongs to this category.

Secession conflicts get even more complicated if the people or ethnic group giving the name to an administrative district such as an autonomous republic are in the position of a minority even in "their own" district. This is the case not only in many republics and regions of the Russian Federation, but also for instance in the Georgian-Abkhaz conflict: the Abkhaz people makes up less than one fifth of the population of Abkhazia (18%). Besides Armenian and Russian inhabitants the majority of the population of Abkhazia consists of Georgians. In such cases secession would mean that either large groups of population would be left as minority or even as possibly discriminated majority or that great numbers of people would leave the "new" state as refugees.

1.2 Anatomy of Conflicts

The rough distinction between territorial, minority and status conflicts does not adequately portray reality. Generally, territorial and border disputes emerge in or about those regions inhabited by (national) minorities. In turn, minority conflicts can manifest themselves in status conflicts, which can escalate to secession conflicts. Conflicts between different nationalities thus show very complex structures and constellations, the different types of conflict overlap in most of the cases or merge in the course of their escalation. Although the conflicts have much in common, in every single case, in every violent conflict as well as in the case of a potential conflict that might become violent, a great number of specific causes, ethnic or religious aspects, specific historical, economic, social and demographic backgrounds has to be considered for analysing a conflict, for preventing a potential conflict from violent outbreak and – finally – in order to solve it.

a) First, it must be asked which *demographic, economic, social, political, and historical backgrounds* have led or may lead to the outbreak of conflicts:

Where, to what extent and for which reasons do minorities exist (for instance as a consequence of deficient congruency of ethnic settlement and administration structures, due to historically grown, extremely mixed settlement of peoples and ethnic groups, arbitrary determination of borders (especially with disregard of ethnic or national affiliation or identity leading to a great number of large "national" minorities in neighbouring states), the settlement of large groups of population outside their places of origin either due to migration policy or (historically) to displacement)?

Where is a long-term deteriorating economic and social situation – a breeding ground for violence conflicts – to be found or to be expected?

Are there democratic traditions or institutions for peaceful conflict settlement or are they lacking?

b) Further questions have to be focused on possible *immediate causes* for the outbreak of conflicts:

Who has territorial claims or demands for border revisions against whom and for what reasons (for instance historical justification)?

Where is discrimination of minorities to be observed; in the sense of, for instance, inadequate possibilities for political participation, economic, social, and educational disadvantage as well as insufficient chances or obstruction to maintenance of ethnic, cultural or religious identity)?

Which groups (minorities) in which countries complain about such discrimination or claim their rights for adequate political participation, equal economic and social chances and the maintenance of cultural and/or religious identity? It has to be considered that not only the factual, but also a supposed discrimination which exists only in the perception of a minority, can lead to conflict.

Where are complaints about deficient political and/or economic competencies for subordinated administrative units such as republics or regions in multinational states or federations, possibly aggravated by disproportions in economic development or distribution of economic goods?

c) Concerning the *conflict process* the following aspects have to be considered:

Which actors or groups of actors are involved in a conflict: respectively, which groups articulate which demands (oppositional or national movements, political parties, national or ethnic authorities/elites, regional/local authorities like governments of subordinated districts or republics)?

What are their intentions or conceptions for the realisation of their demands (besides the concrete demands for border revision – in certain cases this means especially: achievement and protection of minority rights in the sense of political participation, equal economic and social opportunities and the maintenance of cultural and/or religious identity within a state by means of law, achievement or expansion of territorial cultural, economic and/or political autonomy within federal structures, or even national independence by secession)?

What is the respective reaction of the concerned central government towards the demands in question?

d) Special attention has to be drawn to the great number of possible *intensifying factors* in disputes between nationalities, particularly between a minority and the majority composing the central government:

traditional "historical" tensions between peoples of different ethnic origin due to former conflicts, wars or conquests;

traditional tensions between different religious communities;

in this context the obvious attractiveness of ethnic, national or religious ideas for creating collective identity and solidarity, especially in the situation of declining state authority and growing loss of ideology and/or social orientation;

the consequence of overestimating the importance of ethnic, national or religious identity or – vice versa – disregarding its importance, especially in case of conflicts;

as a result the instrumentalisation or mobilisation of ethnic, national or religious identity by new ethnic, national or religious movements, parties or elites striving for political power or economic advantages;

additionally, economic or ecological factors, the struggle for limited or decreasing resources such as for instance water in dry regions.

The following *main characteristics* of conflicts between nationalities can be summarized:

1. The significant characteristic of disputes between different nationalities is the *combination* of conflict of *identity and conflict of interests*.[5] Consequences of the changes in the Soviet Union in the course of reforms (perestroika) were, among others, the decline of state authority as well as a loss of ideological orientation and social identity. For the necessary creation of a (new) collective identity and solidarity ethnic, national or religious identity turned out to be most attractive. Social groups and especially groups and parties involved in a conflict then tend to define themselves primarily on the basis of a (actually imaginary and vague) feeling of ethnic, cultural or religious solidarity and are often easily inclined to overestimate the importance of this kind of identity. A deteriorating economic and social situation and the decline of authority and state structures which form the background for redistribution or reallocation of political power and economic goods, then make it possible for certain pressure groups (ethnic, national or religious movements, parties and new elites or groups just using the ethnic, national or religious label) striving for political power or economic advantages to instrumentalize and to mobilize ethnic, national or religious identity to achieve their own aims and to realize their own interests. Along with the *ethnic component* of conflict comes a "traditional" *struggle for power* and a "traditional" *distribution conflict*. So the ethnic component of such conflicts obviously is not the *cause* of conflict, but as long as people define their identity along ethnic criteria, as long

as this identity seems to be the most attractive, and as long as this kind of identity can be easily mobilized and instrumentalized by pressure groups, especially in case of (for instance external military or internal economic) threat, this factor has to be considered as serious and important.
2. Due to the (subjective and emotional) overestimation of ethnic, national, cultural or religious identity, conflicts between different nationalities are also characterized by a great deal of *irrationality*, expressing itself in a great potential of aggressiveness, brutality, hatred, and enmity even exceeding rational interests and demands.
3. Characteristics of the *conflict process* are a *high potential of escalation* with a *quick escalation* and its typical dynamics, again primarily due to irrationality.
4. Even rational demands escalate quickly, for instance from cultural to economic and political autonomy and finally to national independence, which in some cases must be called irrational as well considering the economic capacity of some of those (potential) new states.

In general, the main characteristic of conflicts between different nationalities is their *complexity* as a whole: the complexity of historical, political, social and economic backgrounds, of immediate causes, of actors, their aims and interests, and of intensifying factors, their overlapping and merging territorial, minority, and status questions and problems.

This complexity shows that it is impossible to find easy solutions for such conflicts. In every single case all specific characteristics have to be analysed.

2 Conflict Settlement: Obstacles and Chances

2.1 *Problems and Obstacles to the Settlement of Conflicts between Different Nationalities*

As seen above, conflicts between different nationalities are primarily an example of numerous obstacles to the settlement of disputes rather than an example for their peaceful settlement. These inherent obstacles are not only a hindrance to the *internal* settlement of such conflicts, for the necessary initiation of negotiations between the parties involved in a conflict by themselves, but also for *international* efforts to influence and solve the conflict either by means of the instruments of peaceful settlement of disputes or by peacekeeping operations or by means of military actions.

The complexity of potential conflict causes and issues obstruct the pure fact-finding: the real reasons, the aims of the involved parties, the matters of conflict. The complexity of historical and political backgrounds hinder the clarification of general questions like the legitimacy of territorial claims, the legitimacy of secession, the legitimacy of national independence or affiliation to another administrative district, republic or state. The complexity of conflict main characteristics and intensifying factors obstruct a peaceful and quick settlement.

The great potential for escalation and the sometimes sudden outbreak of violence (pogroms, fightings and incursions by paramilitary, guerrilla or volunteer troops etc.) makes it difficult to find out at what particular time a dispute becomes a violent conflict, at what particular time a third party could offer help by suggesting negotiations or by means of mediation, or to determine definitely who is the "aggressor", and against whom certain measures should be taken. The number of involved parties (not only regular governments, but also leaders, self made or illegally elected "presidents" of regions and districts prepared for secession, leaders of guerrilla or paramilitary troops etc.) makes it difficult to find the relevant persons to address for negotiations or for attempts at mediation from a third party. The characteristic aspect of irrationality obstructs negotiations because of insufficient willingness to compromise on all sides or could even prevent them if one party does not accept another as negotiation party. In this context, in armed conflicts as well as before the outbreak of violence, it has to be considered who are the "relevant" conflict parties that may, can or have to take part in peace negotiations, that should or must agree with planned measures of conflict settlement, for instance the deployment of peacekeeping forces. If one party is excluded from negotiations or has not been asked for its agreement to certain measures, this may lead to non-acceptance of negotiation results and decisions, for instance of armistice agreements, which then are meaningless, even if international law does not necessitate participation.

The number of armed units involved in fighting is often unclear: regular government forces as well as their opponents (for instance "national guards") are supported by a number of guerrilla, volunteer and paramilitary troops which often leads to completely unclear command structures. Sometimes governments have little or no influence even on the commanding officers of government forces. For that reason armistice agreements, indispensable precondition for instance for peacekeeping operations, are permanently unstable and insecure. Unclear front lines often running through the middle of towns and villages, broken terrain (for instance in Northern Caucasus, in Nagorno-Karabakh or in Georgia) additionally obstruct the deployment of peacekeeping forces as well as peace enforcement actions.[6]

Obviously most of the characteristics of such conflicts are serious obstacles to conflict settlement by negotiation too. Nevertheless negotiations are the only appropriate alternative to solve the complex problems characterizing such conflicts in comparison with military action by the parties involved as well as international military action. Because of the irrationality commonly accompanying such conflicts the parties involved often are not able to go this route by themselves. At this point, the settlement of disputes by negotiations, international efforts should set in.

2.2 Possibilities of International Peaceful Settlement of Disputes in (Internal) Conflicts between Different Nationalities

The conflicts in question usually are internal conflicts or civil wars which can become international conflicts or wars if one of the parties, for instance a minority striving for secession, gets support from another state, especially from a state where the (ethnic or religious) majority or leading nation has good relations with the concerned minority. Furthermore such conflicts could become international if the international community of states accepts the secession of a region (republic, district etc.) and recognises it as a (new) state.

For international action in the case of internal conflicts in general there is a contradiction between territorial integrity and national sovereignty, which means non-intervention in internal affairs on the one hand and the right of self-determination of peoples, the protection of minority rights, the global responsibility for the prevention of war and violation of human rights on the other hand as principles of international law. Therefore in the case of internal conflicts it has to be distinguished between *formal* and *informal* possibilities of peaceful settlement of disputes.

Some remarks concerning the right of self-determination in the sense of the right to secession should be made. In international practice, as well as in the interpretation of international law by the majority of states, the principle of territorial integrity of states has precedence over the right of self-determination of peoples insofar as self-determination should be realized within the constitutional frame of existing states rather than by secession. The right of self-determination does not automatically mean the right of building an own and independent national state.[7] One of the political reasons for this attitude is the idea that a greater number of national states would detract from international cooperation as well as enlarge the traditional dilemma of international security resulting from the existence of national states. Faced with 2,500-6,000 ethnic groups worldwide who could theoretically claim their own national state it seems to be a sensible idea to reject secession in most cases. Without excluding the long-term possibility of peaceful change it must also be considered that secession always means the loss of a certain part of state territory which will normally not proceed without conflict.[8] Of course this must not legitimate the preservation of territorial integrity by force or by military means. Moreover this attitude requires the constitutional and practical protection of minority and human rights within (multinational) states and also international responsibility in case of conflict.

In the case of internal conflicts there are only a few formal possibilities for international intervention or binding regulations for taking measures without the agreement of the concerned state. At the regional level for instance, apart from some (limited) competencies of the High Commissioner on National Minorities, mainly two OSCE-procedures have to be taken into consideration: the "mechanism for consultation and co-operation with regard to emergency situations" and the "Human Dimension Mechanism".[9]

However, considering their long duration as well as their limited applicability and effects, these instruments seem to not be appropriate for *acute* and *violent* conflicts in one of the OSCE-participating states.

Furthermore OSCE-resolutions and agreements are only politically binding, but not binding by international law and cannot be forced.

As long as states remain the actors in international relations, at least those facing internal problems – for instance strong, maybe militant oppositional movements or minority problems – they will not give up the principle of non-intervention in internal affairs nor will they permit establishing binding rules for the settlement of internal disputes. On the other hand, the actual conflicts in Eastern Europe and the CIS, already armed or still latent, are in a stage that does not allow waiting for changes in international law. So the remaining possibility is the *informal* way to influence the conflict parties. This means, primarily, seriously and repeatedly urging the parties involved to use the existing instruments of peaceful settlement of disputes that can be called upon voluntarily and at every time. These are, for instance, *good offices*, where a third party tries to initiate direct negotiations between the conflict partners without participating itself, or the procedure of *mediation* by a third party by participating in these negotiations and making suggestions for solving the conflict, etc. These offers have to be permanently repeated, perhaps accompanied by economic incentives. Intensive negotiations and mediation between the conflict parties, witnessed or at least initiated by a neutral third party, should start as long as a minority (or a region, administrative district, etc.) is not yet striving for secession, but would still agree to, for instance, governmental and institutional guarantees for the protection of their rights or to federal structures; at the latest, however, after a unilateral declaration of independence, for instance. If negotiations have started, the participation of all relevant parties involved in a conflict is desirable. Those who reject one of the parties as a negotiating party (for instance Azerbaijan for a long time rejected the participation of Armenians from Nagorno-Karabakh and only accepted Armenians from the Armenian republic as negotiating partners) should be urged to accept them. If one side feels excluded or isolated, it may undermine decisions and agreements such as armistice agreements so that violence would most likely continue. So, for instance, Russia, mediating in the Abkhaz-Georgian conflict, invited to the negotiations not only Georgian and Abkhaz politicians, but even representatives of the North-Caucasus republics involved in the fightings. Doing so, chances achieving compromises and agreements kept by all sides increase.

For this purpose, however, international institutions and organisations, such as OSCE and UNO, urgently require much more financial means as well as skilled and permanent staff, such as regionally specialized so-called "preventive diplomacy teams",[10] in order to identify potential conflicts, to gather information about each single dispute and to observe it continuously. Then, in case of the outbreak of a conflict, certain groups consisting of experienced experts already familiarized with a conflict would be available for conflict regulation.

The necessary elaboration of long-term plans for conflict regulation should be based on international participation in solving internal conflicts, at least in the sense of employing the mentioned instruments of peaceful settlement of disputes and offering them for voluntary use. Apart from the intensified use of the existing procedures and mechanisms this might also mean their further structural and institutional development in the sense of changing international law and restricting national sovereignty; for instance, by subjecting conflicts to obligatory and binding international arbitration. As already mentioned, these changes in international law are not to be expected in the near future.

2.3 Long-term Preventive Measures for Peaceful Conflict Settlement

Apart from short-term (international) conflict regulation, long-term developments for conflict prevention – or better still: for *preventing conflicts from becoming violent* – are necessary and can and must be supported by the international community. Long-term prevention of violence and violent conflict settlement requires *structural circumstances* that allow for a peaceful settlement of disputes and prevent conflicts from escalation, reducing the causes of violence.

For the long-term stabilization of societies that had been under authoritarian rule for decades, a profound and permanent process of *democratization* is necessary in order to build up institutions in which different social groups – including, among others, ethnic and religious minorities – can express their interests, can realize them peacefully or can come to compromises which are protected institutionally. Such processes, the development of democratic and juridical institutions and procedures, including for instance the elaboration and implementation of a constitution and free elections, have to be supported by the international community of states (as is the task of the CSCE-mission in Georgia, for instance).

Another step to long-term prevention of violent conflict settlement could be the *federalization* of centralized states, especially centralized multinational states, conceding to the members of federation certain competencies for maintaining ethnic or national identity, but also competencies relating to economic and domestic affairs in order to prevent secession conflicts. Federalisation in the sense of vertical decentralisation has two main functions: vertical separation of power and at the same time integration of heterogeneous societies.

As mentioned above, within the territory of the former Soviet Union and in the successor states it is hardly possible to determine the borders of administrative districts in accordance with ethnic settlement. Therefore a third preventive measure for peaceful settlement of disputes is an effective *protection of minorities*. A real improvement and exemplary in this matter is the Copenhagen Document about the Human Dimension of CSCE from 1990, even though it is not obligatory in the sense of international law, but only politically binding.

Another essential precondition for non-violent conflict settlement is the *economic stabilization* of the successor states, the building up of functioning national economies that allow people to provide for their elemental social and economic necessities. Also in this respect the international community has to offer their support.

In certain cases, as in the case of national minorities which are the leading nation in a neighbouring state or district, it is even conceivable to *revise borders* in the sense of *peaceful change*. However, this can only be done in a peaceful manner if the relations between the concerned states are absolutely free from any problems. For the time being, this would not be a solution in or between the successor state of the former Soviet Union.

In general, *integration in international structures* is a necessary support for democratic and economic development in Eastern Europe and the Commonwealth of Independent States. In this sense it can also be a future frame for the peaceful settlement of conflicts.

The above-mentioned measures for the prevention from violent settlement of conflicts have to be necessarily and permanently developed. However, under today's circumstances in Eastern Europe and the CIS they will take far too long to settle the actual violent or potential conflicts in that region. Not only on account of the actual conflict stages, but also on account of the most probably long duration of those necessary processes in Eastern Europe and especially in the CIS, *instruments of peaceful settlement of disputes* additionally have to be employed.

3   Conclusion

The complexity of conflicts between different nationalities, the combination of conflict of interest and conflict of identity, the multiplicity of immediate causes, of demographic, historical, political, and economic backgrounds as well as of intensifying factors make it impossible to find easy solutions. The mobilisation of ethnic, national or religious identity – and not the aspect of identity itself – aggravates such conflicts and leads to a high potential of aggressiveness and escalation.

Besides the limited possibilities of short-term settlement of disputes by international organisations and institutions such as the United Nations and the OSCE, the essential requirement is the creation of structural preconditions for peaceful conflict settlement: democratisation, economic stabilization, and an effective protection of minorities and human rights. Their realization requires not only extensive financial support and the supply of functional knowledge; with respect to Eastern Europe, to the Commonwealth of Independent States, and especially with respect to the Russian Federation it requires first of all the long-term integration in international and European economic and political structures in order to help them create the institutional and economic preconditions for internal and external peaceful conflict settlement.

Notes

[1] See for instance: Jahn, Egbert and Barbara Maier. Das Scheitern der sowjetischen Unionserneuerung: HSFK-Report, Frankfurt a.M., 2/1992; Davidov, Juri P. and Dmitri W. Trenin, "Ethnische Konflikte auf dem Gebiet der ehemaligen Sowjetunion", Europa-Archiv 7:172-192 (1993); Brunner, Georg. Nationalitätenprobleme und Minderheitenkonflikte in Osteuropa: Bertelsmann Stiftung, Gütersloh, 1993; Boucher, Jerry, Dan Landis, and Karen Arnold Clark (Eds.). Ethnic Conflict. International Perspectives: Sage Publications, London, 1987.

[2] "Minority" in this context is to be understood as ethnic or, e.g., religious minority. The term "national minority" means an ethnic group living as a minority in one state, but representing the majority or "leading nation" in another (usually neighbouring) state, such as for instance Armenians in Azerbaijan, Uzbeks in Kyrgyzstan and vice versa, etc. On the whole, the term "minority" is still highly disputed in political debates as well as relating to international law. See for instance Heintze, Hans-Joachim. Selbstbestimmungsrecht und Minderheitenrechte im Völkerrecht: Nomos, Baden-Baden, 1994.

[3] See for instance Gitelmann, Zvi (Ed.). The Politics of Nationality and the Erosion of the USSR: St. Martin's Press, New York, 1992; Simon, Gerhard. Nationalismus und Nationalitätenpolitik in der Sowjetunion: Nomos, Baden-Baden, 1986; Smith, Anthony D. National Identity: Penguin Books, London, 1991.

[4] See Waldmann, Peter. Ethnischer Radikalismus. Ursachen und Folgen gewaltsamer Minderheitenkonflikte: Westdeutscher Verlag, Opladen, 1989, esp. p. 19.

[5] See Senghaas, Dieter. Friedensprojekt Europa: Suhrkamp, Frankfurt a.M., 1992, esp. pp. 117-138.

[6] It has to be remarked that military actions, inititated by the concerned state itself, for instance, in the case of secessional conflicts (as in Chechnya), as well as under international rule, in any case means an escalation and is never likely to eliminate the complex causes of conflicts and to solve the relevant problems.

[7] For the interpretation of self-determination in international law see for instance: Verdross, Alfred and Bruno Simma. Universelles Völkerrecht. Theorie und Praxis: Duncker und Humblot, Berlin, 1984, pp. 319-320; For discussion see for instance: Glotz, Peter. Der Irrweg des Nationalstaates: Deutsche Verlags-Anstalt, Stuttgart, 1990.

[8] See for instance Schlotter, Peter, Norbert Ropers, and Berthold Meyer. Die neue KSZE. Zukunftsperspektiven einer regionalen Friedensstragie: Leske und Budrich, Opladen, 1994, esp. pp. 80-81.

[9] See Bloed, Arie (Ed.). The Conference on Security and Co-operation in Europe. Analysis and Basic Documents, 1972-1993: Kluwer Academic Publishers, Dordrecht, Boston, London, 1993, pp. 31-33 and pp. 40-44.

[10] See Evans, Gareth. Cooperating for Peace: Allen and Unwin, St. Leonards 1993, esp. pp. 71-75.

3 Reducing Ethnic Conflicts
Contemporary Approaches to Conflict Resolution in Western Europe

ALBERT F. REITERER

1 Introduction: Democratic Theory as Theory of Conflictual Convivality

Let me begin with some basic remarks. "Society means conflict about scarce resources. But free society means open, regulated and non-annihilating conflict" (Dahrendorf 1972, 7). We are interested in the specific set of rules for conflict-solving which is authoritatively enforced by the power of institutions. The main framework for internal peaceful conflict regulation in modern societies is the state and its institutions. A theory of democracy, thus, will center around the societal facts of power – it must therefore consider conflict as its paramount concern. But as a *democratic* theory it will aim to investigate conflict solution and its mechanisms: democracy – and this is to be seen as one of its most prominent features which will guarantee the working of democratically organized political systems – is structured as a mechanism for *limiting conflict*.

One of the above mentioned rules is considered to be fundamental for a democracy. It is universally accepted, and is for the most part, unchallenged: the majority rule. In conflicting issues the majority should decide about the direction to follow, and the minority gives in. Here the problems begin.

"Is it possible for minority groups to be secure in a country in which democratic procedures allow the majority to take whatever repressive measures it sees fit?" (Hunt/Walker 1979, 21). The majority-rule is a *procedure*, and not a value. *Self-determination* is to be seen as the fundamental value of democracy. "What is the status of majority rule if (1) the unity of the state is not universally acknowledged, (2) all citizens are not, in fact, politically equal, and (3) the political process is not absolutely open and free" (Walzer 1970, 47). Or, as has been said concerning one of the most thorny issues of contemporary international relations which is at the same time a difficult piece of majority – minority relations: "*'Security'* is the central problem in the Cyprus dispute" (Poliviou 1980, 220).

This is by no means a new problem and not only a problem of ethnic or national minorities. It concerns the very existence of political communities and their stability. We can restate what Locke has said about the only option oppressed people have if reduced to its own force: "Where the body of the people, or any single man, is deprived of their right, ...there *they have liberty to appeal to heaven* [that is: to wage war against the oppressor – italics of Locke], whenever they judge the cause of sufficient moment", that is, when the oppressed have "no judge on earth" (Locke 1965 [1690], § 168).

It is quite clear that personal self-determination and the majority rule contradict each other. If we follow *Weber* and *Luhmann* and define power as one person's ability to decide about other persons' actions and behaviour, then, obviously, the majority exercises power concerning the minority's conduct. There seems to be a priori, a dead-end-situation in democracy. The classical writers were well aware of it and they tried to solve the problem in quite different ways. The best known approach is *Rousseau's volonté générale* (general will) as opposed to the majority will. Another proposal is the utilitarian *maximizing principle*. In contemporary thought Rousseau seems to have developed a void concept; and the utilitarian view seems quite unacceptable, not only to liberals.

So, what are the foundations we are to build upon? Generally we are inclined to accept the majority rule as a valid procedure. However, why should we do this in terms of an ethical-political justification, and not in terms of a pragmatic approach for solving day-to-day issues? In short, we are asking for the legitimacy of our political order and its basic procedures.

Obviously, it is not enough to share the same interests, because interests do change. Today, I may agree, tomorrow I shall dissent on specific issues or with particular institutions. If I am to accept to be in a minority position, that is on the side which loses, there are some basic presuppositions:

1) *First, I must have the chance to become the majority position.*
   While this usually applies to political minorities, it proves to be

extremely difficult for ethnic or national minorities if they define themselves primarily in terms of identity (that is ethnicity) instead of interests.
2) If I should accept to belong to the minority of today I must be sure that my vital interests are not harmed. My chances of surviving must remain intact. In order to be sure, the political majority and the minority must share the same basic values. They must constitute some form, or some degree, of a *community*. Hence, a communitarian element is vital for the constitution of a polity, a political community. This said, I must add hurriedly that community does not, by any means, necessarily mean an ascribed one or a community of birth. Most sociologists agree that modernity demands that communities be communities of choice.

Besides, this reasoning also gives credit to some utilitarian features of democratic theory, opposed as communitarianism seems to be to utilitarianism. In fact, the majority principle as democratic procedure cannot be justified without any recourse to utility maximizing. The necessary condition for such a comparing and accounting of individual utilities is the assumption that there are shared values in the polity. This is critical to every analytical approach to democratic theory.

Ethnic Conflicts

Ethnic conflicts as "protracted conflicts" (Crighton/MacIver 1991) are not only conflicts between competing interests, but are also identity-driven. This means there is an underlying "fear of extinction", fueled often by memories of century-old massacres and other horrible events in the history of mutual relations.

As we are all aware, the national conflict is one of the most enduring conflicts in modern times. It can be considered the crudest and least ideologically elaborated form of political conflicts in emerging democracies. This can be demonstrated best in recent conflicts in Eastern Europe. There are many causes to be enumerated. I want to restrict myself to one aspect. It is the *lack of institutions* adapted to reducing political conflicts in a civic manner in the social systems of these states. So called Socialism has been constructed in such a way as to avoid the emergence of conflicts, although ironically enough it based on the ideological concept of class struggle political as well as social, and all forms of their public utterances. Thus, as the system collapsed, there was no institutionalized possibility for formulating conflictual views of alternatives and, of course, no possibilities of limiting the emerging aggression between social forces with antagonistic views concerning the future of states and societies. As the socialist countries faded away, the newly emerging party system didn't serve as mechanism to formulate competing views. In the process of systemic transformation it served only to sharpen and to antagonize social and political cleavages.

J. S. Mill (1975 [1861]) at his time has enumerated a number of preconditions for a "system of representative government", as he denominates the political regime he is striving for, and we have baptized democracy indiscriminately. First, as an essential condition he speaks of an elaborate process of *civilization*, in the sense this concept is used nearly a hundred years later by *Norbert Elias* (1976); resulting from this process he calls for a "democratic personality" ("the individual qualities of the citizen"); and finally, he cites constraints of a more technical or organizational nature (an efficient system of communications: "physical conditions for the formation and propagation of a public opinion", p. 151). All these preconditions – with the important exception of the almost universal approval of free elections – are lacking in Eastern European countries. Meanwhile people unfortunately tend to also look at free elections with much less esteem than they did five years ago. The widespread disappointment seems so entrenched as to materialize in distrust of democratic procedures, or parliamentary institutions, in general. This is a dangerous point of view leading at best to populism and at worst to a new dictatorship. You need only to think of such authoritarian personalities as Lech Walesa and Boris Yeltsin...

Mill is by far superior to his contemporaries. He conceives of nationality as an *option*: The affiliation to a nation is seen as a voluntaristic act. The counterposition to that conceives nationality as *ascriptive* – and choosing to express nationalism this way means a very rational approach compared to current mythical concepts like community of common ancestry and the like – is pronounced. Thus, we see Mill in the tradition of the enlightenment, above all in the tradition of French rationalism.

"One hardly knows what any division of the human race should be free to do, if not to determine, with which of the various collective bodies of human beings they choose to associate themselves" (Mill 1975 [1861], 381). This reasonable question at the same time shows the wide gap separating *Mill's* reasoning from contemporary political thought. It is the rationalism which springs up to one's eyes. However, this rationalism is his weak point, too. The nation as a possibility to select one's own societal membership is a reality only for a few *individuals*; most human beings consider themselves to be born into a nation with which they are fatally connected – perhaps against their will. The idea that they themselves chose their national allegiance must seem strange to most of them. So nationality for most people must be considered an *ascribed comprehensive role*. The "fight for a national identity" ordinarily is not a struggle between individuals, but between social groups with competing claims. Ethnicities become nations either by becoming hegemonious or by becoming subject to other ethnic nations. If we investigate the seemingly lucid concepts of *Mill*, they reveal themselves as being of normative rather than of analytical value.

This brings us to the most important issue this paper tries to face: If you look at the conditions for representative democracy in general, enumerated by *Mill*, you have many of the features for the political culture that has been called *consociational democracy*.

Consociational Democracy as a Formula for Ethnic Peace?

Arend Lijphart (1977; 1984) has stated a model which is called *consociational democracy*. This model is drawn from the political experiences of some Western European countries lacerated in former times (especially the interwar-period) by fundamental social and political conflicts. *Lijphart* starts with the concept of the *plural society*. Now it is of great importance to know that this concept has been developed by a social scientist formerly employed in colonial administration (Furnival 1939, 1948). The situation there basically could be described by the picture of two sharply divided groups in the population inhabiting the same territory: the colonial masters and the colonial subjects' overwhelming majority. Each group has its own religion, its own culture, and its own habits of life. They don't develop contact as individuals, they meet each other only in their characteristics as sellers and purchasers on the market-place. Few of them acknowledge that there are some common material interests, most of them tend to see their interests as opposed, indeed, as antagonistic (Furnivall 1948, 304). Of course, *Lijphart's* plural society is not the colonial society of the '30s and '40s, but the society he is familiar with in the European history in the first half of 20th century. *Lijphart* is concerned exclusively with democratically organized polities. However, there is a basic similarity between *Furnival's* and *Lijphart's* plural society: "A plural society is a society divided by ... 'segmental cleavages' (Harry Eckstein): 'This exists where political divisions follow very closely, and especially concern, lines of objective social differentiation'" (Lijphart 1977, 3). It seems to me of utmost importance to draw the reader's attention to the point that the concept of the plural society originally has been designed for analyzing problems of ethnic convivality.

The basic preconditions of *Lijphart's* approach to models for reducing conflict in such plural societies are: political elites must be willing to cooperate in a peaceful manner; they must be ready to acknowledge the vital interests of their political counterparts whereby "vital" are those interests which are defined as vital by their opponents. The perhaps politically unorganized but interested masses must follow them in this spirit of tolerance and co-operation, even if there is a clearcut numerical *majority* and *minority*. To state this Liphart's his own words: "concordant democracy [is] a strategy of conflict management by cooperation and agreement among the different elites rather than by competition and majority decision" (p. 3). "Because of the tenacity of primordial loyalties, any effort to eradicate them not only is quite unlikely to succeed, especially in the short run, but may well be counterproductive and may stimulate segmental cohesion and intersegmental violence rather than national cohesion" (p. 24). "Consociational democracy can be defined in terms of four characteristics. The *first* and most important is government by a grand coalition of all the political leaders of all the significant segments of the plural society... The other three basic elements ... are (1) the *mutual veto* or 'concurrent majority rule' which serves as an additional protection of vital minority interests; (2) *proportionality* as the principal standard of political representation, civil service appointments, and allocation of public funds, and (3) a high degree of autonomy for each segment to run its internal affairs" (p. 25).

The terms "majority" and "minority" are meant by *Lijphart* in a political sense. However, if we want to be rational and not give in to the various nationalisms and ethnic ideologies, we must concede that there is only one important difference between political and ethnic/national groups of different size and power: nations and ethnic groups are primarily defined in terms of ethnic *identity* while political parties tend to see themselves in terms of specific *interests*. This difference is a minor one if you consider that many political parties define themselves in terms of a uniquely conceived political identity ("socialism", "christian values", "liberalism", etc.). This was exactly the situation to which the model of consociational democracy was adapted. So, consociational democracy would be the ideal mean of conflict solution in national or ethnic relations.

I want to stress that, in my view, the two fundamental features – namely the will of the political elites to cooperate while tolerating the others and the institutions for this purpose – *are lacking in Eastern Europe*. Let us remember another remark, quoted by *Lijphart* (1977, 142), and which seems to be written especially for nationalist Eastern European politicians and, more generally, for all those who tend to see "communalism", "subnationalism", or whatsoever, as the single most important danger to their societies and states. "The stability of culturally plural societies is threatened not by communalism per se, but by the failure of national institutions explicitly to recognize and accommodate existing communal divisions and interest" (Melson/Wolpe [1970]).

Before taking these examples into consideration, we have to ask: What is ethnicity? What is nationalism?

2   Ethnicity and Identity: Conceptual Premises

Identity and interest are analytical categories, i.e. scientific tools for a better understanding of contemporary social reality. Both influence each other – indeed, the two factors are merely two strategies to face the world and its complexity. The boundaries (that is: the identity-bound *self-definition*) of ethnic groups shift in accordance with the interests of the group: in the short run these interest will decide whether a person is recognized as "belonging" to "us". On other hand, it is identity which engenders certain interests. Identity e.g. is the background for demanding the costly implementation of bilingual education, or of education in a language other than that of the majority of the country. (There may be some social and economic interest related also to questions of bilingual education. Who will teach the children and get the often scarce job of a teacher? etc.)

Ethnicity as Life World

We propose to understand ethnicity as a *universal category* in the historical development of human society (societies). Ethnicity, ontogenetically, is ordinarily the first social identity achieved by human beings. Thus, it can be conceived as "primordial", of fundamental importance for other identities and, if competing with them, taking the first place among them. If we use the term "ontogenetic", we mean by this terminological designation to give a hint to the *microsocial feature* of this identity which, although anchored in communities, have little similarity with ethnicities or with nations. In this sense ethnicity is the single most important structure of collective identity since humankind's beginning.

Identity first is the psychic organization of the individual person used to coordinate his mental and psychic functions. However, identity is not only of personal but of social value too. By socially controlled personal identity the individual person is integrated into society. Identity in this sense is a relation to other members of my own society, and to members of other societies as well. It is the very core of what we ordinarily label *subjectivity*, that is, the human person as constituent part of society. *Life-worlds*, identities, are not incidental to human society, they are indeed unavoidable individual and social realities. They determine how the outer and the social world is perceived and structured. Ethnicity is a *structure of relevance* (Schütz 1982) for the ethnic group concerned.

Ethnicity designates a corporation or group of persons "relating to which we are subjects of a common (social) environment... The persons belonging to this corporation are given to each other as 'fellow-men' and as 'co-persons', they are not objects for each other but subjects who live 'together', are related to each other, communicate with each other" (Husserl 1984, 21 and 25). Only those 'co-persons', those 'fellow-men', who share with each other their mutual life-world, recognize themselves mutually as co-humans of equal value. "All experience of social reality is founded on the fundamental axiom positing the existence of other beings 'like me'... I immediately perceive another man only if he shares a sector of the life-world's space and of world time in common with me" (Schütz/Luckmann 1973). The following rather lengthy quotation, taken from *Schütz* and *Luckmann* (1973, 3-4), is perhaps the best description of ethnicity in its original structure we can find, although *Schütz* and *Luckmann* did not think of ethnicity while writing down these sentences. "The everyday life-world is the region of reality in which man can engage himself and which he can change while he operates in it by means of his animate organism... Only within this reality can one be understood by his fellow-men, and only in it can he work together with them. Only in the world of everyday life can a common, communicative, surrounding world be constituted... In the natural attitude I always find myself in a world which is for me taken for granted and self-evidently 'real'. I was born into it and I assume that it existed before me. It is the unexamined ground for everything given in my experience, as it were, the taken-for-granted frame in which all the problems which I must overcome are placed. This world appears to me in coherent arrangements of well-circumscribed Objects having determinate properties... Moreover, I simply take it for granted that other men also exist in this my world and indeed not only in a bodily manner like and among other objects, but rather as endowed with a consciousness that is essentially the same as mine. Thus from the outset, my life-world is not my private world but, rather, it is intersubjective; the fundamental structure of its reality is that is shared by us... Furthermore, I take for granted that the significance of this 'natural world' (which was already experienced, mastered, and named out by our predecessors) is fundamentally the same for my fellow-men as for me, since it is brought in a common frame of interpretation."

If we take ethnicity this way as a life-world, then all the old misconceptions are not difficult to master. This applies especially to all biological or naturalistic concepts. The "community of birth and ancestry", e.g., dissolves in a common frame of reference into which we are ordinarily born, surely. But this being born into a group of co-humans is contingent to the structure of ethnicity. The same is valid for "kinship". Of course, kinship is the most important structure for analyzing small segmented societies because in this case kinship constitutes the societal structure for these groups. But the moment societies are structured by other devices – as is the case in all societies embracing more than a few thousand men – kinship becomes a micro-social relation which has nothing to do with ethnicity. Thus, *van den Berghe's* foundation of ethnicity on the infamous "egotist gene" – which he calls the "nepotist gene", for the sake of originality – is merely ideology rooted in Social-Darwinism.

In the process of successfully building a nation the micro-solidarity of persons in small groups is transferred from many very small units to a few greater societies. This process means, of course, the weakening of the original solidarity in the sense that it must acquire a more abstract character. This is a necessity because in societies of millions of members the "natural world" of which *Schütz* and *Luckmann* spoke can not be extended to all those millions. Thus, the original ethnicity in segmented societies must not be taken for the form of ethnicity in modern societies, that is, in societies we are ordinarily concerned with. Here, we have to distinguish the identitarian structure of ethnicity and the political structure of nationality as a "community" of shared interests. However, the co-nationals must be recognized as equals as they maintain the same identity. Only the recognition of the fundamental equality in national relations is accepted as fairness and justice: "In a fair society equal rights for all who belong to it are supposed. About these rights based upon justice there can be no bargaining and no compromising" (Rawls 1979, 20).

Drawing boundaries between *specific* ethnic groups, of course, is not, and has never been, a fact of historical necessity. On the contrary, similar to the problems of delimiting the size of nations and deciding who belongs to this nation, it is mostly dependent on political accidents. It is purely a question of *socio-political power*. There is nothing natural or artificial in these processes. Boundaries between ethnic groups are dependent upon social and political interests and can be instrumentalized in their turn for such interests, as stated above. If societies are differentiated and various limited social and political structures can be recognized (this means for the individual person that he/she can select different "roles"), there is obviously a plausible and probable possibility that boundaries between ethnicities are drawn where several or most "cleavages" coincide. As identities are definitions of the possible roles, those roles will tend to coincide into a comprehensive role. Human beings who fulfill these coinciding roles will tend to see them as inseparable and to identify them with ethnic membership. In this moment their interests have become *ethnicized*, although these interests do not necessarily have ethnically tinged features.

The nation gives legitimation to the power of the state. And it especially legitimizes the drawing of borderlines between different populations. It is this legitimation which enables the nation-state to authoritatively regulate social relations. That is to say, it is essential to belong to the ethnonational community. Being or becoming a citizen depends on this fact. You must be included in an ethnic or national society if you want to get all the attributes of political trustworthiness.

"The idea of distributive justice presupposes a bounded world within which distributions take place: a group of people committed to dividing, exchanging and sharing social goods, first of all among themselves. That world [...] is the political community, whose members distribute power to one another and avoid, if they possibly can, sharing it with anyone else. When we think about distributive justice, we think about independent cities or countries capable of arranging their own patterns of division and exchange, justly or unjustly. We assume an established group and a fixed population, and so we miss the first and most important distributive question: How is that group constituted? ... The primary good that we distribute to one another is membership in some human community" (Walzer 1992).

3 Minorities

Ethnic tensions are often expressed in relations of minorities to a majority. What is a minority? It is evidently insufficient merely to answer: "a group smaller in number than the majority". Minority in the first instance does not signify the smaller number, but rather *a group with lesser power*, and sometimes with lesser rights, a group, whom the majority, i.e., the ruling sector, claims to dominate. It is this hegemonic relation between majority and minority which defines a minority, irrespective of its specific characteristics. *Schermerhorn* (1970) thus defines a minority by applying two dimensions: the number, and the power.

Table 1: Relationship between number and power

		dominance	
		powerful	not powerful
number	great	*majority*	*oppressed*
	small	*élite*	MINORITY

It was not until the advent of the modern parliamentary states that minority came to also mean "smaller in number". The fundamental principle of majority rule became the legitimizer of political decision-making. As a consequence, the numerical majority by definition became the dominant group in the population.

Human rights-based minority policy can only have one single comprehensive purpose: the minorities must cease to be minorities in the analytical sense of the concept. An example of the mood in the newly created nation-states in Eastern Europe is an author who writes in a reproaching manner: "It is a characteristic of this group [the Russians in the Baltic States] that it lacks an awareness of being a minority... At present nobody is doing anything to develop this consciousness" (Vebers 1993, 188). Thus, the repressive policies towards the minorities – not only the Russians – in the Baltics will not surprise. The *Language Law* of Latvia (March 31, 1992) mentions the Latgalian Language (considered as ancestors of modern Latvian) to be protected, and that of the Livs; you would search in vain for the Russian in this Law. In fact, Latvian is dealt with like a minority language. [1]

4 Case-Studies in Ethnic Conflict Management

Institutional Means for Managing Ethnic Conflicts

Let me first state clearly: I am dealing here almost exclusively with institutional means for lowering the intensity of ethnic conflict – for permanent conflict-management, and not for "solving", once and for all, ethnic conflicts. That is: I am dealing with the *macro-social and -political* level of ethnic conflict. However, as we all know, ethnic conflict has, more than most other fields of conflict, a micro-social character too. It is very often a conflict between individual persons of popular strata. Of course, we are all aware, at least if actively aware, that ethnic conflict as a political conflict is instrumentalized most times by a small proportion of the population. But it is this small proportion which is responsible for the political culture in a multi-ethnic or -national state. Thus, we must not forget that institutional means will do their work only if they succeed in transforming individual attitudes from open enmity to some sort of rational behaviour between materially competing members of the same "community of communities". If this target is missed, the institutional means applied must be considered a failure.

Nevertheless, institutional means are indispensable in a political system, as the concept itself tells us. An institution, in the sociological sense of the word, is a set of attitudes and behaviour that members of a society have learned, have been accustomed to and regard as regular and to be expected. As the political dimension of society consists of authoritative implementation of a sample of such attitudes, institutions in a more political sense of the word, as differentiated devices with specialized personnel for specific purposes, are the framework within which solutions to problems of social choice are to be found, and by which individual behaviour is to be guided.

This intricate and often complex relation between macro- and micro-level must always be kept in mind. Otherwise any understanding of the possibilities and conditions of conflict management will be flawed.

Cyprus – A Case-Study in a Failure of Ethno-National Understanding

The single most important conclusion we can draw from the failure of the Cypriot history since independence is: consociational mechanisms and institutions not being based on a *consociational political culture* rooted in the concerned population(s), that is, the principle to respect the vital interests of the other side, is doomed to fail. As consociationalism is rather intricate and sometimes makes it very difficult to reach any solution, it can be used in bad faith to paralyse the political process as well as administration. And we must presuppose "bad faith" automatically if there are no consociational attitudes, that is, no trust and confidence that the partner (or enemy) will respect one's own interests. Cyprus must be considered as an example that *consociationalism as a sophisticated system of institutions cannot work at the beginning of a cumbersome and difficult national (ethnic) relation full of distrust*, and burdened by a past full of tensions. Unfortunately, this is exactly what we see to be the reality in Eastern Europe today. Before discussing how to avoid this *impasse*, let us have a look at the Cypriot experience. By the way, it is sometimes surprising how similar some processes and approaches which failed in Cyprus are to the events and the propositions made in Bosnia today by the so called international community and their speakers. It seems as if none of the mediators in this conflict has ever heard of the existence of and the events in Cyprus. They could draw very heavily on the experiences of the 30-year process of the negotiations, interrupted from time to time by violence and armed clashes.

Cyprus gained independence on August 16th, 1960, after a political struggle, intermingled with violence in the last few years, which was conducted by the Greek Cypriot community alone. However, the final settlement (the Zurich and London agreement of February 1959) were not negotiated by the concerned ethnonational communities of the island. This settlement was the outcome of a compromise between the "guarantors" of the island, that is, by Greece, Turkey, and the United Kingdom. The Greek Cypriot community did not like it. However, they had no alternative other than to consent. Thus, from the very beginning, the majority on the island – a minority in the wider frame of regional power relations – was reluctant to accept the rule of the game settled by others. No wonder that after a few years intercommunal violence on a great scale broke out. One of the "guarantors" of the security of Cyprus (!), Turkey, threatened to intervene. Only in the last moment could it be reined in and held back from attacking the island (Panteli 1990).

In the frame of the intercommunal talks between Greek and Turkish Cypriots at the end of the '60s and the beginning of the '70s the concepts of both parties differed widely. After the break-down of the first round of these talks Rauf Denktash expressed his view in the words: "There was no Cypriote nation which had won ... independence and in consequence the Greek Cypriot argument that '(the) democratic rule of one man one vote should settle every issue' was unacceptable to the Turkish Cypriot side" (Poliviou 1980, 93). Seldom has the fundamental problem been formulated so clearly.

The main task of the Turkish side was to ensure that 'the political status of the Turkish community is not reduced to that of a *minority* [my italics – A. F. R.] in a Greek ruled island' (Denktash, a.a.O., 75). The Greek side, on the contrary, always aimed at a "unitary state" and always used the term "democratic procedure" as synonymous with the principle of majority. Thus they wanted to substitute the constitution of 1960 with its sophisticated and, to be sure, rigid consociational mechanisms with a British-type parlamentarianism in which the majority should have its say and its way. However, they did not see that they themselves, the Greek Cypriots, in fact were what has been called a *regional minority* (Crighton/MacIver 1991). Only after the Turkish invasion, beginning July 20, 1974 after the aborted coup of the National Guard, the Greek Cypriot realized their factual position, as Glavkos Clerides, then Acting President of Cyprus (and meanwhile by an extremely narrow victory in the election of 1993 president of the island), formulated it at the Geneva conference (August 10, 1994, quoted in: Poliviou 1980, 170): "What about security for the Greek Cypriots? The true position was that whereas Greek Cypriots were a majority on the island they were a small and defenseless minority in the strategically relevant area given Turkey's geographical proximity and military might. 'So, when one considers the general position of the area, it is clear that it is we who need protection from a territorial division of the island.'"

Thus, the antagonist parties both feared to be treated unjustly: the one side strove to avoid becoming a minority; the other one felt to be unduly hindered in its right to exercise their position of a majority. As we know, the intransigence of the then majority led first to an attempt to force its will and then to the solution it disliked most; to Turkish armed intervention and the factual division of the island, or "taksim".

Anyway, in all the intercommunal talks, the term *minority* has been of crucial importance, whether openly admitted – as for the Turks – or not. To begin with, there were quarrels concerning who should participate at the talks and who was not allowed to. In this aspect the whole problem was stated in a nutshell. Who is or who should be considered a minority? If "the interested parties" were to only be the Greek and Turkish Cypriots, then, clearly, the Turkish side had to play the minority. Then the problems of the talks could be no others but those: what minority rights should the Turkish community be given? If, however, the Greek and Turkish governments were to be involved in these talks, the terms of the negotiations would be conceived in another fashion: under such circumstances, the Greek Cypriots politically became a regional minority within "the wider regional balance of power" (Poliviou 1980, 147 ff.). "The close proximity of Turkey" (ibid., 145) thus was not merely a lofty and unsustainable absurdity in international law, namely, the so-called "principle of contiguity". As Greece (1) was not able militarily to help Cyprus because they were too weak and too far away and (2) was not willing to assist the actual Cypriot government considered disturbing the common (to Greece and Turkey) target of "fighting communism", Cyprus had to cope with its role as a microstate in an inimical political environment.

This shift of positions according to the changing circumstances or, to put it more clearly, the apprehension of it, are demonstrated by the participants of the Geneva talks. Of course, the Turks were participants after the (first) cease-fire. Indeed, the real "interested parties" were both the Turks on the one hand (the Turkish Cypriots playing only a minor role serving mainly as pretext for the adamant Turkish position), and the Greek Cypriots on the other hand. The negotiations which were in fact a continuous pressure and blackmail by the Turks were held between them. And not by chance was there a complete reversal of the political stances. The Greek Cypriot who had always maintained that the 1960 constitution was dead and invalidated by the course of events, now argued that this same constitution as the only legal ground for negotiations. The Turks, on their part, although founding their attack on the treaty of guarantee – (a part of the 1960 constitutional arrangements), denied that this arrangement further existed, quite contrary to the thesis to which Turkish Cypriot had always held. This surprising reversal is nothing as the expression of the now different situation: the Greek Cypriot, under the power relations as they were, now were becoming a virtual minority opposed to a Turkish majority composed of the Turkish Cypriots and the Turks from the mainland.

Three years after the invasion the interested parties resumed negotiations. The Turks, of course, argued from the strength of their status quo. And what did the Greek Cypriot do? One is tempted to find it ridiculous, but they tried to restore the *status quo ante*. The exchanged the word "unitary state" for "integral republic" and maintained "that the republic of Cyprus has not been dissolved as a result of the Turkish invasion", which may be a legal basis for negotiations. However, they went further on this pace by saying, "the political and constitutional reconstruction of Cyprus cannot start from either the premise of the existence of 'two autonomous administrations' on an equal footing or from the preexistence of federated states, *because these do not exist*" (my italics – Poliviou 1980, 218). So, the very problem which has to be dealt with "did not exist" in the eyes of the Greek Cypriots. No wonder that there was no progress until today. Indeed, there was a stiffening of the Turkish positions. They were well aware that the Greek Cypriots wished to go back to the pre-war period. One detail illustrates this quite clearly: as it is known, there was a significant amount of ethnic cleansing in Cyprus 1974. Now it is not only understandable but goes beyond any discussion that the Greek Cypriot side claimed, the refugees should be allowed to return to their homes. Things being as they are, one can suppose that not many of the refugees which have settled either in the Southern part of the island or elsewhere would be inclined to go back in an area under Turkish control. Thus, both the dignified principle of restitution would be honored as the real impact of this resettlement is probably irreversible. And this would be even desirable, because everyone knows that a massive return there would cause new tensions between the communities. However, the Greek Cypriot added to this: "Every possible effort must be made to ensure that as many displaced persons as possible return to their homes". One cannot help: these attitudes are at best foolish...

The Greek Cypriot wanted to avoid by all means a federal system in which the Turkish side had considerable power and autonomy. As one device to have a unitary state while satisfying some demands of their Turkish counterparts they proposed a *cantonal solution* – which the Turkish Cypriots were not prepared to accept. They apprehended, obviously, that by accepting this solution there would be a federal system only on the surface. One has to remember the same fate for the proposals of cantons void of real power in Bosnia.

Belgium – Successful Ethnic Conflict Management

Belgium has devised general consociationalism as the predominant political feature, in fact, as its political culture guaranteeing not only the reduction of ethnic and political conflict but the survival of the state. Constitutional developments since the 1960s have seen this political experience become codified in juridical norms and institutions: "Belgian political life is indeed characterized by a long-standing 'elitist-consensus', the majority (almost) always trying to find a solution which is acceptable to the minority and which will not hamper the latter's vital interest. Whenever this political rule is violated in Belgium, very sharp conflicts arise" (Alen 1992, 17).

Belgium has been labeled a decentralized unitary state moving towards a federal State-system with three *"communities"*, three *"regions"* and four *"linguistic regions"*. Belgium thus has combined two principles for solving national conflicts well known in the political debate in the beginning of this century: the Belgian unitary state of before 1970 is now not only *regionalized*; it is also *communitarized*. By creating communities, a long lasting demand of the Flemish politician had come into reality. Flemings had always been discriminated against especially with regard to their linguistic status. The regions, on the other side, were created in order to meet the Waloon desire for territorial autonomy, to give them more power in economic matters. Thus the *principle of personality*, baptized the *national-cultural autonomy* by Austrian social democrats, as well as the *principle of territoriality*, in some way a proxy for self-determination, have been combined.

There are *councils* both for the three regions as well as for the three communities which serve as legislative institutions, and there are *executives*, that is governments, for these territories and bodies. In fact, there are not six, but five councils and governments, because the institutions of the Flemish region and community have been fusioned although legally they are differentiated. In the last constitutional step to a federal state in summer 1993 it has been decided that the members of parliaments of the federal entities should be elected directly. The political competencies of the regions and communities are ascribed to them by enumeration in the constitution (Chapter IV which comprises the articles 115 to 140).[2] Fields which are not expressly attributed to the regions or communities are in the realm of the central (or now: federal) State.

The approach of institutional regionalism belongs to the classic tools of national regulations according to the principle of *territorial unilingualism*. In the Belgian regions of Flanders and Wallonia it is the majority, not the minority which is protected. (In Switzerland the linguistic policy follows the same path, and it is argued that this will protect the lesser used languages against a shifting of the linguistic boundaries, especially against the most prominent Swiss language, German.) The cause is to be sought in the situation the Flemish experienced in the last hundred and fifty years: although numerically superior to the Walloons since the very start of the new state they did not achieve equal treatment for their language in public use until late in the history. They were treated similar to a minority.

As the two great regions of Belgium are virtually mono-linguistic, the conflicts and the problems may not seem very acute. However, the single most important area for those interested in the workings of the devised solutions and for problems of the protection of minorities or regulating national (or inter-ethnic) relations is *Brussels* as a bilingual region, and of course, the central authorities located in this region. Although there are no questions in the Belgian censuses since 1960 regarding linguistic or national affiliation, it is well know that in Brussels the ratio between Wallons and Flemings is approximately 85:15. Despite this ratio, Flemings are overrepresented in the presidium of the council of the region (with 40 to 60). The same applies for the Brussels executive. As concerns the ordinary citizen, he/she can stick to the principle of monolingualism insofar as he has the right to be addressed in his own language. Thus, in order to guarantee linguistic treatment for each citizen, the administration is strictly bilingual down to certain ranks.

Federalism with its competing competencies is always in need for an *arbiter*. Thus it has been created some sort of a Supreme Court, the *Cour d'Arbitrage*, has been created to deal exclusively with such problems. Half of the personnel consists of judges. The rest of the seats are occupied by former senior politicians. The decisions of this court have been inclined to give extensive powers to the regions.

There are some other institutions on the level of the central state worth mentioning. This applies especially to the *Concertation Committee* as an institutional device and to the job allotment rations in the civil service according to the proportions that the national languages are used in the population. By this regulation jobs of the central administration below a certain (academic) degree are allotted in the ratio of 40:40 to the two communities, the remaining of 20% reserved for bilingual clerks. Similar regulations which are more specific to the local and regional circumstances apply to some communes along the linguistic frontier, in the area bordering Brussels, in the area inhabited by German speaking people and for two problematic groups of localities (Comines, Warneton and Fourons). The Concertation committee – chaired by the prime minister – consists of six members of the central government as well as six members of the regional governments. Its function is to solve conflicts in the framework of petty politics by consensus. Furthermore, there exists a *Standing Committee for the Supervision of Linguistic Matters*. Its aim is the political downgrading of problems specifically related to the complex of the linguistic conflict.

Beginning with April 6, 1992, a process of further federalisation and regionalisation has ended with the until now last revision of the Belgian constitution. This is aimed at making Belgium a fully institutionalized federal state. The senate shall become a federal council instead of remaining simply a second house of representative as it indeed was until now. The procedure for constitutional revisions being very complicated,[3] the same must be said for the promulgation of special laws,[4] this revision and its impact in daily politics will last a certain time. So we have to wait to judge its efficiency.

Belgium thus combines two principles which are ordinarily considered to be antagonistic both in theory as in political practice, that is, the "national-cultural autonomy" (personal autonomy approach) and the administrative features of regional or territorially-based federalism. The "communities" are to deal with culture- and language-specific problems. On the other side, the political administration of the concerned areas are – analytically speaking – thought to be in the competence of the regions as distinct from the communities. The regions are conceived as sub-states, and their concern should be of general politics centering around economic policy and social welfare. This means they are autonomous in a very classical way and familiar to constitutional law. Theoretically this double approach (most times considered as competing) signifies that the communities are conceived as *ethnic units* regardless if we face the Flemish, the Waloon or the German community. The populations, bearers of the regions, on the other side got attributes mostly considered the criteria of nations. However, this more important politico-juridical status belongs only to Flemings and Waloons, not to Germans. They are considered an ethnic minority (labeled as "linguistic region") belonging to the Walloon region. The *Brussels region* in its turn is a *multiethnic federal unit*.

Also in the case of a *multinational state*, that is, a state with several (territorially separable) nations which are subject to the authority of a single political power, there is a need for regulations on the level of the central state. Otherwise there would be no reason for the existence of this common state, especially if we presuppose a representative or parliamentarian system. If there are no common regulatory needs and necessities, a federal state would cease to exist. But existing political conflicts are unavoidable in each situation with different systems of values and political creed. And if there are conflicts there will be ethno-national conflicts as well. To minimize them and to have the possibility of rational conflict management it is advisable to pick out the policies known as dangerous because they are identity-related. Usually, such policies deal with resources for language and educational affairs.

Experience has taught us to be extremely cautious if we come near such questions. Administrative language and language in educational matters have proved to constitute explosive stuff. If we can draw a strategy of de-nationalisation or de-ethnification in policies destined to regulate economic and social affairs it is quite impossible to do the same handling the socialisation of children or the "property" of a specific group in matters of linguistic policies. So, we have to avoid making ethnic/national identity a problem of political quarrels. It is almost unthinkable to apply the same political procedures as usual. There is no compromise about one's own identity.

Why does regional unilingualism receive such a central role in the Belgian communal relations? The Flemish community was discriminated against for a long time, as stated above. The first and foremost condition for peaceful convivality, is in such circumstances, mutual trust. In an abstract sense, surely, bilingualism would be preferred. Unfortunately, bilingualism was in fact always an obligation for the weaker part, put aside some tiny fractions of élites. If the Belgian federation will be a durable construction – there are some doubts in certain quarters about the future prospects although there is not much reason for this pessimism – bilingualism could be a device for better understanding in the not so distant future.

The combination of personal and territorial autonomy is very promising. Until now the above mentioned elitist consensus has helped to avoid dangerous conflicts. In the meantime this consensus raises some doubts and is considered insufficient. Modern politics demands a stronger involvement of the concerned citizens. This demand is to be met by federalization and autonomy.

In Belgium there are no predispositions for *referenda*: "Any form of direct democracy is excluded by the Belgian Constitution" (Alen 1992, 11). In contemporary Belgian history one event has won great fame. We are speaking of the "royal question". In the second World War King Leopold III had behaved in a manner of which a substantive part of the population disapproved. Thus, after the war, a debate about his person, also involving the institution of the monarchy in general, began. The Belgium population was divided, and this division followed more or less linguistic lines. In 1950 a referendum was to decide the king's fate. The Flemish population voted with a majority for the king's returning, the Waloons voted against, approximately in the same proportion. As the Flemings are about 55% of the whole population,

74 *Ethnic Conflicts and Civil Society*

there was an overall majority favouring the return of Leopold. The debate became quite passionate, and the county seemed to be on the verge of civil war. Finally, the king "renounced" to return and saved the peace. This solution is characteristical for Belgian attitudes and for consociational democracy in general.

We have to draw the conclusions from this example: In a multinational state there is no single common "national interest" if one of the nations feel threatened by a majority decision. However, it is the feature of a plebiscite to come to a decision by a simple majority irrespective of whom the votes are coming from. A plebiscite is by definition the decision of a majority against a minority. Thus, plebiscites about vital problems in multinational states are a deadly danger for minorities and must be avoided in any case. [5] "The plurality two-party system like the British raise such high barriers against the acquisition of influence by nationalist movements representing ethnoterritorial minorities that they actually provoke the emergence of extremist tendencies" (Zariski 1989, 264).

5   Criteria of Working Interethnic and Minorities' Relations

You cannot solve once and forever ethnonational tensions and conflicts. However, you can create *favourable conditions for successful ethnic conflict-management*. One of these conditions is: De-coupling ethnic identity and national allegiance. For doing this, formal institutions and, paradoxically, some degree of ethnicization of political instruments have proved efficient. Let me say this that way: As belonging to a minority, you must be sure to have a fair trial.

1) *Arbitration*: The decisive institution for maintaining peace in interethnic and national relation is some sort of *referee* between minorities and the majority. Giving political and juridical competencies to majorities as well as to minorities of one nation, or of one region (e.g. by entrusting a territory with autonomy) there are always some critical, or unclear areas. Thus, such a settlement has to determine what happens if litigation should arise. As the central state is – by definition – dominated by the majority, there is no easy solution. There must be some guarantee of an impartial arbitration. Minorities ordinarily will not simply trust the majority-led government of the central state. International

arbitration courts have until now proved to be the institutions best fitted to these ends. At present, the most important institutions of this sort are the *European Commission for Human Rights* and the *European Court of Human Rights*, both working in the frame of the Council of Europe. The CSCE has instituted a High Commissioner on (!) National Minorities. As he is completely dependent upon the governments he is meant to control in some way there is not much hope for success.

There may be similar institutions within states. Besides arbitration courts or constitutional courts with partly similar aims, sometimes the central government can assume such a function, if the minority is inhabiting a specific area and its immediate counterpart as the representation of a majority is the regional (local) government. In such circumstances the representatives of the majority-dominated central government usually have decisive weight. Thus, the protection of the concerned minorities remains rather precarious, although the very existence of such an institution has to be interpreted as a step in the right direction and is meant to avoid majority decisions fatal for the minorities.

2) *Regional citizenship and restrictions of movement within the state*: Autonomous territories are built following the structure of a state. They are featured as sub-states, disposing of a parliament and a government of its own. This has to be seen as a technical device and says little about the real power the autonomous community disposes. However, it is of symbolic importance. Nonetheless, we have to look for institutions perhaps less visible but of greater real importance than assemblies and "governments".

A "political community" (a state) is "an area (...) the people residing therein permanently or temporarily reserved for the orderly domination of these people, who are willing to guard this privilege by means of physical violence, if necessary, by means of arms" (Weber 1976, 514). Citizenship therefore is to be considered a principle of exclusion. Only those are admitted as citizens who can prove that they "belong" to the co-nationals as "co-ethnics". Freedom of movement is one of the criteria the citizens are disposing of. The national soil is shared in political ownership by all who can claim to be citizens of this state. If the autonomous territory is really to be a substate, this must have consequences for the freedom of movement for those who do not belong to the citizens of the autonomous territory. Thus, almost all autonomy statutes acknowledge some form of territorially restricted citizenship. However, most of these statutes are purely symbolical in this point. There is no factual consequence of this regional citizenship. Sometimes, it cannot be denied that there are political relevant consequences. This is one of the most sensitive questions in majority – minority relations. Exceptions to the purely symbolical concept are to be found in Åland (Finland), and in Southern Tyrol. In Åland a five year uninterrupted period of residence is required also of Finnish citizens to be allowed to accomplish certain economically relevant acts (e.g. buying land). In Southern Tyrol immigrants of the rest of Italy get the right to vote only after four years.

3) Most states are mistrustful of their minorities and are eager to guard their "sovereignty" in cases where there are autonomous areas. Almost all of them have instituted *supervisors* on behalf of the central power. Those prefects have to watch the constitutionality and the good will of minority groups. Although a source of tensions, the aim of this institution is to assure the *majority* not to be threatened by the minorities. Ridiculous as it may sound, most majorities live in fear of their minorities. Thus, a prefect can contribute to lessening such tensions if he is willing to accept the minority's political will.

At this point it is interesting to observe the negotiations and their outcome in South Africa. We can draw a sad conclusion of this case and similar others: Minority protection seldom works if the minority is a real minority, that is, has no power to display. There are a few working solutions, and the South African example promises to count among them. The prospective minority, in South Africa as well as in Zimbabwe years ago, the hitherto dominant white stratum, acts as the power-holder while bargaining. Surely, they are threatened, and if the attempt to solve the *imbroglio* fails, they may be losers too, especially in the long run. Nonetheless, this would be very costly to their adversaries-partners. This way they have an efficient bargaining chip and they can get guarantees for their survival. With this I want to demonstrate the *paradox of minority* protection in a nut-shell. Let us remember that the relation "majority" (which is not a numerical majority in the South African case of *Apartheid*) to minority is essentially a power relation which takes the feature of a numerical ratio only in the framework of a parliamentarian system with equal and general suffrage. If the powerful majority is a numerical minority, the transformation to parliamentarian democracy means it is expected to lose or to voluntarily give up the constituent characteristic of political power. Or to say it more drastically: The majority is expected to commit political suicide. The other way round: If the majority is a numerical majority it is expected to renounce its full entitlement regarding the minority. The powerful is expected to preserve the powerless – it is indeed a paradox!

4) As ethnic relations are not only based on identities but in everyday life, at least in the same measure on interest (often directed against the interest of the majorities, as interests in the short run are almost always a zero-sum-game), *fiscal affairs* are of utmost importance. Autonomy which is not endeavoured with the autonomy of levying some taxes or getting their financial needs elsewhere in an independent wax are not worth of being designated autonomy. This is, e.g., one of the problems of *Corsica* which is almost totally dependent upon Paris. On the other side we can find examples like the *Føroyar*, who are virtually independent in disposing about their resources. However, there can be difficulties. Autonomous areas on the grounds of being inhabited by people of a different ethnic belonging are often peripheral areas. That means, they are dependent upon resources from outside if they claim to have the same standard of living as the core areas. In *Kalaallit Nunaat (Greenland)* 47% of the region's expenses in 1989 have come from Copenhagen. At the same time, the region is aiming for full independence. Of course, Denmark hesitates to fund this government...

Managing ethnic conflict is dependent on political tolerance. This is not meant as a moral category, but as a political one. It is to be understood as a specific obligation of states (and their majorities) to respect human rights which they claim as their foundation. And it is also a question of good political tactics. Stability of the state is best maintained by satisfying the vital needs of its constituents, not by suppressing them. Minority protection, to say the least, thus can be judged as one of the most reliable indicators of a state's (or its majority) democratic consciousness.

78 *Ethnic Conflicts and Civil Society*

Notes

1. In this basic feature there is a striking resemblance with the *loi Toubon* (revised version: *loi no. 94-665 du 4 août 1994 relative á l'emploi de la langue française*).

2. The juridical bases for these regulations are: Special Institutional Reform Act of 8 August 1980 providing the structure and powers of the French Community, the Flemish Community, the Walloon Region and the Flemish Region. – Special Brussels Institutions Act of 12 January 1989 providing the structures and powers of the Brussels Capital Region. – Institutional Reform Act for the German Speaking Community of 31 December 1983. – Constitution de la Belgique du 17 février 1994.

3. If a constitutional revision (by the three "legislative organisms", that is, the senate, the house of representatives and the king) is announced, this implies automatically a dissolution of the parliament, after the publication of this intention in the "Moniteur belge" (the official Journal of the Belgian state). The newly elected parliament is considered to be the Constituent Assembly.

4. They need a consent of two thirds of the members of parliament while half of its members of both the two linguistic groups need to be present.

5. As we are dealing with national tensions in Eastern Europe, we have to remember the policy of the EC vis-a-vis the former Yugoslavian republic and especially vis-à-vis Bosnia. EC stated as a condition for recognizing Bosnia as a sovereign state a plebiscite deciding about independence. At this time, civil war between the three nations in Bosnia was around the corner. We are allowed to ask: Has the Belgian attendant of the EC-council forgot his own history? This decision and the following plebiscite which the Bosnian Serbs must have interpreted as directed against themselves has furthered the break-out of the civil war. Of course, as always in such situations of dependence, politicians in Bosnia-Hercegovinia were eager to execute this dictate of the EC.

Bibliography

ALEN, André, ed., 1992: Treatise on Belgian Constitutional Law, Deventer-Boston, Kluwer

AVINERI, Shlomo/SHALIT, Avner de, eds., 1992: Communitarianism and Individualism, Oxford, University Press

BRANS, Marleen 1993: High-Tech Problem Solving in a Multi-Cultural State: The Case of Brussels. Dutch Crossing 49: 3-27

BREUILLY, John 1985: Nationalism and the State, Manchester, University Press

CRIGHTON, Elizabeth/MACIVER, Martha Abele 1991: "The Evolution of Protracted Ethnic Conflict. Group Dominance and Political Underdevelopment in Northern Ireland and Lebanon". Comparative Politics 23: 127-142

DAHRENDORF, Ralf 1972: Konflikt und Freiheit. Auf dem Weg zur Dienstklassengesellschaft, München, Piper

ELIAS, Norbert 1976: Über den Prozeß der Zivilisation. Soziogenetische und psychogenetische Untersuchungen. 2 Bände, Frankfurt/M., Suhrkamp

FURNIVALL, J. S. 1939: Netherlands India: a study of plural economy, Cambridge, Univ. Press

FURNIVALL, J. S. 1948: Colonial policy and practice: a comparative study of Burma and the Netherlands India, Cambridge, University Press

GELLNER, Ernest 1983: Nations and Nationalism, London, Basil Blackwell

HOBSBAWM, Eric J. 1990: Nations and Nationalism since 1780, Cambridge, Univ. Press, 1990

HUNT, Chester L./WALKER, Lewis 1979: Ethnic Dynamics. Patterns of Intergroup Relations in Various Societies Holms Beach, Learning Publications, 2nd ed.

HUSSERL, Edmund 1984: Die Konstitution der geistigen Welt, Hamburg, Meiner

HUSSERL, Edmund 1985: Die phänomenologische Methode. Ausgewählte Texte I. Mit einer Einleitung hg. von K. Held, Stuttgart, Reclam

HUSSERL, Edmund 1986: Phänomenologie der Lebenswelt. Ausgewählte Texte II. Mit einer Einleitung hg. von K. Held, Stuttgart, Reclam

KEDOURIE, Elie 1986: Nationalism, London, Hutchinson

LIJPHART, Arend 1977: Democracy in Plural Societies. A Comparative Exploration, New Haven/London, Yale University Press

LIJPHART, Arend 1984: Democracies. Patterns of Majoritarian and Consensus Government in Twenty-One Countries, New Haven, Yale University Press

LOCKE, John 1965: Zwei Abhandlungen über die Regierung, Wien, Europa Verlag

MEW: MARX, Karl/ENGELS, Friedrich 1967: Werke. 42 Bände, Berlin (Ost), Dietz

MILL, John St. 1975 (1861): "Considerations on Representative Government". In: John St. Mill, Three Essays, Oxford: University Press, pp. 143-423

PANTELI, Stavros 1990: The Making of Modern Cyprus. From Obscurity to Statehood. Introduction by Robert Browning, New Barnet, Interworld Publications

POLIVIOU, Polivios G. 1980: Cyprus. Conflict and Negotiation 1960 – 1980, London, Duckworth

RAWLS, John 1979: Eine Theorie der Gerechtigkeit, Frankfurt/M., Suhrkamp

REITERER, Albert F. 1988: Die unvermeidbare Nation. Ethnizität, Nation und nachnationale Gesellschaft, Frankfurt/M., Campus

SCHERMERHORN, Richard A. 1970: Comparative Ethnic Relations. A Framework for Theory and Research, New York, Random

SCHÜTZ, Alfred 1981: Der sinnhafte Aufbau der sozialen Welt. Eine Einleitung in die verstehende Soziologie, Frankfurt/M., Suhrkamp

SCHÜTZ, Alfred 1982: Das Problem der Relevanz, Frankfurt/M., Suhrkamp

SCHÜTZ, Alfred/LUCKMANN, Thomas 1973: The Structures of the Life World. Translated by Richard M. Zaner and Tristram Engelhardt jr., London, Heinemann

SMITH, Anthony D. 1983: The Ethnic Origin of Nations, London, Blackwell

SMITH, Anthony D. 1989: The Origin of Nations. Ethnic and Racial Studies, 12: 340-365

TILLY, Charles, ed. 1975: The Formation of National States in Western Europe, Princeton, N.J., University Press

VEBERS, Elmars 1993: "Demography and Ethnic Politics in Independent Latvia: Some Basic Facts". Nationalities Papers XXI, 179-194

WALZER, Michael 1970: Obligations. Essay on Disobedience, War, and Citizenship, Cambridge, Mass., Harvard University Press

WALZER, Michael 1992: "Membership". In: Avineri/de Shalit, pp. 65-84

WEBER, Max 1976: Wirtschaft und Gesellschaft. Grundriß der verstehenden Soziologie, Tübingen, Mohr

ZARISKI, Raphael 1989: "Ethnic Extremism among Ethnoterritorial Minorities in Western Europe. Dimensions, Causes, and Institutional Responses". Comp. Politics 21, 253-272

PART III

CASE STUDIES: DOMESTIC EXPERIENCES OF ETHNIC CONFLICTS

4 Temptations of Transition and Identity Crisis in Post-Communist Countries
The Example of Former Yugoslavia

NADIA SKENDEROVIC CUK

1 Introductory Notes

Many analyses of the present post-communist countries are focused on their status of transition, trying to identify a process of democratization by a simplified criterion of "rule of majority". This kind of conclusion, relying only on a fact of free elections, neglects the essence of democracy, seen as a need for establishing the inherent limits of this rule, embodied in human rights either individual or collective.

It is very difficult to determine the future development of these societies, as they are only beginning to search for possible alternatives. Project of Fukuyama about the end of history lost its attraction after only ten years, and it is still hard to think about the possible improvement of liberal democratization,[1] as a liberal market and democracy are values not adjusted to the context of growing nationalism and poverty, so actual in post-communist societies. The thesis about the clash of civilization is also very provoking and applicable, having in mind the situation in Balkans region, a place with a mixture of cultures where it is difficult to predict the dynamic of political processes. However, it is obvious that within this conglomerate of cultures there is a strong need for energy, wisdom and will to organize a common life or coexistence and to solve possible tensions and conflicts. This will be possible only under the circumstances of universal humanistic and democratic standards of behavior and organization, and this means not only an adequate institutional mechanism but a new political culture.

2   Challenges to Democracy

The failure of real socialism in Eastern and Central Europe caused the establishment of new institutions important for parliamentary democracy like parliaments, free elections, pluralism of political parties, independent media and others. Except for these formal or external elements there were not enough signs to indicate, in a definite way, a presence of stable democracy. There was a lack of substance seen in absence of human rights protection, democratic traditions and civil society values. This ambiguity – or better to say inconsistency – raised doubts about the proper nature of new political regimes.

Nevertheless many authors gave explanations in favor of the democratic character of new regimes and main arguments are found in the existence of freedom for political parties and elections through which a legitimacy for a government obtained.[2] Describing this new kind of democracy familiar with countries of South America and post-communist countries, O'Donnell uses the term "delegative democracy".[3] With this unusual term he embraces both the resemblance and difference between parliamentary democracy in Western Europe and that established in ex-socialist countries. Similarity is visible in a democratic process of elections concerning supreme political institutions and by the present critique of their work. A profound difference exists in the accountability of a president which is vertical – maintaining towards voters but not towards other institutions. A process of decision making, it is much quicker then it is usually in stable democracies. This later feature, has however many disadvantages because of a probability for making wrong decisions, possible obstacles in implementing these decisions, and individualization of responsibility in a case of failure.

According to others,[4] one can speak about "protodemocracy" as a contradiction between legislation and social reality. There are also opinions that there is an actual Post-Communist polyarchy, which means a democracy, but not within the ideal definition of this notion.[5]

Democratization in Eastern and Central Europe occurred in two stages. The first occurs in a moment of abandoning or abolishing the dictatorship, i.e., previous regime, and it is known as a transition to democracy, lasting till first free elections. After transition there is a stage of consolidation which leads, after a certain time, to the status of stable democracy. There is a tendency to accept this later phase as a procedure of giving a legitimacy to the new regime, and according to this it is still not accomplished in the majority of Post-Communist countries. However some of them are closer to this aim – for example the Czech Republic – and some of them are far away because of actual conflicts and tensions in political life – for example in Yugoslavia.

These countries have a common "background"; a past communist regime lasting for more then half a century, being established on the ideas of Marxism, public property and public administration in economy. This heritage will be an obstacle for a long period of time, to satisfying all the requirements of market economy. The above mentioned background of these societies has also had an impact on their members where individuals lived under the "protection" of the state, and were not prepared for the risk and uncertainty of free society and competition.[6] This expectation of "protection" could not vanish overnight, and it is even now very obvious. A spirit of non-tolerance and unreadiness for dialogue, which is today an obstacle for political pluralism, has its origin in a previous habit of political campaigns and oppression of those who had different ideas and opinions. Finally, the lack of rule of law had serious consequences on the main institutions of society as a whole.

After the failure of ancient regimes, as it is said, new institutions were founded as a precondition for further development. These institutions should gain stability and validity in order to enable a consolidation of democracy. For this it is of utmost importance to establish powerful and stable political parties which are capable of expressing, selecting, and articulating the interests of different social groups. By this criteria, some writers differentiate between institutional and temporary parties.[7] In the first group are the parties who prove their continuity by participating in at least three elections; taking into account long intervals between elections. Their permanent presence also correlates to the stability of the political system. According to this classification, political parties in Post-Communist countries are more temporary than institutional parties. That means a longer period of time not only for institutionalization of parties but also for gaining loyalty of members to them. This identification with the party became, in Western countries, a kind of tradition, spreading over several generations. Common heritage which points out the similarity of problems in a process of democratization will soon lose its significance. As one author noted, instead of mandatory equality, peculiarities of different countries will cause a different rate of democratic stabilization of in the future. That means the difference between them lies in the process of gaining the basic consensus, which concerns at least three elements of a political system: political community in general, i.e., state, then political regime and persons of political power.

Consensus is necessary for the first segment, as its absence will be a denial of a state, and it is also needed for all the components of a political regime, as are social values, standards or structure of authority.[8] Stable democracy presumes acceptance of these two basic levels of the political system by all of the relevant political subjects. Opposition to persons or groups with political power is in accordance with parliamentary democracy and is maintained through periodical elections. It will be difficult to understand any possible sideroads of democracy in Post-Communist countries without maintaining one social fact with potentially great influence on further development. Consensus about two basic level is much more predictable in a socially homogenous countries – those where more then 80% of whole population is of a dominant ethnic group. Countries with a smaller percentage of major ethnic groups are considered to be heterogeneous societies, as is the situation in Yugoslavia, considering that in Serbia and Montenegro 1/3 of the population are of different non-dominant ethnic groups. Consolidation is more difficult here as sharp social (ethnic, religious, cultural) divisions cause cultural and political divisions. Those are "segmental cleavages" immanent for plural societies,[9] where, generally, small chances exist for consensus. Maintenance for subsocieties with their own parties, interests and aims lead to the breakdown of multiethnic political communities like SFR Yugoslavia, Czechoslovakia and Soviet Union. Nevertheless, consolidation is not completely excluded and is dependent on nature and mutual relations between relevant political parties. In a case of the denial of policy or its major institutions, consolidation will be impossible.

Relevant political parties are considered to be those which achieve at election, at least 5% of votes. According to the results of parliamentary elections in Serbia, there are only 5 relevant parties. Important parties are considered those not participating in elections, but with a presumed support of 5% of the voters. This happens in the case of a boycott, which is a political demonstration of a disapproval towards a state or political regime. This happened (in Yugoslavia) with the Albanian political parties, and the Party of democratic action of Muslim provenance, showing that 1/5 of the population in Serbia does not participate in political life at all. Beside this there was also a challenge to the constitutional framework of republics (Serbia and Montenegro) and of Yugoslavia as federation.

In Serbia there have been attacks on the Constitution which were made before and not after elections by the previous communist regime, in order to disable the opposition from influencing the Constitution's content. The same was the case with the federal Constitution, which was ratified under even more peculiar conditions.[10] These events slow down the process of democratization, and they are normally accompanied by a lack of confidence in political institutions. Research conducted in Post-Communist countries is proving this notion, so that there is quite a high percentage of unsatisfactory remarks on the development of democratization (In Albania 58%, Slovenia 59%, Estonia 51%, Hungary 74%, Slovakia 78%, Bulgaria 69%, Poland 49%, Romania 56%).[11] An attitude toward institutions is dependent on features of political culture. According to Almond and Verba, there are two main types of political cultures; parochial and participate (civil) political culture. The term, political culture of a country, presumes a distribution of orientations to the political system, its institutions, procedures and the role of individuals in this framework. Civil political culture is a part of a real democracy, although not necessarily considered as a precondition. The experience of transition in Central and Eastern Europe, and of some previous reforms in Southern Europe and Central and South America shows that democratic transformation is not inevitably doomed to failure just because of the present parochial culture. Democratic political culture is not always a condition but can also be a consequence of a successful process of democratization.

This first step in Serbia and Montenegro (FR Yugoslavia) began in November 1989, when the governing communist parties accepted pluralism, and was completed in December 1990, with the first free elections. In other words it can be said that this country is in a period of consolidation, with serious refrains and obstacles which will be mentioned later.

3 New Nationalism and its Consequences

According to unanimous agreement, an exclusive nationalism is endangering the process of democracy. Even if we neglect the extreme examples of cruel conflicts in Yugoslavia and the former Soviet Union, there have been many examples of its spreading, despite the multiethnic character of many countries today.

It is very difficult to determine precisely a definition of nation and national affiliation, as it is hard to discuss terms of "good" and "bad" nationalism. However there have been some attempts to justify this phenomenon, but nor in persuasive way. These arguments were used to explain the new nations being established after the break-down of former federations. Despite all the patriotic feelings and understanding of their own nations, these national democracies have been proved as ethnocraties rather than democracies. Of course one can accept an abstract profile of nationalist "unbiased in favor of any special nationality of their own, and generously preaching for all nations alike: let nations have their own political roofs, and let all of them also refrain from including non nationalist under it".[12] This non-egoistic nationalism is from the aspect of present experience, not very usual and the manner of its expression is not often: "so sweetly reasonable nor so rationally symmetrical".[13]

A distinction can be made between nationalism as a sense of loyalty to the state (nation), and as a sentiment of belonging to the group of people of the same origin. In the latter sense a loyalty is related to the presumed ethnic group, so it is often called ethnonationalism.[14]

Maintenance of the term ethnicity necessitates an explanation of its meaning. According to the definitions given in contemporary literature, ethnicity has few essential elements.[15] First is a combination of factors such as phenotype, faith, language, origin or population concentration in a given region, passed from generation to generation, which demarcates a given collectivity. A sense of solidarity shared by the members of a group and a common subjective identity based on mentioned factors are also very relevant components. The third feature reveals the necessary contacts of a group with another in the same society. That means that ethnicity is "objective and subjective, involving the fact and the sense of membership in a group in contact with another in the same society where each has at least a partially unique normative culture resting upon, reflecting and sustaining its notions of its origin and history".[16] Although ethnic oriented action could be, according to these neutral determinations, useful and rational, in ethnically diverse society there is a dilemma which can be solved in different ways. There is to be decided in what ways ethnic groups should be left free to live by their own standards or in what ways they should live by a common code. Without an adequate and tolerant framework and institutionalized mechanism of solving this dilemma, a subordination of some ethnic groups to others, occurs with weaker groups having to adapt themselves to the common culture or be limited by discrimination.

Recently there have been claims that nationalism has disappeared, because of the successful integration of Western Europe and a strong belief that it is far away from communist countries. This later conclusion was, however, wrong, neglecting the paradox of nationalism in so called real socialism. At the same time it was a powerful weapon against communism and the only instrument for the leaders of previous regimes, to safeguard their position and legitimacy, or to obtain social support.[17] In multiethnic societies it was used for producing inter-ethnic conflicts, enabling regimes to govern more easily.[18]

The revival of nationalism has attracted the attention of numerous writers, and has been explained in various ways. According to one opinion its occurrence is neither new nor original, but is framed by traditional notions of national aims.[19] On the other side, there are analyses founded on the comparison of nationalism (related to ethnic cleansing in former Yugoslavia) with that of the 1930s.[20] New nationalism is therefore described as decentralizing and fragmenting in contrast to earlier unifying and centralizing nationalism. "Earlier nationalisms were culturally homogenizing rather than culturally divisive; homogeneity was largely achieved through assimilation rather than through exclusion...". It is also identified as a "primitive grasp of power" based on "anarchic war economy" "a social formation dependent on continuous violence".[21]

Schierup finds a major distinction in the fact that citizenship is explicitly based on nationality defined in narrow ethnic terms. This is the discriminatory constitutional basis for the form of nationalism called ethnic nationalism according to Kaldor and "a basis for populist mobilization, the ideological legitimization for warfare and for systematic and violent ethnic cleansing of alleged national territories".[22]

Parallels have been made between nationalism and communism, seen as a close relation with the ideas of collectivism and anti-individualism. Arguments were found in a practice of Romania, present Yugoslavia (Serbia and Montenegro) and in some parts of former Soviet Union, where communists took the role of nationalist.[23] This is also related to a conclusion about "ethnically strengthened communism". Discrepancy in such an observation is false, having in mind that communism in this region lost its original content and aims and finally became a process of safeguarding the authoritarian political system.

Historical deviation in the process of transition, visible in many post-communist countries, led to multiplication of "national" parties on their political scene. Their ethnic orientation is determined by their aim to gather all members of one ethnic group and to exclude others. Promotion of so called "national or ethnic interest" was visible also in their names and programs, which frightened different ethnic societies, especially within a multiethnic framework. Elections in Bosnia in 1990 are mentioned as a different example of this type of ethnic identification. Besides three ethnically oriented parties there were three neutral, parties and voters were faced with the "prisoner's dilemma". Instead of a politically gained ethnic option, a coalition of three ethnical parties was created. It was obvious that such a coalition would not be able to govern and it soon felt apart.[24]

There is also a premise that an identity crisis in post-communist countries is intensified by attempts to solve the problem from the aspect of ethnic nationalism.[25] Ethnic identity in post-communist countries is defined as primordial, as essentially an orientation to the past, to a collective origin. "Celebrated in rituals, narratives and histories, ethnicity is the sense of belonging, submersion of the self in something that transcendent self, the awareness of heritage and ancestry".[26] Such an implication of ethnicity suggests its existential import. According to Deveraux, ethnic boundaries are caused by commitment to and identity with the groups, and they are a means of preserving the self-identity.[27]

These primordial sentiments in ethnic identification are explained by a rapid urbanization which had destroyed previous society. It may be also found in establishing new relations under the dominance of politics, with identity closely related to the state and class. Such an identity belongs to a society with huge industrial and urban centers, and inhabitants without urban tradition and identity. Elements of modern identity such as town, civic society, culture, liberal ideology, and a democratic political community do not exist. Identity crisis is present as the old patterns are abandoned and new ones are in a process of development with a nationalistic attitude towards the notion of ethnos.[28]

This observation fully corresponds with one recent research of public opinion in Serbia and Montenegro.[29] In an attempt to foresee the prospective of democracy in this country, inquiry consisted of a set of questions concerning ethnic identity. Primordial elements mentioned above were found in all three segments of inquiry: grounds of ethnical self identification, estimation of their own ethnic identity and their attitude towards other ethnic groups. Ethnical identification was measured by several different elements: by the fact of birth into a certain ethnic group, common history and tradition, common territory, religion, language, state, culture, and economy.

According to survey results more than 37% of the population in Serbia and 24.5% in Montenegro are in favor of using birth into ethnic group as a basic criteria of identity. This is the opinion of all ethnic entities, including minorities as well (Hungarians 34.5%, Muslims 83.3%). Because of a correlation between ethnic self-determination and demands for certain territorial boundaries, there was also a question about the stability of FRY (Serbia & Montenegro) boundaries. According to acquired answers, more than 50% in both republics are convinced that boundaries are temporary and that they should be changed. According to the ethnic background of the inquired population 62% of the Serbs and 64.05% of the Montenegrians share this opinion, while 15% of the Serbs and 20% of the Montenegrians believe that they are permanent and stable. It is interesting that even 45.7% of Hungarians also share the opinion that boundaries are temporary and changeable, which is explained by their general political inclination towards territorial autonomy and the very important role of territory in their ethnic identity, shown also in this inquiry.

Contrary to this, only 14.1% of Muslims expect some changes of boundaries, and 26.9% of them believe in their stability. According to the final analysis of these results, the open question of boundaries reveals an identity crisis of the whole country and a crisis of national identity within major ethnic groups. It is also obvious that the processes of integration and the flexible notion of boundaries are not familiar to the public in FRY. In fact boundaries are more important then ever, and firmly connected with expectations for future.

In addition to this, research of this kind of society showed some other features, among which is a latent xenophobia.[30] Ethnic groups are exclusive entities, unready for communication or cooperation with the outside world. Distance to other groups was analyzed through inquiry about the attitude towards Muslims, an ethnic group often denied not only in politics but in science, too. More than 57% of the inquired population in Montenegro considers them as Serbs who accepted Islamic religion, and more than 33% of them in Serbia have the same opinion. A part of them, 17%, think that they are in fact Serbs and Croats with Islamic religion. According to their ethnic background, 40.2% of the Serb population and 40% of the Montenegrian population denied Muslim ethnicity, calling them Serbs. Only 10.5% of the Serbs and 8% of the Montenegrians accept Muslims as an original ethnic group. The Hungarian population was quite uninterested in this segment of ethnic composition – so 37.1% of them admitted that they have not even thought about them and about 45% support their status as an ethnic group. Within the Muslim group 94.9% consider themselves as an ethnic group like other groups.

Finally, an ethnic survey was completed by the estimation of different ethnic groups. According to the results the Serbs and the Montenegrians are the most popular ethnic groups, and there was quite a negative attitude towards groups which are considered as competitive (mainly Croats and Muslims). In Serbia, 59.5% have "very negative" and 13% "to a certain degree negative" opinions about Croats and 59.1% with "very negative" and 13.4% "to a certain degree negative" opinions about Muslims. Results were even more drastic if they are analyzed according to the opinion of each ethnic group.[31] It should be mentioned that similar results proving xenophobia were obtained in research studies done in other Post-Communist countries, of course related to other relevant ethnic groups.[32]

New, or so called ethnical nationalism, is not so visible in legal regulations of these countries, as for the sake of their international reputation they need an impression of democracy. Some signs are present, however, for example, in the tendency of exclusion which is often hidden in the stipulations of constitutional and other legal acts. According to this, each ethnic group should have its own state, excluding others, as historic anomaly or heritage from the past. This could be expressed by identification of the state as a national (ethnically national) state, described by some authors as a constitutional nationalism (as is the case of Croatia, Macedonia and Serbia). Sometimes there is no clear ethnic identification but the idea is still present (article 4 of Constitutional Act of Romania), or it is presumed in those regulations based on a right of self-determination as a right reserved for ethnos and not for demos (Constitutional Act of Slovenia, Introductory part). There is also an opinion that the similar inclination exists if the state guarantees protection for compatriots of the same ethnic background living in other countries (Constitutional Act of Hungary).[33] Exclusionary ideas have implications on legislation concerning citizenship and it presumes three groups of inhabitants: a group consisting of the members of the same dominant ethnic group, other ethnic groups (ethnic minorities) and foreign citizens with permanent residence. Confusion between ethnic identity and citizenship is even more severe in multiethnic federal countries. Their break-down caused a lot of new ethnic minorities, while previous inherent boundaries became international and, what is more important, ethnic boundaries. Different attitudes towards the right of self-determination and interpretations of what is called ethnical interest led to tense situations and conflicts, as in Yugoslavia.

We speak also about one specific (in Yugoslavia a quite large one) minority group of people who lost their ethnic consciousness during the former ideology and couldn't adapt their behavior to new circumstances. Groups with a constitutional ethnic status in previous multiethnic federation became minorities and some earlier tolerated groups in new circumstances lost their ethnical identity.[34] To this one can add old minorities, which became more isolated because their position was made worse by new national states, but also because they are gathering around parties which are also ethnically oriented or identified only with that particular group. These are very painful and distressing situations, and can be seen as refusals to accept differences. They are even more serious considering that individuals are important only as members of some ethnic groups.

At this point we are again on the main feature of nationalism, seen as a collectivism. Collective rights have become dominant, as the claim for right, in such circumstances, can be protected only within one group or society. Instead of a crossing of cultures, nations and interests, we are facing the reality of separated, distant states and populations.

4   Concluding Remarks

A national question should not be treated as a crucial moment in the break-down of former federations, and it is not the major problem of transition in post-communist countries. We could underline the problem of identity crisis and put it in a context of comprehensive social influences, which together with the heritage from the past, affected their path to democracy. That means that the genesis of present conflicts in some post-communist countries is a complex matter, and that possible mechanisms for solving all these problems should include different social preconditions for building up a new society. Pointing out events and situations which caused actual collisions is useful, however, and illustrates mistakes which should not be repeated and direction of desirable way out.

The origins of the present tragedy of former Yugoslavia were searched for in the repression of national feelings under communism.[35] They were also recognized in different factors which caused the internal instability of the past. According to Bianchini we have to take into consideration at least three facts.[36] First is the phenomenon known as economic nationalism; economic and social changes in 1980s which resulted in companies, municipalities and self governed republics isolating themselves to safeguard their particular interest. It was caused by a huge debt crisis which forced the federal authorities to adopt restrictive policies which affected the importation of advanced technology and prevented the country from taking part in the information technology process. To this was added the constant bureaucratic interference and power decentralization, with sharp contrast between developed and underdeveloped areas in country. He concludes: "The disarticulation of the economic system came to affect the political system, reinforcing the image of the Republics as a repository of national interest...".

Another fact is connected with the system of political representation which was actually in past. Citizens in assemblies and parliaments were represented only according to territory, to jobs or to authorized political organizations, but not as individuals. Decision making depended on convergence among various groups, or in the most important issues, of unanimous agreement among the republics and provinces. "After the decentralization established in 1974, the absence of free debate capable of shaping public opinion, influencing associations and opinion and developing critical awareness, led each ethnic group to believe that the difficulties were the consequence of the other nationalities exploitation of their own resources and entrepreneurial and administrative skill." This can be seen in a political culture burdened by a nation strongly cultivated by all ethnic groups and by intellectuals as this author notices. The sentimental relationship between nation and territory originated and was considered to be totally inseparable. "It was a relationship which ended up in making minorities and endless course of irredentism, a sort of Trojan Horse ready to undermine the stability of the majority, a source of constant suspicion." This formed a political culture which developed the national question to extremes and turned it into an ethnic question.[37]

The background of present conflicts could be found in many other facts, such as, for example, the non-existence of democratic institutions and experience in democratic procedure for handling conflicts. There was an increase in the social and political uncertainty of the population, who in previous authoritarian regime did not have support as citizens and had to search for support in the "supra-individual entity of nation".[38] The idea of confederation which was connected with strengthening bureaucratic centralism at the level of national entities, is also considered a burden from the past and a present deadlock for reasonable solution.

Confrontations involving old-fashioned concepts of federalism and sovereignty diminish chances for compromise.[39] Reasons for regression from multicultural to ethnical community are obviously numerous and it is certain that in Yugoslavia, national antagonism was not predestined. However the speed of this process was unexpected as it ended in conflicts within a very short period of time, over a period of two and half years.

Democratization and transformation of all Post-Communist countries, including Yugoslavia, are possible within the framework of a free, civil society, presuming a long term process. Reforms in legal system or declarations will not be of great importance without all-inclusive efforts and free initiatives, as well as autonomy of all people in these societies. The beginning of this process should be expected only after estimation of all negative consequences and recognition of own mistakes. It is, of course, hard to suggest a certain model of transition, knowing that there is a huge civilization gap between these new born countries and other European countries. With the presumption of necessity of integration of these countries in wider associations and surroundings, their ability to overlap this distance is dependent on their ability to reconstruct their complete structure. That means adoption of universal standards and principles like those of democracy, decentralization, rule of law, protection of individual human rights and minority rights and free market, by which a role of state will be in a function of a free and open society within its framework. Rule of law and human rights protection will be possible with the condition of independent judiciary, division and balance of power, and a stable legal system. Economic transformation needs a state of competition, in the form of a free market, where we consider a rather neutral state which integrates economy and free entrepreneurship and not disrupt it with a great deal of intervention.

These changes also correlate with decentralization of authority on a territorial basis. In multiethnic and multinational societies, a territorial subdivision has great importance, and considering the international position of the state, it is in function of integration. Territorial subdivision may be done in manner which makes it possible for a compactly settled minority to have greater influence over the political, cultural and economic decisions affecting its members.[40]

However, this should not serve to give ethnic groups their own state governments, but rather to bring the institutions of power and state services closer to them. In fact a process of solving problems should be closer to citizens and to the extent it would be done, they will achieve their democratic rights with more success. Regions or other forms of territorial subdivisions on interest basis, should be established on geographic, economic, historic, cultural or multiethnic grounds or their mixture, with differences in their status and rights. In regions with multiethnic populations, minority rights protections should be realized through different kinds of mechanisms, like regulating the number of their representatives in regional parliament, or by minority self-government concerning the matters of entrenched jurisdiction of a region.[41]

Decentralization must be coupled with genuine pluralistic democratic governance in each territorial unit, with the same respect for human rights and minority rights as at the national level. This also has to be established in the constitution or in an international agreement as well as it should presume a certain scope of authority or competence of the regional bodies, which is in the interest of its inhabitants.

The benefits can be several as it reduces government overload, facilitates pluralism within the country by diffusing power, broadens the allocation of prestigious political and administrative functions, and facilitates the organization of mother tongue education.

Structural changes and further development in the whole region of former Yugoslavia will still depend on the ability of its countries, to build up a cultural identity on different, new grounds, and to accept dialogue and tolerance in their mutual communications in the future.

Notes

1. Vasovic, V. 1994/95: From the book: "DrZzavnost i regionalizam", Otvoreni univerzitet Subotica, pp. 48-63.
2. Goati, V. 1994/95: Research project: "Puls Jugoslavije", ECCCR 1994.
3. O'Donnell, G. 1994: "Delegative Democracy", Journal of Democracy 5/1994, pp. 59-79.
4. Mitev, P. 1991: From Communism to Democracy, The New Elites in the Context of Social Change – From the conference on: "New Elites, Social Stratification and Social Mobility in the Course of Antinomenclature Revolution", American University Blagoevgrad, pp. 4-5.
5. Goati, ibid.
6. Sartori, G. 1994: "Repenser la democratie: mauvais régime et malais politique", Revue internationale des sciences sociales, 129: pp. 466-481.
7. Rose, R./Mackie, T. 1988: "Do Parties Persist or Fail? The Big Trade-off Facing Organizations", When Parties Fail, Ed. Kay Lawson & Peter Merkl, Princeton, Princeton University Press, pp. 536-556.
8. Easton, D. 1979: A System Analysis of Political Life, Chicago and London, The University of Chicago Press, pp. 207-231.
9. Lijphart, A. 1984: Democracies. Pattern of Majoritarian and Consensus Government in Twenty-One Countries, New Haven, Yale University Press.
10. Goati, ibid.
11. Goati, ibid: Eurobarometer.
12. Gellner, E. 1989: Nations and Nationalism, Blackwell, pp. 4-6.
13. Gellner, ibid.
14. Connor, W. 1973: The Politics of Ethnonationalism, Journal of International Affairs, no. 1, pp. 45-54.
15. Segal, B. 1978: Ethnicity: Where the Present is the Past, From the book: Ethnic Autonomy – Comparative Dynamics: The Americas, Europe and the Developed World, edited by Raymond Hall Pergamon Policy Studies.
16. Segal, ibid.
17. Dimitrijevic, V. 1993: Neizvesnost ljudskih prava, Novi Sad.
18. Liebich, A. 1992: Minorities in Eastern Europe: Obstacles to a Reliable Count, RFE/RL Research report, vol. 1, no 20, pp. 32-45, Examples of Bulgaria and Albania.
19. Hobsbawn, E. J. 1990: Nations and Nationalism Since 1780, Cambridge University Press, pp. 163-178.
20. Kaldor, M. 1993: Yugoslavia and the New Nationalism, New Left Review, no. 197, pp. 96-112.

[21] Kaldor, ibid.

[22] Schierup, C. 1994: Eurobalkanism – Ethnic Cleansing and the Post Cold War Order. From the book "Religion and war", European Movement in Serbia, Belgrade, pp. 125-146.

[23] Dimitrijevic, V. 1994: pp. 52.

[24] Dimitrijevic, ibid: pp. 55.

[25] Janjic, D. 1994: Project: Puls Jugoslavije 1994, Etnonacionalizam i nezivesnost status etnickih manjina, ECCCR Subotica.

[26] Alverson, A. 1978: The Roots of Time. A Comment and Utilitarian and Primordial Sentiments in Ethnic Identification, From the book: Ethnic Autonomy – Comparative Dynamics: The Americas, Europe and the Developed World, edited by Raymond Hall, Pergamon Policy Studies.

[27] Alverson, ibid.

[28] Janjic, ibid.

[29] Project of European Civic Center for conflict Resolution Subotica 1994: Puls Jugoslavije 1994 (Goati, V. /Janjic, D. /Neskovic, R. /Petrovic, J. /Mihailovic, S.).

[30] Janjic, ibid.

[31] Results from the report in project: Puls Jugoslavije.

[32] Dimitrijevic, V. 1993: Case of Poland, Czeh Republic, Bulgary, Slovenia and others.

[33] Gomien, D. 1991: Discrimination and the Right of Political Association under the European Convention on Human rights and the Constitutions of Eastern and Central Europe" – Seminar: The Domestic Implementation of the European Convention on Human Rights in Eastern and Western Europe, Leiden, Oct. 1993.

[34] Dimitrijevic, ibid: pp. 90.

[35] Dimitrijevic, ibid.

[36] Bianchini, S. 1994: The Collapse of Yugoslavia: Sources of its Internal Instability, War and Religion, pp 84-104.

[37] Bianchini, ibid.

[38] Janjic, D. 1994: Disintegration of the former Yugoslavia and the Tragedy of Civil War, War and Religion, pp. 74-84.

[39] Spadijer, Bl. 1992: Osnove buduceg politickog uredjenja, from the book: Za Novu Zajednicu, Institut za medjunarodnu politiku i privredu, pp. 67-70.

[40] Asbjorn, E. 1993/94: Possible Ways and Means of Faciliating the Peaceful and Constructive Solution of Problems Involving Minorities, Economic and Social Council UN, E/CN.4/Sub.2.

[41] Pajvancic, M. 1994: Pravni aspekti regionalizma, from the book: Regioni i Gradjani, Otvoreni univerzitet Subotica, pp. 109-114.

5 Autonomy as One of the Means of Minorities' Protection

The Case of Slovenia

SILVO DEVETAK

After the collapse of the Soviet, Yugoslav, and Czechoslovak federations more than 60 million people, previously citizens of those federations, were transformed overnight into ethnic minorities, living on the other side of the frontiers of their new "mother nation". Together with 30 million persons in Western Europe who belong to ethnic and linguistic minorities, or to regional cultures and languages, the number of minorities in 53 European "nation-states" has come to close to 90 million.[1] With the recent changes of the political map of Europe the greatest number of minorities in its history has thus been created.

A dormant giant whose move may shake Europe to the bottom is the presence of about 25 million Russians in other non-Russian former Union states, and the existence of a further 40 million of non-Russians who live outside of their ethnic territories. According to Mikhail Gorbatchev on May 14, 1992 to the United States Congress: "... We must also recognize that no Russian government can ignore discrimination against a Russian speaking population. Especially when this leads to armed clashes and to the creation of hundreds of thousands of refugees. If the democrats cannot resolve the problem it will be resolved by totalitarian nationalists...".[2]

The refugees could be the possible future "source" of "new" ethnic minorities in Europe. Starting with 10 million Germans that were uprooted in the aftermath of the war, and continuing recently with a mass population transfer of about 5 million that accompanied the partition of the Soviet, Yugoslav and Czechoslovak federations, Europe put itself on equal standing with other continents in this regard.

The status of ethnic minorities is the crucial issue at stake in the process of nation-building, both in old and especially in the newly created states.

The greatest threat to the security of many states is thus their internal conflict with different kinds of minorities, which is in most cases a consequence of their failure to find strength in diversity. The repression of minorities has been shown to be an unsuccessful strategy which fuels conflicts and retards development. The increasing incidence of ethnic dissent is but one manifestation, though one with far-reaching implications, of the widening gap between state and civil society.

It is increasingly obvious that new approaches to the resolution of ethnic conflicts and to the regulation of ethnic problems should be studied, especially those concerning the dichotomy between integration and diversity; concerning democracy and decentralisation of power; regulation and functioning of multicultural societies; suppression of nationalism, xenophobia; and concerning different practical new scenarios for protection of minorities[3] dealing, for instance, with electoral systems (local balance representation, communal balance representation)[4], minority veto for changing the constitution[5] and autonomy[6].

1   Autonomy – Innovation or a Source of New Conflicts?

In theory the terms cultural, political, regional, territorial, personal, and functional autonomy are used like order to specified different ways and means of participation of the given ethnic, linguistic, cultural or religious minority in managing matters related to the territory where they live or to the elements which constitute their separate identity. Each of this type of autonomy has its own characteristics. In practice all of these types are intermingled and overlapping.[7]

The term autonomy is derived from Greek: auto means self, nomos is law. Autonomy in the legal-political vocabulary denotes self-government. The European Charter of Local Self-government defines self-government as "the right and the ability of local authorities, within the limits of the law, to regulate and manage a substantial share of public affairs under their own responsibility and in the interest of the local population" (Art. 3).[8] Granting autonomy to an ethnically mixed area allows the people inhabiting it to exercise direct control over important affairs of special concern to them, while allowing the larger entity, which retains certain powers over the area, to exercise those powers which are in the common interest of both entities.[9] Autonomy means the legal recognition of minorities and minorities rights. It excludes absolute majority rule in view of the special values of a minority. Autonomy is closely connected with human rights.[10]

Normally, the protected minority inhabits a certain part of the state territory, but other constellations are possible. For instance, where an ethnic minority is scattered over the whole or the greater part of the state, it is conceivable that there will be "personal" autonomy and not "territorial" autonomy.[11] The difference between territorial and personal autonomy has been defined in the following terms: territorial autonomy is established in a delineated portion of the territory of a state and it relates to all the inhabitants within the area; personal autonomy is accorded to members of a certain (ethnic, linguistic or religious) community irrespective of their place of residence.

Territorial autonomy is utilized when the population of the autonomous region (or a predominant element of it) has special ethnic or other characteristics justifying a privileged position. But when ethnic and other groups are interspersed throughout the country, autonomy may be offered to all individuals belonging to a particular community, wherever they live within the boundaries of the state.[12] There is the opinion that personal autonomy did not make sense except as a complement to territorial autonomy.[13]

What does the term "cultural autonomy" mean? There are several entities which have been granted "autonomy", not as a response to desires for political self-government, but rather as a means of guaranteeing certain social and ethnic groups a degree of independence from governmental interference in matters of particular concern to these groups, e.g. cultural autonomy (or religious freedom).[14] The effect of the relevant statutory or other provisions in these cases is to protect certain cultural peculiarities, customs, practices, and societal structures from interference on the part of the central or sovereign government.

The term culture should be defined in a broader sense. It should cover not only art and literature but also a way of thinking, tradition, moral principles, the patterns of living, etc.[15] Culture was defined in a similar way by the UNESCO Declaration adopted in Mexico City 1982: "The integrity which constitute all distinctive spiritual, material, intellectual and emotional elements which characterise the society or the social group".

Culture thus cannot exist without freedom in general, which provides the human spirit with the necessary creativity, or without the freedom of conscience. Culture is oriented towards the "inside" ramified system of values which is oriented towards the "outside" different cultures, and therefore mostly in "defense position" towards other "outside" systems of values. How to overcome this differentiation is one of the global necessities of our times, in which there are strong tendencies not only towards universalisation but towards uniformity as well.[16]

The right of nations to preserve their cultures is included in international legal instruments in different ways. It is a part of the UN Charter, of the Universal declaration (1948), of both Conventions on human rights (1966) and of other relevant instruments adopted within the UN system. In addition it is included in the UNESCO Declaration on the principles of international cultural cooperation (1966), and in the documents of the NGO.

The right to culture is a collective right. Capotorti stated in his UN sponsored study that there are few states which have the right to culture regulated by constitutions and laws, and that this right is implemented most effectively when the members of minorities live concentrated in certain regions or when they enjoy political autonomy.[17] In order to implement this right, the states should adopt a great number of provisions concerning, for instance, financing of literature and art creativity, in regard to the spreading of minority culture, of introducing modern technological and other achievements, maintenance of customs and traditions, the protection of cultural heritage, improvement of education as the most important part of culture, etc.[18] Capotorti is of the opinion that the sense of these obligations is to maintain and develop the cultural identity of minorities, and that the states are obliged to adopt the necessary measures for reaching these goals.[19]

In other words, minorities should have the right to be protected; to maintain and develop their culture; to freely express their culture and the achievements of their culture; to the financial support of the state for the implementation of this right (in accordance with the material possibilities of the states concerned); to the inclusion of their culture on equal basis in the state cultural policy as a whole; to the presentation of their cultural achievements in the international cultural cooperation of the country as a whole.

The granting of only cultural and religious autonomy, even if coupled with certain administrative responsibilities, would not seem to constitute "full" autonomy or self-government. The degree of cultural or religious independence enjoyed by minorities in this model does not include sufficient political or legal control over internal matters to constitute full autonomy.[20]

In considering these issues we must take into account that we live in the complex world in which an insistence on only individualism or state sovereignty could not contribute to the resolution of the problems that emerge in the contemporary world.[21]

2   The Case of Slovenia

As to the Republic of Slovenia, according to the census of 1991, was its population of 1,965,986 was composed of 87.84% (in 1953 of 96.52%!) people who declared themselves to be of Slovenian ethnic origin. 141,422 persons or 7.20% of the total declared their ethnic adherence to the "nations and nationalities" of the second Yugoslavia (Croats constitutes 2.76% of the total number of "non-Slovenes", Serbs – 2.44%, Muslims – 1.37%, Macedonians – 0.23%, Montenegrins – 0.22%, Albanians – 0.18%).

A great deal of those who declared themselves as Yugoslavs (12,370 or 0.63%) or of those whose "descent" was "undetermined" (9,011 or 0.46%) or "unknown or unclear" (53,545 or 2.72%) could be added to the "non-Slovene" faction of the population. The segment of the population with roots in the "non-Slovene" nations and nationalities of the former Yugoslavia is probably around 10% of the total population of Slovenia. That figure does not include the descendants of the "Yugoslav immigrants" who had, in the census 1991, chosen the "Slovene" allegiance and could "change their mind" in other political and social circumstances.

Nevertheless, as the non-Slovene population is treated by the constitution as "non-autochthonous", they are entitled (Art. 62 of the constitution) only to the right to use their languages and scripts "in all dealings with state bodies and other bodies having official functions".

The "manner" shall be determined by the statute that was not yet adopted.

The three "ethnic communities" that are, together with the Slovenes, treated by the constitution as the "autochthonous population" of the republic and thus protected – the Hungarians, Italians and Roma (Gypsies) – numbered, according to the 1991 census, 13,860 members altogether or 0.71% of the total population. In particular, Hungarians – 8,503 or 0.43% of the total population, Italians – 3,064 (0.16%), and Roma 2,293 (0.12%). The status and rights of the Hungarian and Italian "national communities" (the constitutional term for ethnic minorities) represent a mixture of elements of the territorial/political, personal and cultural autonomy, while the Roma (Gypsies) enjoy (Art. 65 of the constitution) a limited cultural autonomy, mainly concerning primary education, which should be determined by the statute (that was not yet adopted).

The territorial/political autonomy of the Hungarian and Italian "national communities" is based on the notion of "ethnically mixed territories" that was established 30 years before by a list of "ethnically mixed locations" enshrined in the statutes of the communes Murska Sobota and Lendava/Lendva (Hungarians) and Koper/Capodistria, Izola/Isola, and Piran/Pirano (Italians). In these communes both minorities had, by the constitution of 1974, among other privileges, the right to participate, through their representatives, in governing these communes as well as participate in the decision making within the local authorities. The participation was exercised in two ways. First, the self-managing communities of interest of the ethnic minorities decide independently on matters of paramount importance for their identity. Second, these communities of interest constitute the third chamber of the communal assembly, thus deciding on an equal basis with the "majorities chambers" on matters of interest for minorities (concerning culture, education and upbringing, space planning, topographical inscriptions etc.).

With the reform of local self-government in 1994, 157 municipalities have been established, replacing 61 former communes, including the five communes with "ethnically mixed territories". The new law on the establishment of municipalities and the determination of their territory[22] has introduced important modifications into the system of local minorities' self-government, at least as far the Hungarian minority is concerned.

Some of the ethnically mixed areas populated with Hungarians have been placed into different municipalities than they were before. The Hungarian national community is now divided between three local communities – municipalities: Hodo-Salovci, Moravske Toplice and Lendava. The ethnically mixed area that has before been on the territory of Murska Sobota has been divided between the municipalities of Moravske Toplice[23] and Hodos-Salovci.[24]

The Hungarian national community has thus been divided into three parts instead of two parts as it was during the socialist regime. The territory of Hungarian settlement is geographically dispersed. The consequences of the further administrative division could harm the ability of this minority to self-govern the matters which are of paramount importance for the maintenance of their identity, or to act jointly when necessary.

Hungarians will in the future have more difficulties cooperating with each other than they had during the former regime. In the new municipalities, except Lendava, the Hungarian minority constitutes a real minority. In the municipality of Hodo-Salovci only two out of 8 settlements are ethnically mixed and in Moravske Toplice 8 out of 28. Obviously, this is a sphere where the special rights of Hungarians are in danger of being reduced.

On the territory of the municipalities of Lendava, Izola, Koper and Piran no changes have been made as far as ethnically mixed areas are concerned. All ethnically mixed areas remained in the same municipalities as they were before the changes of legislation.[25] The law on self-government (Art. 72)[26] provides the "ethnically mixed" and other interested municipalities with the option of establishing a region in order to "resolve the issues concerning the realisation of the rights and statutory provisions prescribed by the constitution". Insofar as neither the "majority" nor the "minority" population had realised this opportunity.

This law (Art. 39) prescribes that the new municipalities which have ethnically mixed territories will, within their competence, regulate the issues concerning the rights and the financing of the needs of the "national communities". The latter will have the right to veto these municipal enactments through their representatives in the municipality's council (at least one member of the relevant "national community"). In this, municipalities commissions for ethnic questions will be established, of which one half will be composed of minorities' and the other of majority members.

The laws on the elections of deputies in the State Chamber of 1992[27] and in the councils of new municipalities from 1993[28] prescribe that the Hungarian and Italian "national communities" are represented, by mandate, by one deputy each in the State Chamber, and (together with Roma) by at least one member of the councils of the new ethnically mixed six municipalities. The minorities' representatives are elected by persons who are on the "electoral list" prepared by both ethnic self-governing organisations.

The law on the self-managing national communities of 1994[29] prescribes special rights for Italian and Hungarian national communities regarding their organising on the territories where they live, concerning relationships between their organisations and state agencies or local bodies as well as their international cooperation. It is an attempt to encompass several important questions regarding national communities with a single norm, especially their role in the decision-making process on different levels of state administration and local self-governing.

According to this law the members of Italian and Hungarian national communities in areas of their autochtonous settlement have a special right to establish self-managing national communities for the promotion of their needs and for organised participation in public matters. This right is guaranteed in the constitution. Herewith it is carried out in details through law.

According to the law (Art. 3) the "self-managing national community" is a public legal person performing following tasks:
- deciding autonomously on all matters within its competence in accordance with the constitution and law;
- giving consent, in accordance with the law, to matters concerning the protection of special rights of national communities;
- discussing and studying matters concerning its status, and adopting opinions and submitting proposals and initiatives to competent bodies;
- stimulating and organising activities contributing to the preservation of ethnic identity of members of the two national communities.

The highest body of the municipal self-managing national community is its council (Art. 7). It is elected by the members of the national community through direct elections. The statute of the self-managing national community defines in detail the tasks and competencies of the community, its organisation, the methods of decision-making process, the modes and forms of representing the community and the procedure for electing the organs of the community.

The statute determines the manner and forms of cooperation of the self-managing national community with organisations, associations and other forms of activities, established by the members of the national community, for the implementation of their special rights (Art. 11). Self-managing national communities implement those tasks by (Art. 4):

- inciting and organising cultural, research, information, publishing Nadia Skenderovic Cukand economic activities essential for the development of national communities;
- establishing organisations and public institutions;
- considering and promoting the development of education and schooling of members of national communities and, pursuant to law, participating in the planning and organising of educational work and the preparation of educational programs;
- promoting contacts with their parent nation, members of ethnic communities in other states and with international organisations;
- pursuant to law, performing tasks which are the competence of the state;
- performing other tasks arising from the statute.

The self-managing national communities cooperate with the representatives of the national communities, elected in the bodies of self-managing local communities and in the State Chamber, with the bodies of self-managing local communities and with state agencies (Art. 5).

The members of national communities who have the general right to vote and are registered in a special municipal register for voters – members of the national community, have the right to vote and to be elected for a member of the council of the municipal self-managing national community (Art. 8).

The Italian and Hungarian national communities have the right to integrate the management of their issues on all territories where they live by creating a regional community for fulfilling their special needs. Self-managing national communities could unite into an Italian or Hungarian Self-managing Community of the Republic of Slovenia. The highest body of self-managing is the council of the self-managing national community (Art. 9).

Self-managing national communities may submit proposals, initiatives and opinions to local self-governing communities on matters regarding the status of national communities and the preservation of characteristics of the ethnically mixed territory. The bodies of self-managing national communities are obliged to deal with such motions and express an opinion on them (Art. 12). From the law it is not clear what the procedure should be in the case when the local communities reject those motions. This means that the national community could not challenge the negative decision of the local community but could probably prepare a new motion.

Self-managing national communities could also submit proposals, initiatives and opinions on all matters within their competence to the State Chamber, the government and to other state agencies (Art. 15). These bodies are not obliged to give their opinion on those motions but are requested to ask for the opinion of the national communities whenever deciding on the matters related to their status. Of course, they are not legally bound to take the opinion into account. In this case, negotiations and political pressure remain as the only means which the national community could undertake in order to put forward its cause. Due to the small number of members of the national community is it a rather weak remedy, probably connected with many political inconveniences.

Personal Autonomy

Is expressed by the right of the members of the Hungarian and Italian national communities to learn their languages, on facultative basis, in secondary schools outside the ethnically mixed territories if at least 6-7 pupils express this wish (until now one case). The second case of personal autonomy is the provision that the members of the "ethnic communities" living anywhere on state territory can vote for mandatory minorities' deputies in the State Chamber, providing that the self-governing national communities organisation had put him/her on the list of voters.

Cultural Autonomy

On the basis of the law on the organisation and financing of education[30] and the law on institutes[31] (both of 1991), the ethnic communities are the co-founders of primary and secondary schools and representation in the school councils is mandatory. In accordance with the latter law the Hungarian national community has established the institutes for culture and for information (TV and broadcasting programs are not yet included, due to different interests of the employees). This action is in accordance with art. 40 of the law on mass media.[32]

The Italian minority has no institutes of this kind but exercise "autonomous influence" on managing its local TV and broadcasting studio (which is formally a part of the national/state program), through the program council, and by giving opinions for the nomination of the director of the program (who is appointed by the Council of RTV) and the editors. Members of the Italian minority are not satisfied with the situation in this regard. Both minorities have the right, according to the law on broadcasting and TV[33], to each nominate one member of the Council of the RTV (Art. 16) and two thirds of the members of the program council for minorities' programs (Art. 22). The law has stipulated that until 1 January 1996 a "minimal Hungarian national program" should be established (Art. 30).

Both national communities autonomously run the publishing of newspapers, periodicals and books in their respective languages. The public libraries on ethnically mixed territories – in the councils of which the national communities are duly represented, on the basis of the respective law – have separate units with literature in the minorities languages.

All the above mentioned rights should be implemented regardless of the numerical strength of the respective national community (Art. 64, par. 4 of the constitution). This obviously applies, first of all, to the implementation of the elements of different intermingled kinds of autonomy, exercised by the members of the Italian and Hungarian "national communities".

3   Conclusions

In the past it has been thought that linguistic and cultural uniformity would lead to greater economic well-being. Yet the flourishing economic developments witnessed, for example, by the Flemings and the Catalans from the time they have been able to master their own autonomous development, contrasts most favourably with former circumstances when their specificity was ignored or even discouraged.

Autonomies have, in principle, a special link with regionalism and especially with cross-border regional co-operation. Should the European governments recognise the special role of ethnic autonomous regions in this co-operation, and of the development of cultural, social and economic links between people who are united by a common language, culture and tradition?

In considering the issues related to the rights and status of ethnic minorities it is not to be forgotten however, that the return to the roots, which is identified with cultural pluralism as response to the homogenised culture of our mass societies, is only one side of the equation.

The other side is equality of opportunity in a society which places a special premium on social mobility.[34] The equality in opportunity could be realised in the circumstances of economic and social development of the societies, what is not the case in many societies of Eastern Europe.

In addition, European integration will, of necessity, have to reconcile the acceptance of cultural diversity and linguistic pluralism with overarching, shared values affecting such things as parliamentary democracy, freedom of the individual, social intervention, economic organisation, etc. If there is to be a Europe, if there is to be a cultural Europe, it must be cosmopolitan or it must not be, said Bernard-Henry Levy.

Nationalist and xenophobic movements of various forms are once more emerging in both Eastern and Western Europe and may eventually pose a serious threat not only to democracy of the states concerned but to European unity and peace as well. Will the democratic conscience of European people be strong enough to open new prospects for the future in which the Four Riders of the Apocalypse will fade as are discrimination, racism, nationalism and hegemonism?

Tolerance is needed in order to handle relations and diversities in any society in proper way. But tolerance does not mean indifference or the renunciation of standards in the face of pressures from demagogic tyrannies. Tolerance should be supported by *guarantees* of intellectual, ethical and social health.

In addition, would the forming of the new European order be based on the traditional (nationalistic) patterns of irredenta, secession and the like, all connected with great risks for peace and security, or will new models will be constructed, emanating from the concept of cooperation and mutual interests and understanding? Would the European governments be aware, when taking their stands toward such questions as are self-determination, plebiscite (as one way of its realisation), irredentism, secession, separatism that they are in this way making their choices between peace and war?

The map and the history of Europe – not just its Eastern parts – is a maelstorm of conflicting forces, warring tendencies. Our task in the last decade of the 20th century will be to come theoretically to grips with them, to see to it that this will not in fact be the widely publicised "end" of European history, nor a desperate return to national atavism, but rather the beginning of a new European civilisation, a civilisation able to maintain differences and dynamism, but without the enemy imagery that has been such an integral part of European history in the past.

Autonomy remains a useful, if imprecise, concept within which flexible and unique political structures may be developed to respond to the increasingly complex interdependence of contemporary world politics. The increasing frequency of claims to autonomy and the incremental effect such claims undoubtedly will have upon the international legal order make the concept of autonomy ripe for review.

Notes

1. For the basic data consult:

   Murdock, G.P. 1987: Ethnographic Atlas, University of Pittsburgh Press, Pittsburgh.

   Heraud, G. 1968: Peuples et Langues d'Europe, Paris.

   Stephens, Meic1976: Linguistic Minorities in Western Europe, Gomer Press.

   The preparatory documentation of the Council of Europe for the European Charter on minorities' and regional languages and cultures.

2. Moynihan, Daniel P. 1993: Ethnicity in International Politics, Oxford University Press, New York, p. 6.

3. Francis, E. K. 1976: Interethnic Relations, New York: Elsevier, pp. 386-429.

4. Chapman, David 1991: Can Civil War be Avoided? Electoral and Constitutional Models for Ethnically Divided Countries, London: The Institute for Social Inventions, pp. 62-83, pp. 88-90, pp. 146-49.

5. Lijphart, Arend 1984: Democracies, Pattern of Majoritarian and Consensus Government in Twenty-One Countries, New Haven, Yale University Press, pp. 189-90.

6. National Separatism, Ed. Collin/H.Williams 1982: Cardiff: University of Wales Press, especially p. 96, p. 101, p. 110, p. 115, p. 173, p. 389, p. 391.

7. For broader information on this topic see Minorities and Autonomy in Western Europe, Compiled and edited by Minority Rights Group, Manchester Free Press, London, 1991.

8. European Charter of Local Self-government, European Treaty Series No. 122, Council of Europe, Strasbourg, 15 October 1985.

9. Sohn, Louis B. 1981: Models of Autonomy Within the United Nations Framework, in: Dinstein, Yoram (Ed.), Models of Autonomy, New Brunswick – London, p. 5.

10. Bernhardt, Rudolf. 1981: Federalism and Autonomy, in: Dinstein, Yoram (Ed.), Models of Autonomy, New Brunswick – London, p. 27.

11. Bernhardt, ibid p. 27.

12. Dinstein, Yoram 1981: Autonomy, in: Dinstein, Yoram (Ed.), Models of Autonomy, New Brunswick-London, p. 292.

    See also: Redslob 1931: Le principe des nationalites, Recueil des Cours 1, 37, pp. 48-49.

13. Dinstein, ibid, p. 293.

14. Hannum, Hurst/Lillich, Richard B. 1981: The Concept of Autonomy in International Law, in: Dinstein, Yoram (Ed.), Models of Autonomy, New Brunswick – London, 1981, p. 246.

[15] Devetak, Silvo 1988: Manjine, ljudska prava, demokratija (Minorities, Human Rights, Democracy), Oslobodjenje, Sarajevo, p. 256.

[16] Devetak, ibid, p. 257.

[17] Capotorti, Francesco 1979: Study on the Rights of Persons Belonging to Ethnic, Religious and Linguistic Minorities, UN Press Office, New York, p. 99, p. 591.

[18] Capotorti, ibid, pp. 99-100, pp. 593-598.

[19] Capotorti, ibid, p. 100, pp. 599.

[20] Hannum/Lillich listed the following elements of full autonomy: locally – elected body with some independent legislative power; locally-chosen chief executive; independent local judiciary; powersharing between the central and autonomous government. Ibid, p. 252.

[21] Dyke, van Vernon 1980: The Cultural Rights of People, in: Universal Human Rights, 2, p. 21.

[22] Official Gazette of the Republic of Slovenia, No. 60/94 adopted on 3 October 1994.

[23] The municipality of Moravske Toplice now encompasses settlements Berkovci pri Prosenjakovcih, Ivanjsevci, Lonèarovci, Motvarjevci, Pordasinci, Prosenjakovci and Sredisèe.

[24] The municipality of Hodos-Salovci encompasses settlements Hodos and Krplivnik.

[25] In ill Priorske novice, Official announcements, No.9/95 of 25 May 1995.

[26] Official Gazette of the Republic of Slovenia, No.72/93 and 57/94.

[27] Official Gazette of the Republic of Slovenia, No.44/92.

[28] Official Gazette of the Republic of Slovenia, No.72/93, adopted on 31 December 1993.

[29] Official Gazette of the Republic of Slovenia, No. 65/94 of 20 October 1994.

[30] Official Gazette of the Republic of Slovenia, No. 12/91.

[31] Ibid.

[32] Official Gazette of the Republic of Slovenia, No.18/94, adopted on 8 April 1994.

[33] Official Gazette of the Republic of Slovenia; No.18/94, adopted on 8 April 1994.

[34] Zubrzycki, J. 1987: Multiculturalism and the search for roots, Papers in multicultural studies (Centre for multicultural studies, The Flinders University of South Australia, p. 17.

6 Ethnic Conflicts in Croatia?

DRAGO ROKSANDIC

1   Is Ethnicity the Focus of the Current Conflicts in South-Eastern Europe and Elsewhere?

This is no doubt the most important question to deal with at the conference for ethnic cooperation. It is almost trivial to say that interpersonal (and/or group) relations are always, in different ways, conflictual ones. Sometimes, while following a certain number of recent international discussions about current conflicts and/or wars in multiethnic regions like that of South-Eastern Europe, it looks like that triviality has been either forgotten or ignored.

In such an approach, overestimating "ethnicity", human beings participating in those conflicts and/or others affected by them in innumerable ways do identify themselves only with a certain "ethnicity". Experts reduce their individual "characters", their personalities to a supposed national "character", "willingness", "aspiration", etc. Since "characters" have been involved in conflicts, causing heavy human losses and large-scale destruction, "good" and "bad" guys have had to be identified, etc.

It will be very important sometime in the future to investigate the "reinvention" of stereotypes, in particular, South-Eastern "ethnicities" in Western mass media in Europe in the period 1991-1995, in order to understand the controversies of the attitudes toward the "reinvention" of ethnicities.

This is not to laugh at somebody, just creating a new group of "stereotypes" along prevailing types of perceptions of the nature of conflicts in similar circumstances. Unfortunately, effects of such an approach to ethnic conflicts and/or wars have been disastrous in many ways.

This is just to insist upon the fact that a long tradition of critical thinking in European and American social and political sciences and humanities cannot be marginalized and just put aside while dealing with such complex realities as "ethnic conflicts".

What makes the Western tradition distinctive in the world, in a long-term modern historical perspective, is a rational attitude toward conflicts and continuous and practical efforts to manage them.

One of the most important expectations in the "other" Europe after 1939 was related to that particular feature of the Western tradition. Actually, the major concern of the majority of "dissidents", later on of mass movements, including a certain number of reformed communists "returning" themselves to social democratic "roots", was how to establish a society of free individuals, who are willing to respect each other in their distinctiveness, including differences of interests, etc.

There is one essential question to be answered. How did it happen that processes of ethnic homogenizations and sometimes confrontations of different kinds in that "other" Europe overcame the other ones based on reconstructions of societies on civil values, the closest ones to the constitutive values of the European Community – in spite of the generally proclaimed aim to integrate the "other" Europe with the European Community – this remains an open question which includes a large variety of problems.

It is quite clear that there has been a lot of historical illusions in the process of "deconstructing" totalitarian structures of power in the "East", as well as in the "West". Both parts of Europe were not ready to confront themselves with the challenges of the future under new historical circumstances. How to try to understand it?

After realizing that the collapse of "leftist" totalitarianism made it possible to *recognize real differences of all kinds all over the continent*, it became of the utmost importance in the "East" as well as in the "West" to learn to manage the process of *rapprochement* of distinctive regions, within a continental framework, in a long-term perspective. It has been beyond capacities of either the "West" or the "East" to cope with it within a relatively short time. *"Europe now!"*, a slogan from 1989, turned out to be as illusionary in a short-term perspective as so many others in the 20th century history of the continent.

Instead of *"Back to normality!"* from 1989, the new slogan became *"Back to the history!"*, meaning, *"Back to traditional values!"*, of course understood as the "invention of traditions" (E. Hosbawam). It made it possible to "rehabilitate", in the public opinion, two currents in different political traditions intending to restore a certain status quo ante; both pretending to present themselves to be the only ones able to "protect national interests", to "save the nation".

The first one, having more chances to succeed in the immediate-after-1989 was related to traditional pre-Communist nationalisms. These were mostly outlawed and persecuted by Communist authorities because they were at odds with the realities of the totalitarian systems, particularly when these systems attempted to present themselves publicly in terms of "national communism".

The other one was and has been related to the successors of the once ruling Communist parties, newly "adjusted" to the constitutional realities of the collapse of the totalitarian structures of power, interwoven in many ways in the structures of powers, etc. and identify with recently discovered populist "historical national interests" in opposition to "illusions of European liberalism".

Both currents, although hostile to each other for the last half a century, quite often "reconcile" themselves in their traditionalist "antimodernism" and "national fundamentalism". Their competing modernizing political currents have been oriented toward processes of global structural changes and European integrations. In a long-term historical perspective, such different traditionalist currents will represent cores of populist/nationalist "revivals", rooted in a more or less discredited policy of the "rush toward Europe".

Such "revivals", incompatible with many of major European objectives, do and will not necessarily contradict at least temporary interests of the European integrationalist policy, including all its complexities on a different basis, in particular continental regions and/or countries of transition in that "other" Europe. Having in mind that, from the point of view of the European Union, many of the challenging problems that the "other" Europe has been continuously dealing with are relatively "insoluble" within a shorter period of time, it is quite realistic to assume that in some cases authoritarian systems, guaranteeing either geopolitical stability or the "rule of law" (in an ironic sense), under different covers will be at least tolerated by "Europe" for certain periods, as well as some other authoritarian systems that will not be treated in comparable ways under certain circumstances. It is the same with the American policy in the "other" Europe to the extent it is different from the Western European one.

Europe, as the project for the 21st century, is still in the making and traditional nationalisms, sometimes more to the right and sometimes more to the left, will be unavoidable from the pragmatic, instrumental standpoint in that long-term process. From that point of view, ethnonationalism is and will be "structural" both from inside and outside, nationally and internationally. As was generally the case of communist strategies in the 20th century, the "national question" in the "other" Europe appears to be again the "instrumental" one. Instead of interrelating political democracy and national interests, following some of the most successful Western experiences, the "other" Europe is confronted with the challenge of the old-fashioned clientalist ethnonationalisms on a longer transitional way to the world of liberal democracy and prosperity. It is doubtful whether it will function. The gap between the "West" and the "East" of Europe is going to be bigger than in the past, in spite of different kinds of systemic adjustments of the "East" to the "West".

It means that it is quite realistic to expect new types of ethnonational frustrations and conflicts in the near future, related not only to traditional lines of ethnic tensions either within or outside particular societies, but also to unfulfilled expectations of the future and directed against "responsible" ethnically identified structures of power in "Europe", "America" etc.

2 Positive Approach: Is it Possible in the History of Interethnic Relations?

The most controversial problem of the "positive approach" to ethnic conflicts is how to rationalize conflicts, to make it possible to understand what "produces" and "generates" them. This is the problem affecting policy-makers as well as scholars and scientists, intellectuals of different backgrounds, not to mention a democratic public opinion. I can try to contribute to it from the standpoint of a social historian interested in using history to study cultural impacts of pragmatic objectives of ethnic policy making.

There is one aspect which is particularly important within such an approach. Ethnonationalists regularly do instrumentalise history and have in mind a conflictual character of interethnic relations. Regularly, they do not pay appropriate attention to critical evaluations of the historically articulated context of particular cases of conflicts. Quite to the contrary, linking different cases of conflicts, quite often irrespective of time and space, into voluntarily constructed "continuities", they perpetuate them into ethnically based structures of eternal war, obliging every new generation to contribute to reach its final outcome. *"Either we or they!"*

Are there actually "continuities" of that kind in the history of Croato-Serbian/Serbo-Croatian relations in Croatia since the 15th century, the period of the first historically relevant Serb migrations into medieval Croatian territories until now? Ethnonationalists on both sides do insist upon them along different lines (social, cultural, religious, etc.), better to say, along practically all those constituting a complexity of interethnic relations. Respecting *"quasi-immobile"* structures of history, one has to admit that it is not that easy to ignore that an example of religious intolerance from the 16th century is particularly interesting for everybody inclined to reduce realities of both concrete historical situations to "features". That is why I find that the culture of historical thinking is directly related to the culture of interethnic relations.

Within such a reductionist construction of history of interethnic relations, in the case of Croats and Serbs, the climax has been reached in the 20th century, of course perceived in different ways on opposing sides. All the atrocities committed either on the one or on the other side do represent the main arguments for the legitimation of the use of the most drastic measures against the other side as the only appropriate ones in the multisecular continuity of conflicts.[1]

If one reconsider only some aspects of the history of Croato-Serbian/Serbo-Croatian relations in Croatia in a long-term perspective, it can be found that instead of a one-dimensional, "reductionist" perception of its heritage, as has been aggressively imposed on public opinion on both sides, there is another, to a large extent still uninvestigated history, based on innumerable research of generations of scholars.

It has been dominantly *border history*. (The exact notion should be determined!). For the last half a millenium, in particular from the 16th to the 18th centuries, Croatian territories have been divided between such powers like as Hapsburg Monarchy, the Ottoman Empire and the Venetian Republic. One has to take care of processes and developments within all of them, in particular in different kinds of interactions and interdependencies, in order to try to understand, either in Rankean or in any other way of historical thinking, what actually happened in the one or the other Croatian territory at a certain period. In the 19th and the 20th centuries, within the process of nation-building, a problem of *territorial integration* has been continuously overshadowing and determining the other ones related to modernization of the Croatian society within its larger inter-regional framework (Pannonia, Alpine region, Adriatic/Mediterranean, Dinaric/Balkan region), shared with neighbors. Again, *border history*. Not for the last time.

In order to legitimize frontiers in regions historically populated by different ethnicities and to affirm a national territorial unity within an area including parts of different European regions, as is the case in both Serbia and Croatia, it is very important to continuously regenerate a historical consciousness based on the assumption that either the one or the other is particularly important for the stability of the European civilization as such. (Again, *border mentality*.)

Due to the fact that frontiers of national territories, derived from the history of the medieval state law, have not coincided with ethnic ones, perceptions of national interests were subjected to those arguments which made territorial aspirations under new historical realities more viable. That is why even frontiers from the classical period, as well as religious ones from early modern ages, having nothing to do with Croats and Serbs, used to be introduced to interethnic disputes in the processes of modern nation-building.

Interethnic relations have been often intermediated either with their heritage or with aspirations. The weakest point actually became its capacity to link competing national ideologies with realities of interethnic relations. That lack of capacity on both sides to put the appropriate questions on the reality of interethnic relations within the Croatian society in longer periods in the 19th and 20th centuries has helped to create many myths, stereotypes, etc. on both sides, limiting the ability to study in a more pragmatic way. It is in the interest of both policy-making and historical research to distinguish properly between history of interethnic relations and their realities and new potentials in future-orientated project(s). It is to a large extent dependent upon political willingness of elites as well as lower strata of the population to be ready to agree upon such a turning point. It is hard to believe that it is possible with the actual situation in Croatia. The positive approach includes, two quite contrary attempts to either forget the past or to "deethnicise" interethnic relations within a broader perspective of modernization, necessarily including an open, complex and, in particular, interethnic dialogue of past, present and future interethnic relations in varieties of conflicts, conflict management, reconciliations, cooperations, etc.

It is in the interest of the international community to participate in such a long-term project of establishing interethnic research and education in Croatia. Positive outcomes might be of positive impact not only in that country.

3 What Does a Positive Approach in Historical Research and Teaching Constitute?

One of the most important obstacles to affirming such an approach is a general lack of readiness to accept the culture of thinking in comparative terms. It is probably not convincing for so many who are sure that obsession with comparisons is one of the most striking features of cultural identities of "small nations" in Central Eastern Europe.

The problem is a lack of capacity to compare in concrete, verifiable terms. There is a general ignorance about neighbors among "small nations" in that part of Europe.

I shall try to identify some of the most important fields of research which do have enormous psychological, cultural and political implications in the reality of Croato-Serbian/Serbo-Croatian relations in Croatia. Since it is impossible to register neither all of them nor to describe in depth controversies within every particular one, this list is supposed to present the complexity of the historical argumentation in both ideologies of interethnic conflicts.

1. *Mutual denials of ethnic identities.* Both ethnic names are relatively old ones, in particular in relation to names of quite a large number of other ethnic communities in Europe succeeding to constitute themselves as modern nations. The oldest Byzantine and Western sources do make distinctions between them along with migrations of numerous Slavic tribes to the area of the Roman Empire; but sometimes they interchange one with the other and sometimes even include the one with the other. Every such source implies territorial consequences and it has always been a question of innumerable disputes. Since there is generally not a larger number of older sources, and what is even more important there is an extremely small number of written oldest sources, ethnonational imaginations have been very fertile until the most recent period. In spite of the fact that there is a long continuity of efforts to establish a critical approach to sources, going back to the 17th

century in the case of Croats and to the 18th century in the case of Serbs, it is obvious that the oldest, medieval period of Croato-Serbian/Serbo-Croatian relations will, for a longer time, be for both professional historians and interested public a motive for ethnically competing and conflicting interpretations

2. *Christianization.* One of the most popular beliefs on both sides is that, from the period of migrations, Serbs were under the influence of Eastern Christianity and Croats under the influence of Western, reducing the enormous complexity of the religious history out of interest. That includes conclusions that Croats, from their arrival to the territory of the Roman Empire, do represent "antemurale christianitatis", of course of the Western Church, as well as Serbs of the Eastern Church. It is very well known among experts of that period that such a deep division had nothing to do with realities of the time and that in spite of discontinuities and changing sociopolitical realities, a Byzantine political influence was an important one along the Eastern coast of the Adriatic until the beginning of the 13th century and ecclesiastical influence from Rome was an important one among Serbs as well until the same period. Not to mention that the oldest Christianization of Serbs was probably realized primarily from ecclesiastical centers along the south-eastern Adriatic coast, which continuously belonged to the Western Church.

There is a long list of questions related to interconfessional relations between Croats and Serbs, Catholics and Orthodox, which make simplifications of all kinds and, in particular, identifications of Serbian identity with the Eastern Christian Church and Croats with the Western Christian Church. These views, which prevail today among intellectual and political elites on both sides, are totally inappropriate to historical realities.

Unfortunately, there has never been anything done on either side to relativize the importance of religion in ethnic and/or national relations from the "instrumental" point of view. To the contrary, military disintegration of the Yugoslav federation and "ethnic cleansings" in Croatia, Bosnia and Hercegovina and Serbia were and are to a large extent related to the religious justifications. Ethnonationalism and religious nationalism on both sides have been profoundly interwoven. Historical research and teaching which contribute to rationalization of

Croato-Serbian/Serbo-Croatian relations are particularly responsible for the development of comparative religious history within that framework, including not only ecclesiastical history but also popular beliefs, etc.

3. *Serbian migrations to Croatia.* Historians who insist that under complex historical circumstances, since the earliest periods of settlements until now, there have always been migrations (in different directions!) of communities of different kinds, families and individuals belonging to different ethnic communities in border regions populated by both Croats and Serbs, as well as different processes of acculturation, are still a minority among professionals. Perceived within such a complex network of migrations over a large mountainous region of Balkans open to both Pannonia and Mediterranean, controlled by the competing political authorities of the Habsburgs, Ottomans and Venetians, migrations of Serbs to Croatia since the 15th century is an extremely complicated historiographical problem which could be investigated and understood better only in cooperation with a large variety of experts involved in long-term projects. There is no doubt that these migrations do not include only Serbs and Croats. Since there has never been a continuously established publication of sources and research in social history on ethnodemographic changes in Croatian territories from the 15th until the 20th century, there are mostly disputes and conflicts on everything related to the topic: Who actually migrated? Under what circumstances? Invited? Refugee? What legal status did the migrating groups enjoy, etc.? (Doesn't it sound familiar to recent experiences?)

4. *Ethnodermographic changes.* Again a problem including a large variety of disputes. Both historiographies are inclined to identify data "favorable" for national ideological and pragmatic objectives. The fact is that there is only a continuity of Serbian immigrations and emigrations to/from Croatian territories, as well as moves within Croatian territories. Since Serbs used to be mostly frontiersmen, merchants, etc. (mobile populations), the intensity and spectrum of ethnodemographic changes have been more dynamic than in the case of Croats, although this has always been related to certain differences in cultural patterns, mentalities, etc. Of course, this is a topic for serious investigation, not for

speculation, in particular due to the fact that ethnodemographic changes among Croats have also been enormous ones. Those changes have regularly been related to forceful "stimuli", not only of the political and military type, but also relating to exhaustion of fertile lands, lengthy droughts, famines, epidemic diseases, etc. Cultural and religious pressures of different kinds, related to the customary established ways of life, have also been extremely important.

If there is a long-term tendency in ethnodemographic changes in Croatian territories, the uncertainty is due to the lack of reliable statistical sources until the 18th century. I presume that it is possible to establish a hypothesis that, including all oscillations, from the relative point of view, there is a growing number of Serbs in Croatia until the beginning of the 19th century and a declining number since that period until 1991. This means that if there would be no war, the number of Serbs would continue to decline under the impacts of urbanization of rural populations, globalisation of effects of national culture, etc. Since it has been the case with Croats in Vojvodina and Serbia in general, alternative approaches have been needed, not military and violent ones. This is the point which mostly relates historical research with current trends.

5. *Language and characters.* In spite of the distinctive character of Croatian and Serbian culture and literary language, there is no doubt that either at the level of the popular, mostly agrarian culture, or at the level of the elite culture, there is a large variety of similarities, analogies, etc., in comparison to each other. It has always been a motive to insist upon either integralist identities or on fundamental differences related to spiritual, cultural and civilisational incompatibilities between the Eastern and Western world. Both attitudes are recognizable ones on both sides, mostly in different periods, since there has always been a prevailing pattern of opposing reactions in the 19th and the 20th centuries.

There is no doubt that from the linguistic point of view there is a lot in common among Croats and Serbs, Bosnians and Montenegroes and that, in particular, the modern literary languages of all of them converge to a large extent. But, there is also no doubt that cultural traditions in the long-term perspective do distinguish from each other, even if one does not accept such oversimplifications like the Cyrillic alphabet as a particular Serbian feature and Latin as a particular Croatian feature, not to mention all kind of distinctions constituting an "arsenal" to wage a war of "small /cultural/ differences" in order to prove that these are two communities having nothing to do with each other.

4   Instead of Conclusions

Obviously there is no alternative to "scientization" of the heritage of Croato-Serbian/Serbo-Croatian conflicts in Croatia and elsewhere in the areas populated by both of them. Many of us today are finding out that such an "enlightened" approach is far from a reality. No doubt that is not enough to "solve" such problems as the existing ones in Croatia, as well as all over the territory of former Yugoslavia.

Everyone should remember that everywhere in Europe the establishment of civil structures and cultural patterns took a long period. It is quite obvious that in the case of Serbs and Croats this is a challenge for all of us, in particular in the case of Croatia on its way to Europe.

It is a fact that deruralisation and urbanization of both ethnic (better to say national communities) took part to a large extent within a very short period of two generations. The majority of the population on both sides, as well as newly emerging elites (regarding their mentalities) are "somewhere" between their rural past and urban aspirations, at least regarding cultural patterns, moral values, and understanding of civil rules and institutions. This is primarily because the heritage of the "socialist self-management" – which is deeply divided between the totalitarian nature of the "dictatorship of the proletariat" and the continuous failing attempts to establish "socialism with the human face" – made all those problems of interethnic relations more complicated due to the instrumental use of the "national question" by Communist structures of power. Due to all those controversies, the case of Croats and Serbs in Croatia, burdened with far-reaching tragic effects of the war against and in Croatia, does represent one of the essential points of reference for every attempt to look for a way out of the biggest catastrophe in their millennial common history. If there would be no European, civil alternative for the future, it will surely reemerge in the more or less near future as a motive for another war.

Note

[1] That is why "ethnic cleansings" and mass destruction of properties belonging to individuals of the other ethnic identity do constitute the core of the actual war conflict. The "ratio" is very simple: If they are not among us, there will be no conflict and we could be even good neighbours (*"Scandinavisation of the Balkans"*). Since it is not that easy to reach such an objective, the appropriate price has to be paid (militarisation of the society, mass repression, limitations of human and civil rights, reinvention of the institution of "collective" responsibility", etc.).

7 Ethnic Politics in Ukraine

ZENOVIA A. SOCHOR

The potential for ethnic tensions in Ukraine is obvious. There are multiple ethnic groups in Ukraine, with one group, the Russians, comprising about 20% of the population. Russia, which has not reconciled itself to the loss of Ukraine in 1991, has made it abundantly clear that it views itself as a protector of the Russian minority in Ukraine. Political leaders in one of the regions of present-day Ukraine, Crimea, have openly agitated for some form of reunion with Russia. Moreover, the latest presidential elections in Ukraine, June 1994, produced a sizable and distinct split in the body politic, with the eastern and southern regions voting for Leonid Kuchma, perceived to be more pro-Russian, while the western regions voted for the more nationalist Kravchuk.

And yet, Ukraine is a striking example that facile assumptions cannot be made about ethnicity and conflict. Despite dire warnings of "suicidal nationalism", a civil war, and a scenario worse than Yugoslavia, Ukraine has survived its first three years of independence in relative peace. A host of questions arises. How are the potential sources of tension being managed? Is ethnicity an important factor in contemporary Ukrainian politics? What are the long range prospects?

This paper proposes to analyze the ethnic situation in Ukraine by looking at (a) the ethnic composition, (b) the Soviet legacy, (c) the first steps of independence, and (d) the new Kuchma regime. An underlying theme of the paper is that ethnicity in and of itself does not have an automatic political implication; if there is a relationship between ethnicity and conflict, it must be investigated rather than assumed. Ethnic tensions can exist within a political system without engendering ethnic conflict; only in conjunction with political, economic, and situational factors can ethnicity be used as a mobilizational force.

1 Ethnic Composition

Official Soviet policy, as well as unfavorable economic conditions, prompted the out-migration of Russians into non-Russian parts of the Soviet Union. In 1926, about 6.2 million Russians lived outside of Russia, rising to 23.9 million in 1979.[1] Ukraine felt the impact of this out-migration. The following is the ethnic composition of the population according to the 1989 census:

Total population:		52.8 millions
Ukrainians	72.7 %	37.4 millions
Russians	22.1 %	11.4 millions
Other ethnic groups:	5.2 %	2.7 millions
Jews		486,000
Belarussians		440,000
Moldovan		325,000
Bulgarians		234,000
Poles		219,000
Hungarians		163,000
Romanians		135,000

One other group should be added to the picture: the Crimean Tatars, who were permitted to resettle in the Crimea only in 1989. As of 1994, 250,000 did so.

The largest ethnic group, the Russians, is scattered throughout Ukraine, although the heaviest concentration of settlement is in the eastern and southern regions. In Kiev, for example, there are 72.5% Ukrainians, 20.9% Russians (6.6% other), while in the western city, Lviv, there is a clear predominance of Ukrainians (90.4%). In contrast, Luhansk, an eastern city, shows a distribution of 51.9% Ukrainians, 44.8% Russians (3.3% other); Odessa, a southern city, is one of the most ethnically variegated: 54.6% Ukrainians, 27.4% Russians, and 18.4% other (in particular, Bulgarians, Moldovans, and Jews). Taken as a whole, Ukrainians make up the majority of the population across all regions, except for Crimea, where they constitute 25.8% of the population while Russians represent 67% of the population.[2]

If a transparency of the ethnic map is placed over a socio-economic map of Ukraine, we find no clear overlap, thus mitigating the impact of ethnicity. The Russian minority does not uniformly hold a more privileged socioeconomic position. While Russians in Ukraine are better educated and over-represented in the white collar positions, Ukrainians have made considerable gains since World War II. By 1970, the Ukrainian share of the working class was 73.6%, 93.3% of the collective farmers, and 59.9% of the white-collar staff.[3] In fact, the areas of the heaviest Russian concentration are also the areas of the now-aging industrial base, with declining indexes of economic development—Donetsk, Zaporizhzhia, Dnipropetrovsk, Luhansk (previously Voroshylovhrad), and Kharkiv.[4] Unemployment figures suggest some regional variation. In July 1992, 18.7 % of the population was registered as unemployed; Donetsk, the coal-mining base, showed a slightly higher figure, 22%. Of the unemployed with a higher educational-level (34.5% for all of Ukraine in May 1992), the regional variation was not significant, e.g. 43.8% for Donetsk, 39.8% for Lviv.[5] Even in Donetsk, however, there is a mix of ethnic Ukrainians (51%), including those who are predominantly Russian-speaking, and ethnic Russians (44%).

At the social level, a considerable amount of assimilation and acculturation has occurred, which is perhaps not surprising given the linguistic and cultural similarities between Russians and Ukrainians. There is a high percentage of inter-marriages between Russians and Ukrainians (33%) and of linguistic acculturation. By 1979, 63% of the Ukrainians claimed a knowledge of Russian, while 31% of Russians living in Ukraine claimed a knowledge of Ukrainian.[6] By 1989, nearly three-fourths of Ukrainians claimed to be bilingual, and one-third of the total population of Ukraine gave Russian as their mother tongue.[7] Researchers consistently found little ethnic animosity between Russians and Ukrainians. One scholar, writing in 1986, stated that "[ethnic] relations are least strained in the RSFSR, Moldavia, and the Ukraine, and worst in the Baltic republics, followed by Central Asia and Kazakhstan".[8] A Stanford University research project in Ukraine in 1992, led the author to conclude that "As peoples, Russians and Ukrainians exhibit a low sense of ethnic schism".[9]

2 Soviet Legacy

Among the factors which led to the break-up of the USSR was the flawed Soviet nationality policy, which contained a paradox at the core: "At the same time that it attempted to efface ethnic distinctions and fashion a new supranational group consciousness, the Soviet regime recognized, legitimized, institutionalized, and politicized ethnicity to an extraordinary degree".[10] The very structure of the USSR encouraged an ethnic-territorial identification while modernization raised the expectations of the ethnic elites in the 15 republics. In terms of political power, Ukrainians have steadily improved their position vis-a-vis Russians in Ukraine. In 1920, there were only 23% Ukrainians in the Communist Party while by 1990, the figure rose to 67% (admittedly, still lower than the 72.7% share of the population).[11] In the post-Stalin period, the First and Second Party Secretaries in Ukraine (unlike most other non-Russian republics) were typically Ukrainian, as were top positions in the republic-level Politburo, Council of Ministers, and KGB. In fact, over 75% of leading jobs in both party and state sectors, between 1955 and 1972, were held by Ukrainians.[12] Finally, some Ukrainians found their way up the Soviet political ladder, with Pidhornyi (Podgorny), Shelest and Shcherbitskyi in the Soviet Politburo. The promotion of Ukrainians to positions of political power, even if only as "junior brothers" in the over-all Soviet scheme, nevertheless perpetuated a dual sense of loyalty; their Ukrainian base was the rationale and framework for career advancement in the Soviet Union.

Outside of the political sphere, a new generation of intellectuals arose in the post-Stalin period, with a sense of competence and empowerment but also grievance. They raised their voices to demand what was "rightfully theirs", that is, republican-level rights guaranteed in the Soviet constitution but not implemented in practice. The underlying question was the future: would it represent autonomy (cultural, political or economic) or a blending into one Soviet state and one Soviet people?

Language became a matter of particular concern to Ukrainian literary figures, compelling Ivan Dziuba to write a book *Internationalism or Russification* warning of the gradual eradication of the Ukrainian language and eventually, the distinctiveness of Ukrainian culture. He was concerned less by the natural erosion as by the specific policy of Russification which limited the use of Ukrainian in schools, libraries, publications, and government corridors.

In Ukraine, the 1960s witnessed an increase in demands both within and outside the Communist Party for a change in linguistic policy. The arrest of at least thirty intellectuals who were defending the Ukrainian language only served to escalate the conflict, giving rise to a human rights movement which protested the repression of intellectuals. Ultimately, even the First Secretary of the Communist Party in Ukraine, Petro Shelest, was caught up in the maelstrom and removed from office for displaying "nationalist tendencies". Under the new Party Secretary, Volodymyr Shcherbytskyi, a much harsher policy of repression and Russification ensued. In 1976, the Ukrainian Helsinki Group was founded, protesting the suppression of language and intellectuals. In the 1980s, the cause was taken up by the Union of Writers of Ukraine. Once again, defense of the Ukrainian language was prominent, but now it was joined with a higher political consciousness (thanks to perestroika and glasnost) as well as a set of ecological (post-Chernobyl) grievances. Under these circumstances, it was difficult, even for Shcherbytskyi, to prevent the formation of a popular front movement, Rukh. The future status of the Ukrainian language, and a sense of urgency in preventing its daily demise, became a galvanizing and mobilizing force within Rukh. Ukrainian poets and writers were soon joined by an expanding network of teachers, professionals, and young people. Perhaps the most colorful (and vocal) manifestation was a series of rock concerts where songs were performed in Ukrainian, with increasingly bold political lyrics, by young people who had until recently been indifferent to the language issue.

It is worth noting that the new-found interest in all things Ukrainian did not automatically translate into ethnic conflict with the non-Ukrainian speaking population. Resentment of Russification was not the same as resentment of ethnic Russians living in Ukraine. The reason had to do with the structure of the USSR. It was patently clear to everyone that decisions were not made at the local (republic) level. Nationality policies, including Russification, were introduced and orchestrated at the center. Therefore, the protests were directed not at Kiev nor at the local Russian population but at Moscow.

In October 1989, the Supreme Council of Ukraine adopted a Language Law which pronounced Ukrainian as the official state language. Over the course of ten years, Ukrainian was to be extended to include all public employees as well as mass media and education. Provisions were made for the use of other languages, particularly Russian as a "language of international cooperation". Wherever a non-Ukrainian ethnic group constituted a majority, another language could function as the official language alongside Ukrainian. Some resentment was immediately expressed by the Russian speakers who were used to thinking of Russian as a world language and Ukrainian merely as a provincial language. They understood that the change in language status also entailed a potentially diminished status for them. Precisely because of these concerns (as well as limited resources), the expansion of the use of Ukrainian proceeded very gradually. From 1988 to 1992, the proportion of schoolchildren receiving instruction in Ukrainian grew by less than 2%. In eastern cities such as Donetsk, Luhansk or Dnipropetrovsk, there were only one or two Ukrainian-language schools, even though at least half of the population was Ukrainian.[13]

It was, however, the general economic failure of the Soviet Union as well as specific tragic blunders such as Chernobyl which unified the population of the Ukrainian SSR, eliminating ethnic, class or religious lines. Rukh, which had become a potent political force by 1991, included Russians and other ethnic groups. Russians joined Ukrainians in the December 1991 referendum to vote for independence in overwhelming numbers.[14] Lviv voted 97.45% for independence, but eastern cities like Donetsk or Dnipropetrovsk were not far behind (83.90% and 90.36%, respectively). Even Crimea, with a majority Russian population, voted for independence 54.19%.[15]

3 First Steps Towards an Independent Ukraine

The first steps taken to establish the legal basis of sovereignty and independence were accompanied by an explicitly liberal policy towards ethnic minorities in Ukraine. Thus, in July 1990, the Declaration of State Sovereignty committed the government to respect "the national rights of all peoples" and guaranteed "to all nationalities living on the territory of the republic the right to free national and cultural development". The Declaration of Independence in August 1991 was followed in short order by the Declaration on the Rights of Nationalities in Ukraine, November 1, 1991, which specifically stated that all citizens had the right to use the Russian language, and created a Ministry of Nationalities and Migration as an institutional mechanism of implementation.[16]

The cornerstone of the policy towards ethnic minorities was the Citizenship Law, passed in October 1991. In essence, any resident in Ukraine at the time of the passage of the law was granted Ukrainian citizenship. Lest that seem obvious, it is worth recalling the more tortuous version of citizenship adopted in the neighboring Baltic states, especially Estonia, which restricted the extension of citizenship to large numbers of ethnic Russians. Just this point was made by Leonid Kravchuk, chairman of the Supreme Council, shortly before Ukraine's declaration of independence: "I must note that the Russians in Ukraine cannot be compared with the Russians living in the Baltic republics. In our republic, they are part of the indigenous population, they have lived here for hundreds of years... We do not tolerate any discrimination against them. Therefore there is no need to try and play the Russian language card. It is a dangerous game".[17]

In essence, there was a political consensus in the early days of the new Ukrainian state that it should be founded primarily on the principle of "civic nationalism" rather than "ethnic nationalism". The former conceives the nation as "a sovereign people", emphasizes "voluntary political choice as a key characteristic of national identity" and is "receptive to the inclusion of individuals of diverse ethnic and cultural backgrounds". The latter, on the other hand, views the nation "as a unique people", emphasizes "an exclusive notion of national identity based on ethnic criteria", and rejects "personal political choice as a means by which individuals may become members of the nation".[18]

To be sure, civic nationalism is a more nuanced concept and difficult to implement in a fledgling new state still struggling to define and assert its national identity. Ethnic nationalism arouses more passion and perhaps more fervid loyalty. Indeed, prior to independence, voices were raised to secure "Ukraine for the Ukrainians". Especially in the western regions, the more radically-inclined nationalists were eager to reassert political leaders, organizations, and symbols from earlier independence struggles – all of which had been condemned by the Soviet regime. Any manifestation of Ukrainian nationalism had been branded "bourgeois nationalism", or even worse, "fascism". As one author remarked, it was possible for Galician (western) Ukrainians to remain Ukrainian, "but only if they were specifically Soviet Ukrainian", which meant "forgetting everything that previously had been considered positive in the Galician past", that is, "all the former institutions, national symbols and historical events ... associated with a Ukrainian self-identity". (Western Ukraine had been at various times part of the Austro-Hungarian Empire, hence, Galicia, and part of Poland.)[19]

Under the conditions of glasnost, western Ukrainians attempted to reclaim their historical memory and their uniqueness, to rectify past injustices. At the same time, however, eastern Ukrainians did not readily empathize because they did not share the same aggrieved history of independence struggles, especially during World War II. Eastern Ukraine had been incorporated into the USSR in 1922, after the Red Army nullified Ukraine's brief period of independence, while western Ukraine had not incorporated until the Molotov-Ribbentrop Pact of 1939.

What saved the popular national movement of 1990-91 from disintegrating into separate camps is the broad consensus, among leaders of all the major political parties, to pursue an inclusive rather than exclusive national identity. The positions of Rukh, the Popular Movement for Perestroika, and of Leonid Kravchuk were critical in this regard. Rukh held sway in the country at large; Kravchuk, at the pinnacle of power, in the parliament. Both were sensitive to the ethnic minorities within Ukraine, especially the Russians, and the importance of not creating divisions between eastern and western Ukraine. Mindful of the ethnic tensions in the Baltic republics and "the mistakes made by Baltic nationalists", Rukh leaders "always tried to concentrate on territorial, as opposed to ethnic, conceptions of nationalism".[20] Moreover, Rukh succeeded in winning the support of minorities in Ukraine because it "incorporated and hegemonized the democratic discourse in the widest sense of the word", leading the battle for the democratization of political structures and extension of civil liberties to all citizens of Ukraine. That is to say, the national movement in Ukraine was also the democratic movement.[21] Rukh traced its legacy to the 1960s dissident movement, with some of the earlier dissidents reemerging as newly elected political leaders. Hence, the inclusive concept of "the people of Ukraine" was "a genuine element of an indigenous tradition, not a tactical device intended to dupe Ukraine's Russians into passivity".[22] The very name of Rukh, a popular movement designed to promote perestroika, showed its initially modest goals, which were to support Gorbatchev-type reforms against the highly conservative Shcherbitskyi regime. Its leadership was an amalgam of dissidents, writers, and ex-Communists, representing both eastern and western Ukraine.

As events became more heated in late 1990 and early 1991, the entire political spectrum became more radicalized. Gorbatchev was clearly losing his hold over the republics; first sovereignty and then independence became mentionable goals in Ukraine. Kravchuk played an important role at this critical juncture. A polarization within the

Ukrainian body politic could have occurred, with Rukh pursuing an increasingly more nationalist line and the Communist Party courting the potentially disinterested or alienated eastern regions of the country. In an ironic turn of events, Kravchuk, the former ideological secretary of the Central Committee of the Communist Party in Ukraine and vociferous opponent of Rukh, leaped across the barricades and joined forces with Rukh. As chairman of the Supreme Council (parliament), Kravchuk managed to outmaneuver the die-hard ("imperial") communists, and to form a new parliamentary bloc with "sovereignty" communists. The declaration of sovereignty was passed almost unanimously on July 16, 1990.[23]

More important was the March 17, 1991 referendum on the fate of the union. Gorbatchev proposed a referendum in order to test (and more than likely, assert) pro-union sentiment; the Ukrainian parliament, under Kravchuk's leadership, inserted a second question which emphasized Ukrainian sovereignty and basically negated Gorbatchev's question. About half of the communist members of parliament voted in favor of the second "Ukrainian" question. In the country at large, 70% of voters responded favorably to the first question while 80% supported the second. (In the western regions of Halychyna-Galicia, a third question was proposed, asking for outright independence for Ukraine. It received 88% support.)[24]

Referendum results were both confusing and contradictory (e.g. Donetsk voted 85% in favor of the first question and 88% in favor of the second; Crimea voted 88% in favor of the first, 85% in favor of the second).[25] Kravchuk took the lead in interpreting the results as an endorsement for Ukrainian state-building. This step further ostracized the conservative communists in Ukraine and built bridges to Rukh. On the eve of the failed coup in Moscow, August 1991, Rukh and Kravchuk forces had effected a rapprochement, representing the majority point of view in Ukraine. At a minimum, Ukraine should have a vastly expanded autonomy within a new commonwealth of republic; at a maximum, Ukraine should seek independence.

Kravchuk, of course, made a gamble. Unlike the first secretary of the Communist Party of Ukraine (whether Volodymyr Ivashko or Stanislav Hurenko), Kravchuk decided his political fortune lay in Kiev, not in Moscow. Against a background of a crumbling Kremlin, an increasingly irrelevant Communist Party, and an aroused local population, it was not an unreasonable political calculation. (Kravchuk's uncertainty on how to react to the August coup indicates that he was conscious of the risks involved and was hedging his bets almost until the last minute.)

Kravchuk's gamble paid off. In the presidential elections of December 1991 (coupled with the referendum on Ukraine's independence), Kravchuk won with 62% of the vote. He fared well in all the regions of Ukraine, except for the western region of Halychyna. His main contender was a former political prisoner and leader of Rukh, Vyacheslav Chornovil, who garnered 23% of the vote but placed first in Halychyna.[26]

The vote for Kravchuk was a conservative one; it was for an ex-communist (Kravchuk resigned from the Party after the August coup), steeped in Soviet practice and more predictable than a vote for a radical democrat and nationalist. (Ukraine's neighbors, Poland, the Baltic republics, and even Georgia, all chose in the first instance a more radical alternative.) His five-point campaign program was intended to be innocuous and broad-based: statehood, democracy, well-being, spirituality and trust.[27] Kravchuk was careful to emphasize moderation over any form of divisiveness, whether ethnic or political. Therefore, under "spirituality", he prescribed "the spiritual rebirth of the Ukrainian nation", while at the same time guaranteeing "the free national-cultural development of all the nationalities which constitute the people of Ukraine". Under "trust", he emphasized "harmony above all", warning that "immaturity, alienation, impatience, just like a cancer, devour a social organism".[28] In less oblique terms, Kravchuk claimed that his contenders in the presidential election "would immediately like to sack everyone... nothing but the walls of the Council of Ministers will be left standing". He countered rhetorically: "Should we chop the heads off everyone who used to be in the party? That is not what Ukraine is waiting for. It is waiting for national consensus and unity".[29]

The vote for independence also was probably more conservative than it appeared at first glance. Certainly, 90% support for independence seemed a radical departure from Ukraine's previous status. Nationalists, however, were joined by communists whose decision may have been motivated by calculations similar to Kravchuk's, i.e., how to prevent a collapse of elite privileges alongside the collapse of the USSR. An independent Ukraine, especially one headed by a member of the nomenklatura, might preserve some of their power positions.

Moreover, it is likely that the support for independence, which united Ukrainians and Russians, eastern and western regions, reflected a hope for a better economic future more than a cohesive national consciousness. In the last gasps of the Soviet Union, attachment to the Soviet economy seemed a burden not a boon. Calls for a Ukrainian economy, free of the exploitative (colonial) relationship with the USSR, were issued across the political spectrum, by radical democrats, students, and even members of the government. Prime Minister Vitold Fokin was driven to declare that "economic independence" was a pressing need. Decisions taken at the center had led to a crisis situation, most evident at the ecological level. The guiding principle should not be that "the Union which creates affiliated republics but republics, as sovereign states, on a completely voluntary basis, create their own union".[30]

A leading article in *Literaturna Ukraina*, arguing that independence was the only safeguard for Ukraine, emphasized a substantial gap between Ukrainian contributions to the USSR and Soviet allocations, in turn, to the Ukrainian republic. "National expenditure, in 1988, for one inhabitant of the USSR amounted to 761 rubles; in Russia, the figure was 938, in Ukraine, only 569." In addition, the article asked "Isn't Chernobyl enough? Would we have allowed such an occurrence if we had been masters in our own home?".[31] Just prior to the vote on independence, an opinion poll indicated that 78% of the population listed "escape from economic crisis" as their chief concern, with political or cultural concerns much further down the list, eliciting about 20% of the vote.[32]

A politically moderate consensus, with firebrand nationalism limited to the fringes, augured well for the origins of a new state within an ethnically-mixed community. At the same time, the reliance on "instrumental nationalism", that is, a commitment to Ukrainian independence contingent upon economic performance and the preservation of power positions, raised questions about the viability of the Ukrainian state over the long run.

4 Kuchma Regime

Elections in 1994 were a dramatic sign that the problems associated with Ukrainian nation and state-building were far from over. A general and growing disenchantment with the Kravchuk regime coupled with specific grievances, such as the miners' strikes, precipitated early parliamentary and presidential elections. The first round of parliamentary elections, in March 1994, produced a strong leftist bloc in parliament. Presidential elections, in June 1994, led to the ouster of the incumbent and the victory of a candidate who declared in his inaugural speech that the state should not be treated as "an icon". Leonid Kuchma, a Russian-speaking Ukraine from the eastern city of Dnipropetrovsk, also pledged a restoration of closer ties with Russia and the elevation of Russian to official language status.[33]

Nationalists from western regions feared the worst; elections showed a decisive split in the country, with eastern Ukraine voting for Kuchma and western Ukraine supporting Kravchuk. Political commentators in the West also echoed the sense of crisis emanating from the election.

All the analysts would be dumbfounded by the opinion polls, within six months after the election, showing that President Kuchma enjoying high popularity ratings, and scoring even higher in western than in eastern regions of Ukraine. Why this turn of events? How should the elections be interpreted?

The first and foremost point to be made about the 1994 elections, both parliamentary and presidential, was that they were about economic reforms. They were not a manifestation of ethnic conflict, much less a split in the society as a whole. They were not preceded by a debate over fundamental issues such as the independence or territorial integrity of Ukraine. They presented little evidence that political extremism, in terms of either Ukrainian or Russian nationalism, made much headway among voters.

What the elections did, however, indicate were regional political alignments, a much stronger showing by the left than of the national democrats, and fundamental economic grievances. They also revealed a heightened sensitivity on the language issue and different assessments about the threat that Russia posed.

5   Economic Factors

In one of the many opinion polls prior to the elections, respondents were asked to list their three most important concerns. The results were as follows: 71% named economic crisis, 47%, relations with Russia, and 43%, crime. The people polled were urban dwellers from the four main regions of Ukraine. All other concerns placed much lower on the list. "Guaranteeing security of Ukraine" came in fourth place (19%), "status of Russian language in Ukraine", (9%) was in fifth place. Nuclear weapons, Crimea, and the Black Sea Fleet appeared to be of relatively little concern (7%, 5%, and 5%, respectively). Although there were some regional differences in the first category (78% in eastern regions, 67% in western regions listed economic crisis), the most significant regional differences came in the second category. Twice as many respondents were concerned about relations with Russia in the eastern regions (57%) than in the western regions (26%); the figure was still higher in southern regions (61%).[34]

There is an important link between the first two concerns. As noted above, the very high vote for Ukrainian independence in 1991 reflected a belief, or at least a hope, that independence would bring about economic relief and even an improvement in the standard of living. When the opposite occurred, and the economy took a nose dive, there was a reassessment of the relationship with Russia. Many were convinced that Russia was doing better economically and that a restoration of ties with Russia would help improve the economic status of Ukraine. Not surprisingly, the areas most populated by ethnic Russians or Russian-speaking Ukrainians were more likely to share this conviction. More Russians than Ukrainians stated that the economic difficulties in Ukraine were due to the collapse of the USSR (43% vs. 30%).[35]

A similar division was displayed in the question on the optimal foreign policy course for Ukraine. Russians were more likely to suggest "unification of the CIS republics into one country" (32% in comparison to 17.5% Ukrainians), while Ukrainians sooner opted for "withdrawal from CIS and pursuit of an independent policy" (26% vs. 13%).[36] Pensioners and the unemployed in the eastern Donbas region were even more favorably predisposed towards a restoration of the USSR (59% and 63%, respectively).[37]

The conclusion one can draw from the above statistics is that the presidential candidate who launched a campaign platform placing economic issues in first place, closely tied with a promise of improved relations with Russia, stood an excellent chance at winning.[38] Kuchma adopted exactly this platform, and won handily in eastern and southern regions. His campaign pitch was consistent: "Ukraine stands at the threshold of a national catastrophe". The reason was economic crisis. The way out of the crisis was "strong executive power, a single economic space with all of the republics of the former Union, and in the first place, with Russia".[39]

To be sure, economic concerns were high across all regions in Ukraine. When asked "What would propel you to take part in protest activities?", the highest response was "a lowering of the standard of living for my family", with no difference between Ukrainians (63%) and Russians (62%). More Ukrainians, however, declared that they would protest for the sake of Ukrainian independence and territorial integrity (29%), than Russians (8%).[40]

In the western regions there was a greater mistrust of Russia and sense of fragility in the newly-independent state. Precisely these points were played up by Kuchma's main contender, the incumbent president Kravchuk. After delaying until the eleventh hour his decision on whether he would run or not, Kravchuk announced that he felt compelled to run for president when he saw who had entered the race and "understood that these people could either ruin our independence or steer the country on a wrong course".[41]

Much of the press adopted the official line, i.e. that Kuchma represented an extreme position, that he would split the country, and that he would compromise Ukrainian independence. There was "no real alternative" to Kravchuk wrote the newspaper *Uriadovii Kur'er* (State Courier). Only Kravchuk was able to prevent extreme outcomes in Ukraine along the lines of Yugoslavia, Northern Caucasus, Azerbaijan, or Armenia.[42] In another typical commentary, Kravchuk's "political experience, international authority" were lauded, contending that he was the only one capable of "safeguarding peace and harmony, avoiding bloodshed, and consolidating (rather than splitting, as some would prefer) the people of Ukraine".[43]

These themes were likely to find a sympathetic echo in western regions, much more than in other parts of Ukraine. In the western regions, there lurked a residue of fear about Russia and its intentions. Thus, 79% of respondents in western regions were worried about a military confrontation with Russia, while only 23% expressed this fear in Crimea and still less (14%) in the eastern region of Donetsk.[44] Interestingly, the sharp regional distinction was diluted considerably when the calculations were made on the basis of ethnic identification for the country as a whole; thus, 37% Ukrainians and 18% Russians believed a military conflict with Russia was possible.[45]

Most people, despite the campaign rhetoric, were not convinced that military or even ethnic conflict was likely. Kravchuk, nevertheless, focused on this angle because he wanted to change the terms of the electoral debates – softpedaling his weak points, i.e., lack of economic reforms, and emphasizing, instead, political stability, peace and harmony, continuity. His platform, in the end, fell short of popular expectations.

If the combination of economic reform plus better relations with Russia meant a vote for Kuchma, it is equally important to recognize what the vote did not mean. Once the economic factor was removed, there was much less evidence of support for Russia and/or CIS. Less then 3% Russians supported regional parties which proposed regional autonomy or separation from Ukraine. Only 6% Russians and 3.5% Ukrainians wished to see a restoration of the USSR for the purpose of building socialism.[46] The population at large was willing to entertain almost any solution to economic problems. While 82% thought economic integration with CIS was the answer, almost as many (75%) favored economic integration with the West.[47] Moreover, the same regions which overwhelmingly favored an economic union with CIS, e.g. 87% in the eastern region of Donetsk, were more hesitant in suggesting a military-political course of action. A large bloc of respondents in Donetsk suggested a seemingly incompatible solution, i.e., 45% were in favor of entrance into NATO together with CIS countries; 24% thought neutrality might be the answer; 14% independent entry into NATO, and another 14% CIS union as an alternative to NATO.[48]

Generally speaking, people in eastern and southern regions of Ukraine had a weak sense of national consciousness; they did not respond strongly to Ukrainian nationalism nor to Russian nationalism, both of which had been castigated under the Soviet regime. When asked "What group of the population do you generally identify yourself with?" 34% answered "the population of Ukraine in general", 27% said "the population of the former Soviet Union". Almost as many (23%) fell back on a purely regional identification, and very few (3%) identified with the population of Russia.[49]

On the touchy subject of Crimea, most of the same respondents thought that Crimea "must remain an inherent part of Ukraine" (48%) and only 10% believed it should become a constituent part of Russia.[50] To add to the confusing profile of the people in eastern and southern regions, only 24% responded that they would vote for Ukrainian independence if a vote were held today (May-June 1994), while the greater majority, 47% would vote against independence.[51] Since the same regions voted overwhelmingly for independence in 1991, the main reason for the change was clearly related to the collapse of the Ukrainian economy. The much higher level of national consciousness in western regions showed that independence was not as closely associated with material benefits. There were far more respondents willing to endure economic difficulties for the sake of Ukraine's independence in western regions (52%, for any time necessary, 33%, for 1-2 years, 12%, not at all) than in eastern regions (e.g. in Donetsk, 6%, for any time necessary, 20%, for 1-2 years, 70%, not at all).[52] The importance of economic factors was reflected in the fact that a much higher percentage of the population was willing to endure economic difficulties for the sake of economic reform, e.g. in the Crimea, 49% were not willing to put up with any economic difficulties but 44% were willing to do so for 1-2 years.[53] At a minimum, this suggested a window of opportunity for the new president who had embarked on a bold package of economic reform shortly after his election.

6 Linguistic Factors

Language became an issue in the presidential elections, given the stark comparison between Kravchuk, who spoke Ukrainian fluently, and Kuchma, who usually spoke Russian and only occasionally ventured into broken Ukrainian. For the nationalists who had struggled pre-1991 to salvage the Ukrainian language in the face of persistent Russification, the espousal, by Kuchma, of elevating Russian to an "official language" (while maintaining Ukrainian as the "state language") seemed like a huge step backwards in reclaiming their cultural identity.[54]

For Russians who felt threatened by the policy of Ukrainization, or at a minimum, resented the loss in status of Russian as the self-evident and preeminent language of choice, Kuchma's favorable attitude towards Russian was bound to be comforting. Indeed, some Western commentators considered language as the key to the elections, contending that the pro-Kuchma vote in regions where the Russian language was widely used "was more an expression of cultural estrangement by an electorate protesting a perceived increasing isolation from the Russian/Eurasian world".[55] Language was one issue which consistently reaped a wide gap in responses by Russians and Ukrainians in opinion polls. More than twice as many Ukrainians (61%) as Russians (27%) favored an expansion in the use of the Ukrainian language.[56]

Nevertheless, linguistic factors are far from straight-forward. Ethnic identification and linguistic identification do not overlap, thereby softening the contrast and perhaps muting any potential conflict. The fact that the two languages are mutually intelligible also contributes to some commonalty.[57] The overwhelming majority of Ukrainians are bilingual; some who claim one or the other language actually speak a hybrid derisively labeled "surzhyk". Although Russians primarily speak Russian, 77% of those living in Lviv claimed knowledge of Ukrainian, 88% in Kiev, and 16% in Simferopil.[58] Particularly interesting over the long-run is the reaction to the statement "I would prefer that my children were fluent in Ukrainian". Russians in Lviv and Kiev fully agreed (88% and 81%); even in Simferopil, 24% fully agreed, 31% agreed versus the 24% that fully disagreed and 11% that disagreed.[59] Far fewer Russians, however, were willing to back up this statement by preferring to send their children to Ukrainian schools.

Since being elected president, Kuchma has always used Ukrainian in official functions, although he maintains a highly tolerant attitude towards the use of Russian. (His wife is Russian and they no doubt converse in Russian at home.) His example sets the tone and helps diffuse the situation, although language will undoubtedly remain alive as an issue.[60]

By itself, language is rarely a source for ethnic conflict; only coupled with political and/or economic grievances does it have the potential to be transformed from tension (which every society has) to political mobilization.[61] Thus far, extremist appeals have found a narrow audience, as can be seen in the political alignments emerging in the wake of the parliamentary and presidential elections.

7 Political Alignments

Elections to parliament, in March 1994 and subsequent run-offs, produced 400 deputies (out of a 450-seat legislature). They organized themselves into nine parliamentary factions, as follows:

Communist Party:	91
Socialist Party:	30
Agrarian Party:	52
Unity:	34
Center:	37
Inter-Regional Bloc for Reforms:	34
Reform:	31
Rukh:	27
Statehood:	30

Independents formed yet another group, with 34 members. The first three factions created the leftist bloc, which remains the largest, although somewhat reduced in comparison to the "Group of 238" from the previous parliament. Statehood represents the rightist position, with the others varying in terms of a more centrist orientation.[62] The national democratic forces, represented by Rukh, showed a poor showing in comparison to the communist forces. This was true for both parliamentary as well as presidential elections, where the leftist bloc predominated.

The presidential elections themselves revealed a distinct political alignment, with the leftists voting for Kuchma and the center-right voting for Kravchuk. Although it may seem curious that leftists should vote for someone who represented economic reform, Kuchma's economic platform was vague enough to attract a wide net of supporters while his position on closer ties with Russia and CIS was firm enough to persuade leftist parties to throw their vote behind him. Since the political parties are still very much regional-based, with the leftist parties in the industrial belt of eastern and southern regions, and center-right parties in western regions, the result was an east-west split in the vote (the central regions divided their votes between Kravchuk and Kuchma). The presidential vote, therefore, was above all an indication of political alignments – a separate dimension, albeit related to ethnic alignments.

Parliamentary debates indicate that the main issues revolve around economic reform and delineation of authority between the president and parliament. Ethnic politics, outside of the contentious Crimean issue, do not register as a priority issue. Nor can the line-up in parliament be related purely to ethnic or linguistic factors.[63] The Inter-Regional Bloc, for example, is composed of Kuchma supporters, mostly Russian-speakers from eastern regions; it is far more likely to vote with the

Reform, Center, and Rukh factions in support of economic reform than with the leftist pro-Russian bloc. On average, the president's legislative initiatives have encountered between 150 to 180 votes in opposition.[64] The leftist bloc, which had helped elect Kuchma, has been the main source of opposition, suggesting once again a political rather than an ethnic and linguistic alignment. After the first round of elections, when 338 deputies had been elected, 253 were Ukrainian by nationality, and 70 were Russian by nationality.[65]

Extremist parties which emphasize an exclusively pro-Ukrainian or pro-Russian policy exist on the margins of politics. They have vocal regional supporters who are radical in orientation but small in numbers. Foremost among the "Ukraine for Ukrainians" forces is the Congress of Ukrainian Nationalists, which elected seven members to the parliament. Foremost among the pro-Russian forces is the Civic Congress of Ukraine, which elected two members to the parliament.[66] The very fact that ultra-nationalists were elected to parliament, according to one commentator, shows that they are "moving from the margins into the center of the country's political arena" and this could have "inflammatory results".[67] Indeed, in one of the earliest sessions of the new parliament, in July 1994, some deputies broke out into a fight over the use of Russian in parliamentary speeches. The fisticuffs, however, were between a Socialist and a Rukh deputy, and not the ultra-nationalists. Despite the emotions, parliamentarians rejected a proposal to grant Russian equal status as a parliamentary language.[68] When President Kuchma initiated a series of tough measures, in March 1995, against the Crimea to make its constitution fall in line with Ukraine's constitution as a whole, parliament backed him almost unanimously.

Perhaps it was the disappointment of the pro-Russian groups with the moderate policies followed by Kuchma since his election that a movement was initiated to hold a referendum for the renewal of the Soviet Union. A petition was started by the Communist and Socialist parties of Ukraine together with the Civic Congress of Ukraine to hold a referendum on a new political, economic and military union with Russia, Belarus and Kazakhstan. President Kuchma quickly denounced the movement and the Chairman of the Parliament, Oleksander Moroz, reaffirmed his support for an independent and sovereign Ukraine (Moroz is leader of the Socialist Party).[69] Recently, the Peace-loving Forces Congress, with 720 members meeting in the Donetsk region, denounced

President Kuchma for "bourgeois nationalism", an ironic twist considering the election debates when the nationalists feared betrayal on the part of the pro-Russian Kuchma. For good measure, the Congress also condemned Parliament as well as the Donetsk local government for "bourgeois nationalism".[70]

These sentiments do not seem to be reflected nationally given the high approval rating accorded to Kuchma (72%), with a particularly dramatic reversal of opinion of western regions vis-a-vis Kuchma.[71] Despite the continued economic downfall, 64% of Ukrainians polled also said they continued to favor their country's independence.[72]

8   Conclusions

Ukraine faces numerous problems as it attempts to create a viable state, both politically and economically. In the short term, Kuchma will have to deal with such "hot spots" as Crimea and the eastern region of Donbas. Ethnicity in these regions is interwoven with political and economic factors. Thus far, however, neither region has become a focal point of ethnic mobilization. If there is unemployment in the aging industrial belt, Russian and Ukrainian workers have been affected equally. The Communist Party may appeal to the "good old days," but to most workers, it is dismally clear that even if the USSR and the Communist Party were restored, the old mines could not be resuscitated. The Donbas region voted overwhelmingly for Kuchma as their best hope; both his future and the strength of separatist sentiments depend on the success of his promised economic reforms.

Crimea is a unique situation because of the number of ethnic Russians involved, the strength of Russian nationalism, and the willingness of Crimean political leaders such as Iurii Meshkov to play the "Russian card" in order to buttress their own political positions. Nevertheless, Crimea also voted in Kuchma which gives him some legitimacy in trying to sort out the complex political situation which has arisen there. The tensions are between the president and the parliament within Crimea; between Crimea and Kiev (with almost unanimous parliamentary support for Kuchma on this issue); and, most importantly, between Ukraine and Russia. There have been remarkably few ethnic clashes between Russians and Ukrainians in Crimea itself. Crimea is really not a case study of ethnic conflict; it is sooner a case study of two states, Russia and Ukraine, coming to terms with their new-found status in the post-Soviet world, i.e., non-imperial for the former, independent for the latter.

Over the long term, Ukraine needs to develop a national identity which can weave together different historical and cultural traditions into an acceptable and recognizable tapestry for the diverse segments of Ukrainian society. Thus far, ethnic, regional, linguistic or religious differences have not coalesced into serious protest movements to disrupt the coherence of the state. Extremist opposition has remained on the margins of society. The election of Kuchma has also helped to prevent nationalism from swamping the political agenda; instead, economic issues, which are vital to all sectors of society, have been given top priority. Kuchma's "window of opportunity" is critically important for the long-term prospects of social, political and ethnic stability in an independent Ukraine.

148 *Ethnic Conflicts and Civil Society*

Notes

1. Ralph S. Clem, "Ethnicity", in James Cracraft, ed., *The Soviet Union Today* (Chicago: Chicago Univ. Press, 1988): p. 311.
2. *Natsional'nyi sostav naseleniia SSSR, po dannykh vsesoiuznoi perepisi naseleniia* (Moscow: Finansy i statistika, 1991). For a map showing the Ukrainian presence throughout the country, see Susan Stewart, "Ukraine's Policy toward its Ethnic Minorities", *RFE/RL Research Report* 2, no. 36 (September 10, 1993), p. 56.
3. Bohdan Krawchenko, *Social Change and National Consciousness in Twentieth-Century Ukraine* (Edmonton: Canadian Institute of Ukrainian Studies, 1987): p. 206.
4. Alexander J. Motyl, *Will the Non-Russians Rebel? State, Ethnicity, and Stability in the USSR* (Ithaca, N.Y.: Cornell Univ. Press, 1987): p. 64.
5. *Ukraina: sotsial'na sfera y perekhidnyi period: Analiz Svitovoho banku*, (Kyiv:vyd. Osnovy, 1994): pp. 216, 211.
6. Rasma Karklins, *Ethnic Relations in the USSR: The Perspective from Below* (Boston: Allen & Unwin, 1986): p. 233. Hajda considers this to be an inflated figure, "reflecting more the high degree of mutual intelligibility among the East Slavic tongues than actual fluency". See Lubomyr Hajda, "Ethnic Politics and Ethnic Conflict in the USSR and the Post-Soviet States", *Humboldt Journal of Social Relations* 19, no. 2, 1993, p. 234.
7. Bohdan Krawchenko, "Ukraine: the Politics of Independence", in Ian Bremmer and Ray Taras, eds., *Nation and Politics in the Soviet Successor States* (Cambridge: Cambridge Univ. Press, 1993): pp. 85-86.
8. Karklins, p. 70.
9. Ian Bremmer, "The Politics of Ethnicity: Russians in the New Ukraine", *Europe-Asia Studies* 46, no. 2, 1994, p. 264.
10. Hajda, p. 255.
11. Bohdan Krawchenko, "Changes in the National and Social Composition of the Communist Party of Ukraine from the Revolution to 1976", *Journal of Ukrainian Studies* 9, no.1 (Summer 1984): pp. 33-54.
12. Grey Hodnett, *Leadership in the Soviet National Republics: A Quantitative Study of Recruitment Policy* (Oakville, 1978): p. 105.
13. See Roman Solchanyk, "The Politics of Language in Ukraine", *RFE/RL Research Report*, no. 10 (March 5, 1993).
14. Krawchenko, "Ukraine: the Politics of Independence", p. 86.
15. Electoral Commission, official results.
16. For the Declaration on the Rights of Nationalities in Ukraine, see *Holos Ukrainy*, November 2, 1991.
17. *Pravda*, July 16, 1991.
18. Karen Dawisha and Bruce Parrott, *Russia and the New States of Eurasia: The Politics of Upheaval* (Cambridge: Cambridge Univ. Press, 1994): p. 59.
19. Paul Robert Magocsi, "A Subordinate or Submerged People: The Ukrainians of Galicia under Habsburg and Soviet Rule", in Richard L. Rudolph and David F. Good, eds., *Nationalism and Empire: The Habsburg Monarchy and the Soviet Union* (New York, N.Y.: St. Martin's Press, 1992): p. 101.
20. Taras Kuzio and Andrew Wilson, *Ukraine: Perestroika to Independence* (New

York, N.Y.: St. Martin's Press, 1994): p. 144.
21. *Vechirnyi Kyiv*, February 2, 1991.
22. Roman Szporluk, "The National Question", in Timothy J. Colton and Robert Legvold, eds., *After the Soviet Union: From Empire to Nations* (New York, N.Y.: W.W. Norton & Co., 1992): p. 102.
23. See Roman Solchanyk, "Ukraine and the Union Treaty", *Report on the USSR* (July 26, 1991): pp. 22-24.
24. Electoral Commission, official results. Also see Krawchenko, "Ukraine: the Politics of Independence", p. 82.
25. Ibid.
26. Electoral Commission, official results.
27. In Ukrainian, the program translates into the five "d's": derzhavnis't, demokratiia, dostatok, dukhovnis't, dovir'ia. See *Literaturna Ukraina*, November 28, 1991.
28. Ibid.
29. *Pravda*, November 6, 1991.
30. *Literaturna Ukraina*, April 5, 1990.
31. *Literaturna Ukraina*, November 21, 1991.
32. *Holos Ukrainy*, November 1, 1991.
33. *Holos Ukrainy*, July 21, 1994.
34. Valeriy Khmel'ko, "Peredvyborchi nastroii mis'koho naselennia Ukrainy", *Politychnyi portret Ukrainy*, no. 6 (January 1994): pp. 5-6.
35. Vasyl' Kremen', Petro Sytnyk, Mykhailo Mishchenko, Viktor Nebozhenko, "Sotisal'no-Politychna Sytuatsiia v Ukraiini na kinets; 1992 roku: Stan i Tendentsii Rozvytku", *Politolohichni chytannia*, no. 1, 1993, p. 76.
36. Ibid., p. 77.
37. Iurii Iurov, "Stavlennia naselennia Donbasu do politichnykh partii ta iikh prohramnykh zasad", *Geneza*, no. 1, 1994, p. 197.
38. Interestingly, Khmel'ko made just this observation, although on the eve of the elections, he forecast Kravchuk as the winner by a narrow margin. See Ibid, p. 7.
39. Kuchma's meeting with journalists, July 4, 1994, *Ukrinform*, July 5, 1994.
40. Iryna Bekeshkina, "Hromads'ka dumka shchodo hotovnosti naselennia do sotsial'noho protestu", *Politicnyi portret Ukrainy*, no. 4, December 1993, p. 16. Bekeshkina points out that both Russians and Ukrainians are passive; despite their answers on opinion polls, neither are actually likely to take part in protests. As she points out, shortly after the opinion poll was taken, there was a substantial increase in prices but the predicted demonstrations never materialized, p. 17.
41. *Ukrinform*, June 4, 1994.
42. *Uriadovii Kur'er*, June 23, 1994.
43. *Holos Ukrainy*, July 8, 1994.
44. Viktor Nebozhenko, "Pohliad hromads'kosti na hlovni prioretety zovnishn'oii polityky Ukraiiny", *Politichynii portret Ukrainy*, no. 5, December 1993, p. 9.
45. Ibid.
46. Kremen' et al, pp. 76-77.
47. Nebozehnko, p. 3.
48. Ibid., p. 6.

49 *Political Portrait of Ukraine*. Results of a public opinion poll of citizens in South and East of Ukraine, May-June 1994, p. 10.
50 Ibid., p. 8.
51 Ibid., p. 3.
52 "Societies in Transformation: Experience of Market Reforms for Ukraine", May 19-21, 1994, Democratic Initiatives Center, Kyiv, p. 9.
53 Ibid., p. 9.
54 See, for example, articles in *Literaturna Ukraina*, July 28 and 29, 1994.
55 Dominque Arel and Andrew Wilson," Ukraine under Kuchma: Back to 'Eurasia'?", *RFE/RL Research Report* 3, no. 32 (August 19, 1994), p. 12.
56 Kremen', op cit, p. 76.
57 Serbs and Croats essentially spoke the same language but this did not prevent the outburst of violence. Clearly some intervening factors must be taken into account rather than language alone as an explanatory, even less a causal factor.
58 See Bremmer, pp. 268-269.
59 Ibid., pp. 267-77.
60 A recent visitor to Donetsk thought that language conflict was greatly exaggerated. Most citizens were indifferent to the language problem; "arousing interest in this problem was difficult, practically impossible" especially given existing socio-economic conditions. *Vechirnyi Kyiv*, February 17, 1995.
61 Those seeking a restoration of the Soviet Union frequently advocate as a first step the establishment of Russian as an official language. See, for example, the report from Chernihiv in *Holos Ukrainy*, February 25, 1995.
62 *Eastern Economist*, January 1995, issues 49-52. Also see *Ukrainian Weekly*, September 18, 1994.
63 For a discussion which emphasizes the language factor, see Dominique Arel, "Voting Behavior in the Ukrainian Parliament: The Language Factor", in Thomas F. Remington, ed., *Parliaments in Transition* (Boulder, Colo. Westview Press, 1994): pp. 125-58.
64 Chrystyna Lapychak, "Back on Track", *Transition* 1, no. 3 (March 15, 1995).
65 IFES (International Foundation for Electoral Systems), "Ukraine's New Parliament", April 1994, Kiev.
66 Dominique Arel and Andrew Wilson, "The Ukrainian Parliamentary Elections", *RFE/RL Research Report* 3, no. 26 (July 1, 1994): p. 12.
67 Bohdan Nahaylo, "Ukraine", *RFE/RL Research Report* 3, no. 16 (April 22, 1994), pp. 46, 49. On the whole, however, Nahaylo concludes that so far political extremism has not been a major problem.
68 *Ukrainian Weekly,* July 31, 1994. Actually the fight had to do with translating into Ukrainian the speeches which are delivered in Russian from the floor, without any hindrance from the parliamentary leadership.
69 *Ukrainian Weekly*, January 22, 1995.
70 *UNIAN*, February 27, 1995.
71 IFES Press release, January 18, 1995.
72 Poll conducted by the International Sociological Institute. See *Ukrainian Weekly*, January 15, 1995.

8 The Relationship Between the Majority and the Minority in a Composed Region

The Case of Vojvodina[1]

MIRIJANA MOROKVASIC

There were few regions that had not been affected by the Balkan powder barrel. Those regions who suffered most and who were most threatened had been ethnically mixed regions. The dissolution of the nations which had composed Ex-Yugoslavia, the mythologization of the past, the rupture of the relations between people who had been living side by side as neighbors for a long period of time and whose families have been inextricably mixed, and the unsuccessful attempt of Europe to mediate the dispute have engendered the violent escalation.

The tragedy of Bosnia and Hercegovinia has shown how fatal the source was, on behalf of which Yugoslavia dissipated. The European "solution" regarding Yugoslavia has consisted of a series of "ad hoc" decisions – inconsequent, applied in a selective manner and contradictory to the EU's principles. Moreover, the priority attributed to national consciousness and the dissipation of formerly mixed communities have driven the supranational and regional as well as the individual ideas into the background. In this region the "tyrannic" fascination of the unrealizable notion of "NATION-STATE" – as emphasized by Michel Roux – has not been able to overcome this idea.

Even the relatively calm Serbian province of Vojvodina in the north-east of the country (consisting of a mixed population), which has been spared up to now from major conflicts, is threatened now by the potential powder barrel (Markotich, 1993). They talk about deterioration when talking about neighborhood relations (Oltay, 1993).

This kind of speculation is based on the postulate of "historical hate" resulting in the impossibility of living together among different ethnic-national communities. However, the war in the Balkans showed clearly various other – both internal and external – factors leading to the conflict. Internally, the weakness of the economy and government leadership, which had then already begun and which became more prominent in the late '80s, stimulated the growth of ethnic conflict as separatist movements in the individual republics and provinces threatened the viability of the nation. Externally, new power relations developed in Europe after the collapse of the Soviet Empire and after the Cold War. Yugoslavia, or rather what remains of it, serves as a symbolic demonstration field for new influences, the reckoning up, the regained solidarities, and so on. When it became obvious that none of the powers were able to save the country and thus not even the federal entity was able to articulate itself, the value of the country decreases. The decrease related to the media level, political and others, it concerned all kind of groups – power, intellectuals, politicians, journalists, authors etc. – no matter whether interested in solutions or benevolence in this terrible drama. For this reason we disapprove of the postulate of "historical hate" or the "communist refrigerator" which would have been able to "freeze" the relations between the nationalities; if this had happened, all the multinational regions would have been set into flames by the conflict. It did not happen that way and even if manipulations could exist everywhere they wouldn't find the same fertile ground and the population would be able to resist successfully.

We wanted to examine closely the multinational region of Vojvodina and particularly the way they organized their life within the relations between the numerical majority (the Serbs), which is more and more the dominating one, and the first group of the minorities (the Hungarians). Our previous knowledge and the first observations on site allowed us to form some simple theories to define:

The conflicts show more on the daily level, on the level of direct relations between people than on a symbolic level where abstract relations, as for instance "WE – THEY", and the level of memories count, which are easily manipulated.

We have also postulated that it is less the ethnical pertaining than the ancient history in the region which is determining the relations (Elias, 1990). It is notably important to distinguish between the Serbs – the "ancients" and the "newcomers" – Serb colonists from the interior of the country. It is the third time since the creation of the state of Yugoslavia that the government has used those colonists to modify the profile of a region favoring the majority. This strategy of the government includes a double advantage. It reduces the security of the Hungarian population in front of a real Serbian majority in the provinces and thus introduced a division within the traditional population, both Serb and Hungarian, which is critical for a government on the way to democratization. The government established itself by means of Serb colonists, traditionally loyal to the established government and thus neutralized the others, the "ancients" on site, whom the media have been quick to stigmatize as "bad Serbs". That is a well known strategy, which consists of using a transplanted population, radicalized by its own experience, to be discriminated in their own country, by their role of being victim in the past and its social and geographical uprooting.

1 Vojvodina: A Traditional Cohabitation

Vojvodina is an agricultural and relatively prosperous region of multinational character. For centuries there had not been any dominant ethnic group in this region until the Habsburgs acquired the region from the Ottomans in the 17th century and encouraged farmers and traders of different origins to populate their Empire's borders. At the end of the 17th century, an increasing number of Serbs started to migrate to Vojvodina, progressively settling there beside German, Ruthene, and Slovak settlers. The Serbs in Vojvodina, however, never completely isolated themselves from their compatriots who stayed under Ottoman domination. The Serbs of the other side of the Danube (the "Precani") progressively developed another cultural way of life. The Serbs in Vojvodina, farmers or traders, were very attached to their Serbian-orthodox religion and although they lived in a multinational context, "they had understood the necessity of respectfully living together with other ethnic groups" (Weill, 1938).

However, Vojvodina was the scene of several overthrows that marked the 20th century: the World Wars, the creation and disintegration of the states of which it was made a part.

Since the beginning of this century this province has changed into its fourth state accompanied by overthrows and important movements of populations which have changed Vojvodina's national configuration. After World War I a part of the German and Hungarian communities left the region. By then, the government encouraged and even organized the settlement of Serbs – the latest population of Vojvodina. These were particularly former World War I fighters coming from the south, mainly from the Southern Serbian province of Kosovo. Nowadays, there can still be found territories where descendants of colonists of this period represent the majority of the population. Agricultural reforms and the fiscal legislation gave preferential treatment to the Slavic farming settlers, which caused the emigration of about 15,000 Hungarian growers (Mesaros, 1989). According to the national census of 1931, the province of Vojvodina was inhabited by 1,628,000 residents, composed of Serbs (33 %), Hungarians (26 %), Germans (21 %), Croatians (7 %), Romanians (5 %) Slovaks (4 %) and other ethnic groups.

Between the two wars, the minorities' status, including that of the Hungarians, was established in law by international conventions in force, but in fact was much dependent on the state of bilateral relationships between Hungary and Yugoslavia. Although the power in office often had doubts about the loyalty of Vojvodina's Hungarians (since, for example, 3,500 Hungarians had been expelled after the assassination of King Alexander) until the World War II, neither confrontation nor any fundamental disruption in Serbo-Hungarian relations were evident. After the German aggression against the Yugoslav empire in 1941, Hungary annexed Backa and a part of Banat (the north and northeast of Vojvodina). Serbo-Hungarian relations were damaged severely for the first time, above all when, in winter 1942, Serbs and Jews were slaughtered by Horti forces (3,800 civilian victims). Immediately at the end of the war, numerous innocent Hungarian civilians, for their part, became victims of prevailing communist repressive measures. So the war and post-war period were the times of "ethnic cleansing" applied by both sides: certain sites were purged of Hungarians after the war, especially those sites which had seen significant losses of their Serbian population in massacres (Zabalj, Curug). These events have left traces in the Serbs' and Hungarians' collective memory, recently utilized as the mainspring of the emerging nationalist forces. As our studies reveal, the major part of the population has not been infected, however, mainly in those regions where national plurality has never been called into question.

After World War II, Vojvodina's multinational structure changed once again: nearly the whole of the German population (over half a million) were deported and their property confiscated. In its place, Serbian colonists, coming from Krajina, Bosnia, Montenegro, Serbia's south and from the back area of Dalmatia, were installed there as part of the agricultural reform at the end of the forties. The number of colonists who settled in Vojvodina is estimated at about 200,000. Several colonists were not able to adapt themselves and returned, others continued to immigrate in the fifties, sixties and seventies.[2]

The migrations of the Serbs not only caused a new recomposition for the Serb's profit, but the introduction of a new cultural and political dynamism, too. In fact, the colonists, most of them former resistance fighters of World War II, and their families were hardly attached to agriculture and ideologically hostile to the values of the urban society. They compensated for the lack of adaptability to Vojvodinian life-style by joining the party and entering the new stratum of bureaucrats and the system's rulers. They were of crucial importance for the forced collectivization of agriculture to which the native population was severely opposed. Besides, while rejecting the urban life-style and the society's values (our informants observe a "systematic destruction of all that remembered of bourgeois tradition and life-style"), they oriented towards the towns. They marked the process of advancing urbanization to an important extent, which was characteristic for "Second Yugoslavia".

The period of federal and socialist Yugoslavia had a strong impact on the relations between Vojvodina's nationalities. For more than forty years of stability the national question was certainly of use for the calming of social conflicts and the consolidation of the communist power in place. At the same time conditions were installed which allowed the cultural and political expression of the region's different nationalities. So this was a period when the expression of the national consciousness was ruled by state institutions. This expedient use of the national question helped avoid upheavals, but made any sensibilization concerning the peoples' historical dimension in Yugoslavia impossible. The near past was under a taboo.

While supervising the expressions of national feelings and their potentially harmful consequences, the state put under its control the transgressions of the national feelings throughout the union, too. In front of this state monopoly of "Yugoslavism", any autonomous attempt to create a trans-republic, independent trans-national organization was banned or scorned. This is a reason why, by the end of the eighties, no serious opposition to nationalist powers could be established or articulated.

The communists in Vojvodina controlled the process of the reestablishment of confidence between the different national communities. Their motto "fraternity and unity" was aimed to discharge the populations from collective guilt of crimes committed in their name. There could not have been any enemies but the class enemy, and the governments of both people's democracies, Hungary and Yugoslavia, at least agreed about that.

Claiming the ownership of the national questions, Josip Broz Tito's power was able to avoid national conflicts, and, in former times, to marginalize the expression of national sentiments. On the other side, the exaggerated emphasis put on the national question later raised the question about the power's authorization. A renaissance of the nationalities' representative institutions (of national minorities) could be realized, each of them under ideological surveillance of the party, with none of them receiving any preferential treatment. In this context, the Hungarians of Vojvodina employed their own theaters, publishers, press, radio and television programs. Education in the Hungarian language from childhood until graduating from university was their initial demand. The province's capital, Novi Sad, became the Hungarians' cultural capital, too.

Harmonious relations between the nationalities, accompanied by a certain political liberalization symbolic for Second Yugoslavia, allowed a decisive step towards the society's democratization. Meanwhile, in the eighties, the confrontation between Tito's heirs, struggling for power, obtained national characteristics. In order to remain in power, they knew they could count on the populist ardor of the masses, which, in the period of crisis, was ready to regard the "others" as a reason for their doom.

The constitution of 1974 guaranteed a large-scale independence to Vojvodina, compared with its mother republic, Serbia. This autonomy caused fractions with Belgrade, mainly after Milosevic took office. Vojvodina's rulers were hostile to tendencies of centralization by Belgrade and the policy of Milosevic. They underlined that any preference given to only one ethnic group, the major one, would cause a deterioration in the relations between the communities. In fact, Milosevic's policy produced feelings of insecurity and fear within the minorities, particularly among the Hungarian community, who was largely represented in the national power's structures. After the overthrow of "autonomist" rulers in Vojvodina in 1988 and the autonomy's abolition, the excesses of Serbian nationalism (under its pretext that the Serbs were threatened by the "privileged status of minorities"), could not always be controlled and led to a homogenization among the minorities. In this nationalist atmosphere, the party that could profile itself and express the Hungarians' claims the best was the national party DZVM (the "Hungarian Democratic Union of Vojvodina").

The tensions, which were limited to political structures, became more vigorous particularly between 1991 and 1992, during the period of the Croatian war. A large number of Croatians left Vojvodina because of the pressures and the intimidation of certain Serbian "refugees", who have been utilized by the power (the case of the village of Hrtkovci, for example). On the other side, tens of thousands of young Hungarians and Serbs, shunning the mobilization of the army for the war, have found refuge in Hungary, in Germany, or elsewhere.

This was the last important movement of populations incidental to the current war. According to the Hungarian ambassador in Belgrade, some 40,000, mainly young people, have left the country, some to avoid the mobilization, while others left for economic reasons or fearing political pressures. The number of refugees in Vojvodina is estimated to be more than 200,000, of which the majority are Serbs from Croatia and Bosnia. Thus, the heterogeneous region of Vojvodina has to face once again the strategy of homogenization and the obsession to have "all Serbs unified in one state" (Morokvasic, 1992; Samary, 1994).

Conforming to the census of 1991 (of which the dates have to be taken with caution because of the war), Vojvodina counted little more than two million citizens, of which 57% were Serbs and 17% Hungarians. 8.4% of the population consider themselves as Yugoslavians, 3.7% as Croatians and 3.2% as Slovaks. More than twenty different nationalities could be made out (see the following table).

2 The National Structure of Vojvodina's Population According to the 1981 and 1991 Census

	1981	1991
Albanians	3,814	12,959
Bunjevci	9,755	21,552
Croatians	109,203	74,226
Hungarians	385,356	349,946
Macedonians	18,897	16,641
Montenegrians	43,304	44,721
Muslims	4,930	6,079
Roma	19,693	25,895
Romanians	47,289	38,832
Ruthenians	19,305	17,887
Serbs	1,107,375	1,151,353
Slovaks	69,549	63,941
Slovenians	3,456	2,563
Sokci	199	1,866
Ukrainians	5,001	2,057
Yugoslavs	167,215	168,859
others	12,239	13,404
undetermined	3,361	11,317
regional ident.	1,643	2,516
unknown	3,188	5,906
Total	2,034,772	2,032,520

As a matter of fact, the question of the nationalities' equal rights, and particularly the situation of the Hungarians as the largest minority, has to be examined under the aspect of a constantly growing major group (and diminishing minorities).

3 The Inquiry: Method and Place

Apart from collecting written documents in the local press and consulting statistic dates or examining the national question in Vojvodina, we undertook *semi-directive*[3] interviews in three representative localities of Vojvodina, each of them nationally mixed to different degrees: a little town adjoining the capital Novi Sad, a kind of suburb located at 18 km from the center, Temerin; a Hungarian dominated village which is situated halfway between the capital and the second largest town of the province, Subotica, and which is called Mali Idjos; and finally, Subotica, the cosmopolite border town, where three main ethnic groups, the Hungarian community (as majority), as well as the Croatian and the Serb communities have lived side by side together for a long time, tightly connected by family ties (see map).

4   Three Typical Communities

4.1   Temerin

The community of Temerin is situated south-east of Backa, not far from Novi Sad. The community includes the town of Temerin and the localities Staro Djurdjevo, Backi Jarak and Sirig. Among the total of 25,000 citizens, 48% of the Serbs, 44% of the Hungarians, and further 5.6% of the inhabitants consider themselves as Yugoslavian. There are a smaller number of Slovaks, Croatians, Romas, Ruthenes and other ethnic groups. 80% of the 13.500 inhabitants of the capital city of Temerin are of Hungarian descent and there are others of Serbian origin as well as of other ethnic groups. The foundation of Staro Djurdjevo took place in 1920 by the arrival of about one hundred families coming from Bosnia, whereas Sirig was created in 1927. At the beginning of the war, under Hungarian occupation, a part of the Serbian population was massacred. Nowadays, 850 families (mainly Serbian) are living there. Backi Jarak (alias Mali Temerin) was inhabited by German settlers between 1780 and 1790. After the war, most of the Germans in this community, being considered as collaborators of the fascists, were relocated or deported. Nowadays, 2,500 persons who have lost all during the war in Bosnia and Hercegovinia have settled in former German places of residence. There are now about 6,000 people living here, of which 97% are Serbs of Bosnian origin – "Kolonisti" (colonists), or the "Dodjosi" (the newcomers), as they are still called in this place.

Agriculture is only a secondary economic activity within the population, of which 90% work in enterprises of Temerin or Novi Sad. We are dealing with one of the most developed communities of Yugoslavia.

As a result of their coalition, Milosevic's party SPS (Serbian Socialist Party) and the extreme nationalist party SRS (Radical Serbian Party) have obtained the majority in the community's assembly – to such an extent that the capital city of Temerin, where those parties are of less importance, is actually hardly represented (due to the constituency of Backi Jarak and Sirig).

4.2 Mali Idjos

Like the community of Temerin, Mali Idjos is situated at the international route Belgrade – Novi Sad – Subotica – Budapest, mid-way between Novi Sad and Subotica. With its 14,000 inhabitants it is one of the smallest communities of Vojvodina, and one of the least developed, too. Agriculture, and to a certain extent, services, are the sectors that employ the majority of the active work force.

The community today consists of Mali Idjos, Feketic and Lovcenac.[4] These are Serbian or Serbianized names of localities mentioned in Hungarian literature of the 16th century as well as the communities of Nadjhedjes, Kishedjhes, Seghedj and Feketehedj. The Turkish invasions of the 18th century and the Serbian migrations changed the profile of the sites. Later settlements of different peoples changed the national structure of the population once again: the settlement of the "Donauschwaben", then Hungarians and Serbs which took place mainly after the First and the Second World Wars. The powers in place gave preferential treatment to the newcomers compared to the established residents. The Germans were granted property tax relief for a much longer time than the Hungarians, which led to an impoverishment of a part of independent Hungarian farmers. The installment of Montenegrins was considered by the native residents as a concession of privileges, too. At present, the Hungarians are the majority (59.2%), followed by Montenegrins (23.5%), mainly in Lovcenac, and Serbs (11%). Up to now, mixed marriages between Hungarians and Montenegrins have been very frequent.

It is important to underline that the community was able to overcome the conflicts even in the most difficult periods of its history. World War II only demanded four dead within the community of Mali Idjos. Thanks to the extraordinary courage of a Hungarian Bishop at the beginning of the war and some Serbian village people at the end of it, there were neither any massacres nor reprisals suffered by the civil population. Even nowadays, this is often proudly mentioned by our interviewees.

4.3 Subotica

The community of Subotica covers 809 square kilometers and totals 154,000 inhabitants spread over 19 localities. 46% are Hungarians, 21% Croatians, 13% Serbs and 11% Yugoslavians. It is one of the few Yugoslavian towns where the population has stagnated for the last century. The community is, at the same time, of agricultural and industrial structure, and it is located at the cross-roads of the north-south and east-west routes, oriented towards Hungary. It is provided with an important market where, during the period of peace in Yugoslavia, tens of thousands of sellers and buyers of many eastern states met. Subotica is an important cultural center, too.

It is a multinational, Hungarian dominated town, characterized by harmonious interethnic relations. Until 1987, when Milosevic partisans began to organize meetings, the Serbo-Hungarian relationship had been very good. Since then, fear has settled within the population without turning into conflicts, however: For a few years, to be the majority (by numbers) has automatically included power with accordingly more rights. Within the new power structure, the attention paid to numbers ("We are so many, you are so many") plays an important role. So the Hungarians have felt afraid because they have presented a minority in Vojvodina and in Serbia, whereas the Serbs have been fearful in places where they are minorities.

The population of Temerin (according to the 1991 census)
Serbs	13,303
Hungarians	9,661
Yugoslavians	1,262
Croatians	145
Total	24,901

The population of Mali Idjos (according to the 1991 census)
Montenegrians	3,372
Serbs	1,611
Yugoslavians	457
Hungarians	8,500
Total	24,901

The population of Subotica (according to the 1991 census)
Croatians	16,282
Serbs	22,463
Yugoslavians	22,486
Hungarians	64,274
Bunjevci	17,527
Total	150,266

5 Lectures About the Splitting of WE and THEY

In spring 1993, several years after the abolition of Vojvodina's autonomous status and one and a half years after the dissolution of Yugoslavia as a state, we undertook our interviews, right at the moment when the war in Bosnia and Hercegovinia began to extend. It was a period of degeneration of the economic situation and of a rapid deterioration of relations between the nationalities in Vojvodina; the acceptance and perception of the "others" had been strongly influenced. The supra-national and regional consciousness as an important element of the peoples' identification, in Yugoslavia in general and in Vojvodina in particular, more and more gave way to the national consciousness.

Are we obliged to adopt the national scheme as the only lecture prism for the intercommunitary and interpersonal relations, as did the conductors of the war, their media and after them, a more and more important number of indirect protagonists of the Yugoslavian conflict (international media, politicians, certain intellectual discourse)? If we consider the nature of the powers in office on the territory of Ex-Yugoslavia and the mediatization of the drama being experienced by the population, to be "Serbs", "Hungarians" or "Croatians". These facts appear to be evidence which has shown with such unease that those attributes gradually have obtained a certain legitimation.

Even what concerns research, the splitting, or better, this whole pattern of splitting in lecture, seems to go their own way (speak for themselves). It is the matter of a recent inquiry about the interethnic relationships in Vojvodina, executed by the Belgrade Institute of Political Research (Brankovic, 1994). In this study, the "Serbs", the "Hungarians" and the "Slovaks" (three communities as the subjects of this research) are regarded each as indubitable entities. They appear only as object of research. The author induces prefabricated answers limited to such an extent that the interviewees are forced to talk about their nationality only. In this way, he takes part in the nationalist logic. Even more serious is the fact that, in a compound region, this method ignores the achievement of fusion (in 1991, nearly one of ten Vojvodinians claimed to be Yugoslavians, in an environment, however, that has shown a rising Serb nationalism).

Contrarily, our qualitative approach shows the volatility of identity definitions, explains the inquiries and the fluctuations of definitions in different contexts. During one interview with one person, definitions of "we" and "others" changed steadily.

The consciousness of "we" and "they" is always dependent on one another. That means that the national gaps are only divisions which the "we" and "they" may count on. While the including "we" (the "Yugoslavian we") had existed before the change (before Milosevic and the upswing of nationalism, before the new Yugoslavian constitution, before the abolition of autonomy and, above all, before the war), it is now an excluding national "we" ("we without the others", "we, the Serbs", "the Hungarians") that has been imposed since then.

"When I was in the army, I had never realized that the national belonging would be of any importance, especially not for the relations among us, the recruits and our superiors. Only the Albanian troops, which were not very numerous in our unit, stayed more by themselves and did not take much confidence towards 'us'."

While talking about the past period, this young Hungarian (29 years old, his wife a Hungarian, his parents Hungarians) makes use of the compounding "we" in order to express "we all", the Yugoslavians, excluding the Albanians.

All those "Serbs" or "Hungarians" who were not in the position to be Yugoslavians at the same time because it was not their prerogative to define themselves as such, felt betrayed; they were forced to turn their allegiance from a multinational state, where no one group had the absolute majority, to another, in which the Serbs were of absolute majority. This is a situation they could hardly accept or not accept at all, especially if they are Hungarians or of mixed origin, but also if they are of Vojvodinian origin, too.

In these three localities a strong polarization of statements could be observed: on one side, the native Serbs and Hungarians (and even several Serbs coming from colonist families, if they had been integrated within the *native* population, though of an inferior number), and on the other hand, the answers of colonists, particularly if they were coming from regions predominantly populated by Serbs or Montenegrins. With the people of Mali Idjos we noted a local identification, above all with the village, particularly with those from Fecetic (village of mixed nationalities), an identification with the entire community of Idjos, and finally, with Vojvodina, too.

The expression "we" covers those who share the values of fusion, of mingling, of a gregarious life to which the majority of Mali Idjos adheres; "they", on the other hand, are destructive elements seeking division, the youth from Lovcenac (of Montenegrin majority) or from elsewhere.

The mobilization in Croatia is the factor that contributed to the redefinition of "we and they" in national terms. Not as many Hungarians as Serbs of Vojvodina were recruited. Meanwhile, the feeling persists that this happened:

"It is true that the Serbs were mobilized, too, but in the end, it was 'their' war with the 'Croatians'. But why do 'we, the Hungarians', participate in a war of the others on a territory that does not belong to us? Nobody attacked Yugoslavia. The army to join in was no more the same as it had been, you have seen the symbols it bears ... we are afraid of this army, this does not correspond to the Yugoslavia we had known. And when three soldiers of our community had been killed in one single day (two Hungarian and one Montenegrin), it provoked open resistance."

Here, the "we-Hungarian" opposed the others: Serbs, Croatians, on a territory that was not "ours"; at the same time, an allegiance to a state was expressed that did not exist any more, but which would have been defended if it had been attacked.

The attachment to Vojvodina or to the Yugoslavian idea reveals a citizen's sense of community:

"I feel like a Yugoslavian, even if I am of Hungarian nationality, because I consider this territory as a community. I am not a Hungarian from Hungary."

"I do not distinguish the people for the sake of their Hungarian, Serbian or other nationality, I do not see why I should. Until one or two years ago, I did not realize that in Bosnia, for example, there had lived Croatians, Serbs or Muslims. I regarded them all as Bosnians. As a doctor, I see up to 50 patients a day, I do not see why I should make any difference between the nationalities. I am going to work with the young crippled of this war. I never look at their names or national appearance... It is the humanity that counts."

The following Hungarian, an owner of a large restaurant in the center of Subotica, thought that the situation had never been that serious: "I have grown up as a Yugoslavian patriot; we were all prepared to defend this country. But who to defend in a war like this where everybody kills each other!? I helped my son to escape, and I will leave, too, if this situation continues."

Our participants in the discussions admitted their weakness towards those powers obliging them to decline their identity towards the national consciousness – which they regard as a regressive step concerning civilization:

"We are pushed into this vicious circle by forces that are overwhelming us, but we are taking part in it. Some years ago we would not have been here to discuss national questions but ordinary issues."

"We are not allowed to be Suboticani anymore. We have to accept ideas reminding of a lower level of civilization, something that belongs to the logic of tribal life. We are not strong enough to keep emotionally distant. One day or another, we will be seized by the situation. We are asked to be Serbs, in a kind imagined and propagated by the extremists supported by the government. Without this support, these extremists would not be but what they are in western states: 10% of the electorate. Here, they represent 50%. These 50%, left without alternatives, have been forced to think so ..."

The exaggerated emphasis put on the national belonging for a certain time contributed to the worsening of the relationship between nationalities:

"As a matter of fact, all the time we talked about the Hungarians being in danger, or the Serbs being in danger, feelings of insecurity had been spreading. People who never have thought of that confusion, started to believe that they were really persecuted. This belief has been already a step to make the 'others' responsible for the 'dangers' in which 'we' are drawn ...."

In this context, even the very strong and transnational resistance against the civil war could be manipulated. When mothers from Temerin went in the streets in order to demand that their sons be returned from the war, there was no difference between Hungarians and Serbs. Meanwhile, their demonstration was boycotted by the Serbs of Backi Jarak, which is of Serb, colonist majority. Our partners in discussion estimated that the population had been manipulated by the power which had misrepresented this demonstration as an only Hungarian demonstration, "organized by the Agoston party" (Hungarian Democratic Union of Vojvodina). As a result, the population has been divided, however.

6 Deterioration of the Relationship Between the Majority and the Minority

The Serbo-Hungarian relations have effectively deteriorated compared to the situation before the civil war and the dissolution of Yugoslavia. The subjective evaluation of this situation makes the difference, and we find again the polarization of answers of the native Serbs and the Hungarians on one side, and on the other side the Serbs of colonist descent. They are those declaring themselves responsible for the propaganda of the party in power. In consequence, the majority talked of deterioration while the others talked of a refund balance, of a justified re-establishment of power relations. The tensions were only due to the non-acceptance of this matter of fact.

The difference was made, too, by the evaluation of the question about Vojvodina's autonomy: the colonized Serbs welcomed the cancellation of the autonomy, like the elimination of an obstacle against the unification of the Serbian people, whereas the Hungarians regretted the past: "They take away all we had". In any case, the native Serbs, like the Hungarians, have been reluctant to the centralization resulting from the interpretation of the Serbs' state as a national state (in a way, the new constitution principally defined Serbia as a peoples' republic). With the change of the Serbian constitution, however, engagements had been undertaken concerning the minorities' rights – under conditions that they had not to be put in question, they had been restricted. Though the practice proved the contrary and our interviewees found that certain rights had been cut in a senseless way, they estimated these circumstances as dangerous and provoking.

They were conscious of the fact that in a real heterogeneous environment, the relationships with the others would not run their own way. They had to be cultivated, and, until now, the results of a long process of learning have been put in question. They remembered that even in the serious moments of World War II, the civil population knew how to keep the acquired tolerance.

A Serbian 63-year old woman from Feketic, has still remembered the citizens' courage:

"We have always had a mingling, here. It is our tradition of living ethnically mixed together. We all still remember the Hungarian bishop Agoston, who stood before the Serbs in order to protect those who were shot in 1941. His son in law, a communist, was said to be amongst them. And just the communists killed him after the war! And in 1944, it was my father and some others who stopped the Serbs taking revenge on the Hungarians of Feketic. The current situation frightens me: there are people who have come 'to rescue us, to protect us', but we do not need their protection at all!"

While the population within the little community of Mali Idjos was still able to exercise a kind of sufficient control or self-control in order to maintain peace (even better as the ruling parties are opposition parties), it appeared to be more difficult in the urban environments. In any case, a clear difference could be realized between Subotica, where the opposition has won the elections, and Temerin, or as in the capital of Novi Sad, where the SPS and SRS coalition (Socialist Party and Serb Radical Party) has been in power.

The Hungarians in Temerin practically disappeared from head offices, though they represented half of the population. The senior judge of Temerin, for example, was "relieved" of his office despite his competence. At the hospital, the only persons who were laid off were two Hungarian women. Hungarian editorial offices of radio and television were "purged", too.

In the educational sector, the changes, the pressures and discriminations could be perceived the most. The decrease of hours taught in the native language, the tendency to teach technical subjects more and more in Serbian were mentioned. The least welcome measure was the introduction of Cyrillic letters in official documents. These facts were considered as an unnecessarily provocative measure, because "the people are able to read well the Serbian language in Latin letters, and the Hungarians show reserves in front of the Cyrillic".

Concerning Radio Temerin broadcasts, the programs have been shifted from the afternoon to the morning hours, which has limited the audience. The explanations given stated an increase of demands for broadcasts in Serbian language. As a matter of fact, the Hungarians applying for interviews would express themselves easier in Serbian when talking about professional subjects. In the end, what concerns publicity spots, the demand for publicity in the Serbian language is stronger.

At the time of our interviews, the state of terrorization of the population was revolutionized. These certain excesses (threats of bombs, shots in the night, etc.) were generally attributed to the "others", strangers from outside of the community. Therefore, the tensions and conflicts were imported.

But more than the discriminations was the feeling of fear which could be found characteristic of the situation:

"We are expecting the worst. Because we have lost all hope for progress, all confidence. We are the silent witnesses of the disaster. And we are unable to do anything", explains a Serbian professor in the Philosophy faculty. "We have been informed that we are threatened, but in fact, we weren't. They have spread fear, and afterwards they have sent us protectors. Absurd, but true. Though we have had salaries of 1,000 German marks and more, we have been told that the federal government exploited us. I would really like to have exploiters who pay me as much today. Then they found their enemies: there were more and more, until the day when everyone was an enemy of the Serbs! The next ones in the string will be the Serbs who do not agree with them. They are already about to purge the schools and educational institutions: only patriots are accepted. These are therefore the most dangerous compatriots among us!"

Compared with the worsened global situation, great efforts have been made to preserve an understanding in direct personal relationships in order to prevent tensions from merging and uncontrollable occurrence from gaining the upper hand and transforming into conflicts. In spite of this, the hope is about to lessen in Subotica that the power's scheme will succeed in dividing the population and turning the tensions into open conflicts.

Our partners in the discussion agreed that the tensions had taken place on a political level and that the people were not prepared to dispute.

Mainly at the work-places and in public areas, the strategy of avoidance became the rule of conduct which ought to be respected.

"I'm working with Serbs and Hungarians, and no tensions can be perceived, everybody does his job. Sometimes there is a *charged atmosphere*, but these are personal misunderstandings ... In the end, we tell them what they want to hear, and they do the same; and everyone thinks quietly in his corner what he likes to. Where quarrels have always existed, they obtain now a national coloration."

Regarding every day direct contacts (friends, neighbors), they were suffering where Serbs and Hungarians had lived together for a long time. The atmosphere was revealed to be more tense and the relations were *radicalized easier* in communities with a large Serbian or Hungarian majority. In other places, traditionally mixed communities were better prepared to resist and the people's capability to surmount the present difficulties still existed.

The most intimate relationships seemed to be the least troubled. In fact, one of three marriages takes place between partners of different nationalities in Vojvodina: in 1991, 28% of all marriages. We are talking of by far the highest rate compared with other regions of Ex-Yugoslavia, which has been constant for several decades (Petrovic, 1985). Our interviewees considered this as a normal fact and an advantage within a society as heterogeneous as the one of Vojvodina.

For the majority of the mixed couples of our examples, the problems, if there had been any, belonged to the past, caused by obstacles coming from their families, and, as it seemed, more on the side of Hungarian families. The couples we interviewed made up part of the generation which overcame the doubts and prejudices of their surroundings without larger difficulties. It was the matter of couples understanding each other with bilingually educated children. For many years, they said, they had not realized "that they had been different to other couples".

We took notice of the fact that the mixture was present in all social classes. It could not be found in environments that were more cosmopolitan than others – just because of their level of education and their life-style. For a hotel owner of Mali Idjos, the mingling had been desirable, because "the different cultures complement each other". He was born in Mali Idjos, and after graduating in Novi Sad, he returned to work in his father's *motel restaurant*. "Who am I? My mother was born in Sekic, now called Lovcenac, descendant of a Germano-Hungarian family. My father is a Serb from Macedonia; my wife is a German from Mali Idjos. Then, in the end like my sister who lives now in Australia, I speak Serbian, Hungarian and German. I want my personnel to do exactly the same. This is the normal case."

Only one out of eleven couples interviewed seemed to suffer directly by the change of attitude in their Serbian environment, mainly in the wives' family (of Serbian colonists of Bosnia). Their history, although exceptional within our examples, was absolutely possible. On one hand, it illustrated nationalism intruding into the people's private life, and on the other hand the willingness and courage of the couple which had been necessary to resist, particularly in the social milieu into which nationalism had most easily found its way.

For several years, the rising nationalism and the logic of exclusion had contributed to the stigmatization of those marriages as not normal. Certain interviewees underlined the changes of behavior and the avoidance of exogamy marriages: One part of the people preferred to avoid the problems connected with the environment. On the other side, it could be recognized that in former times, the majority of people got married in a registry office, whereas nowadays, they prefer to celebrate their marriages in church.

We have not found out if celebrations of those marriages were less numerous than they had been before. Quite on the contrary, an obviously "mixed" marriage as the one between the granddaughter of Subotica's orthodox cleric and a Croatian showed that the norms of national exclusion had not been imposed to such an extent, yet. This marriage happened at the time of our study in the place.

7 Which are the Perspectives for the Future?

"I dream of everything that doesn't remind me of my everyday life and present situation, I dream of all which makes me a man and not an Hungarian."

The political scene has been strongly dominated by national parties, former government parties, which have even influenced opposition parties.[5] The participants in our discussion accused the present powers of having caused the society's destabilization, having created insecurity among the population by the use of the "Dodjosi" (colonists) as well as by the help of "people of the society's ground-levels". The dividing and tensions had been introduced either by extremist gangs, or by media "without which there would have never occurred any excesses". The strongest radicalization had taken place under nationally homogenous conditions and in sites where an increasing number of refugees arrived from Bosnia and Croatia (about 200,000 in Vojvodina).

The possibilities of articulating claims without emphasizing the national aspect were very rare, difficult and boycotted in a violent manner by the peoples' "legitimate" representatives. Those other voices not being in the minority were weak within the present circumstances: "The moderate voices cannot be heard – the extreme ones are favorized by television!"

Attempts were made: parties with regional tendencies, associations for Serbo-Hungarian friendships, like the one created in Temerin with its objective of observing the maintenance of the acquerement of conviviality and tolerance.

Teachers, on their part, especially in mixed schools, had tried to preserve the spirit of tolerance. For them, "it is the question how to teach their pupils to think as autonomous individuals and to resist against the propaganda".

On the level of municipality, especially in Subotica and Mali Idjos, they tried to preserve the acquirements, too: In spite of the homogenization's intensity, the relationships could not be disturbed by a simple provocation. We do have an unwritten law that each conflict, each misunderstanding has to be individually examined, case by case. They must not be collectively attributed to certain groups. But these are just the occasions the power hoped for to manipulate and provoke the conflicts.

Often, the statements given about the future development include a kind of nostalgia of the past, the desire "that all will become as it was before". In Vojvodina, the confidence in the people's common sense ("they will understand to where all this leads", "the most important thing is to look towards the future and not to look always back", "our town has not been involved in conflicts, yet, we would have to be afraid of", etc.), were always shown by the reality and hopelessness in front of the tragedy in Bosnia and Hercegovinia: "I remember we said the same thing, we had the same confidence compared with the situation over there".

Sometimes we felt that the possibilities of dialogue were exhausted or were limited to a little circle of friends or the family. The consciousness and pride of living in a developed region has weakened; a region where the apprenticeship of multinational life has been present for centuries; a region which has always been able to integrate newcomers without animosities. Mixed couples, in particular, still resist, just like the majority of the people who talked to us frankly. But we must realize a shift towards increasing national identifications, breaking through against the will of our discussion partners we met: This is not the way they would have chosen, but men and media have been facing them with fear and intimidation. Even if this scarcely has happened, it has already begun to be established as a reality they have to expect one day.

The ruinous economic situation was due to the propagation of nationalism of which our interviewees are conscious:

"We are living under worsening conditions. The formerly very high standard of life has declined to an African level. The only successful are the profit-seekers, the profiteers of the war, the criminals." They had the impression that this insecurity about tomorrow would concern all of them. It could unify them, but at the same time, was to constitute a breeding-ground for the spreading nationalist hate campaign.

If this situation remained, the youth, especially the grammar school pupils we have interviewed, would not wait much longer for an amelioration of the conditions. "Subotica was a town of young people", they say. "Can you still find any young people, here?" Several tens of thousands of youngsters have already left: Hungary is mentioned most frequently, but Australia, New Zealand, Israel, Denmark and Germany, too. Even if these departures are considered as individually legitimated acts, they caused an augmentation of feelings of insecurity and fear for the development, emptying the region of a social class without which the democratization of the society would be unimaginable.

Among those who stayed in Vojvodina, new homogenizations appear: "If everyone turns to his proper surroundings, I do the same, even that I know that it is not good to act this way. This only deteriorates the situation. But there I do not see any other possibility. I turn myself towards the DZVM."

The situation was even radicalized among the children. In a primary school, for example, the graffiti spoke for itself: formerly, that graffiti had reflected the children's problems due to their age (7 to 14 years), now we can see more and more symbols of the parties, messages they heard within their families or in the street. They became increasingly violent, too. In discos, we met groups nationally separated, something that could not be found before.

In areas where one or an other group is a large majority, there was a stronger tendency for national consciousness. This is exactly the situation in Lovcenac, the place which belongs to the community of Mali Idjos and which is of Montenegrian majority, where the motto was adopted: "You are with us, or you are with the others!"

At the moment, national tensions seem to be more important than the serious decrease in the standard of living. The majority of our interviewees had a clear and critical attitude about the power and its methods of manipulating the memories and national sentiments. Most of them developed a strategy of avoidance, being aware of the disastrous effects of provocation. They seemed to be conscious of their situation which they regarded as a time bomb which only *they* could deactivate.

Despite the context becoming more and more clear, even as subject of our dialogues, the dividing of "we and they" did not always show national characteristics. The strong uneasiness often seems due to the rising consciousness of their inability in front of the nationalist forces ... Fear is spreading.

174 *Ethnic Conflicts and Civil Society*

Notes

1. In the year 1993, Pierre Kende and I led the research on "The stability and the instability in Central Europe. The Evolution of the interethnic relations between the Hungarians and their neighbours". The following text with the main topic on the Serbian region of Vojvodina is a part of these studies. We would like to state our gratitude to DATAR, from which we received great cooperation.

2. It has to be mentioned that the balance of migrations has always been negative, except for the period of the fifties and the beginning of the sixties. In fact, the number of people arriving made up for the departure of others who left for the big towns like Belgrade or Zagreb, or went abroad (Curic, 1979)

3. The fieldwork and the collection of material have been entrusted to a Serbo-Hungarian team on the spot, in Novi Sad, that I employed for this purpose (four missions in all, at the end of 1992 and 1993).
In Temerin, twenty-four semi-directive discussions have been engaged with twelve Hungarian, nine Serbs, two Yugoslavian and one Montenegrian. It has to be added that four of them were mixed couples. Husband and wife were interviewed together. Fifteen people have been interviewed in Mali Idjos, of which there had been seven Hungarians, the rest had been Serbs or "of non-declared nationality"; four of them represented mixed couples. In Subotica, nine of twenty-one persons are Hungarian, two are Croatian, ten Serbs. Three couples are mixed Hungaro-Serbian.
This description is only given as a note, which already misses the reality, however: it privileges the national belonging, because our research demands it. Thus on one hand, such national belonging is not shown as distinguishing identity features, and on the other hand, as our interviews reveal, the mingling is much more important than this article admits to assume.

4. Name given to Sekic (originally Seghedj) by Montenegrian Kolonisti who arrived in 1945, after the symbolic mountain of Montenegro which is named Lovcen. In the 18th century, this village with a Slavic majority was inhabited mainly by Germans until the end of World War II, when they were expelled from Vojvodina.

5. Apart from the extremist party of Seselj (Radical Serb Party), certain other opposition parties are national Serb parties, too. Concerning the Hungarians, the majority of our interviewees consider the Hungarian Democratic Union of Vojvodina (DZVM), which pretends to be everyone's representative, as "too nationally coloured" or even "extremist". They dissociate themselves from this party.

Bibliography

BRANKOVIC, S. 1994: Fattibilita del vivere commune nella regione multi-etnica della Vojvodina; Cultura del confine e rapporti inter-etnici nella formazione degli stati degli Slavi del Sud, ISIG (Istituto di Sociologia Internazionale), Gorizia, pp. 10-13

CURCIC, S. 1979: Promena broja stanovnika Vojvodine tokom poslednjih sto godina (La modification du nombre des habitants de la Vojvodina au cours de derniers 100 ans), Zbornik Prirodno-Matematickoq Fakulteta, Novi Sad

ELIAS, N. 1990: Etablierte und Außenseiter, Suhrkamp: Frankfurt a.M.

MARKOTICH, S. 1993: Vojvodina: A Potential Power Keg, *RFE/RL Research Report*, Vol. 2, No. 46

MORIN, E.: Penser l'Europe, Gallimard: Paris

MOROKVASIC, M. 1992: La guerre et les réfugiés dans l'ex-Yougoslavie, *Revue européenne de migrations internationales*, Vol. 8, No. 2, pp. 5-25

OLTAY, E. 1993: Hungarians under Political Pressure in Vojvodina, *RFE/RL Research Report*, Vol. 2, No. 48

PETROVIC, R. 1985: Etnicki mesoviti brakovi u Jugoslaviji (Les mariages ethniquement mixtes en Yougoslavie); Institut de Sociologie, Belgrade

PROTIC, D. 1987: Opstina Mali Idjos (La municipalité de Mali Idjos); Prirodno-Matematicki Fakultet, Novi Sad

ROUX, M. 1992: Nations, Etats et territoire en Europe de l'Est et en URSS, l'Harmattan: Paris

SAMARY, C. 1993: Sans patrie ni frontière, l'Odyssée des réfugiés des l'ex-Yougoslavie; *Le Monde Diplomatique*, Janvier 1994

WEILL, G. 1938: L'Europe de XIXe siècle et l'idée de la nationalité, Albin Michel: Paris

9 The Media
Social Constructions in Inter-Ethnic Communication in Romania

CARMEN DUMITRIU-SEULEANU

1 Introduction

Inter-ethnic tensions emerged in many post-communist countries as a "new" issue after the collapse of the communist systems. The issue was not only new for Western European spectators, but also for the local societies. The media started to report about "minorities", and about the emergence of new NGOs. They also reported about increasing tensions, debates and even violent conflicts. The information available to us includes data about Romania as a whole, but more importantly about local communities and their ethnical composition as well as performance data about ethnical tensions and problems. We will limit our presentation to the Romanian situation. In December 1989 (26-29) several minorities created their own organizations; in February 1990 the other ethnic minorities followed. At that time we had about 14 NGOs in Romania representing: Hungarians, Poles, Greeks, Turks and Tartars, Armenians, Bulgarians, Slovaks and Czechs, Jews, Serbs, Ukrainians Lipovans, Gypsies. Of course, the persons who were among the initiators for each of the ethnic organizations had a certain social status recognized by the entire society, such as poets and journalists (the Armenians, Czechs and Slovaks, Bulgarians), actors or movie directors (Greeks), scientists (Albanians, Bulgarians, Jews), and managers (Ukrainians, Gypsies, and others).

The social change in 1989 not only led to a confusion in the entire society and provoked the establishment of all the ethnic organizations, it also produced a tremendous activity in the media. About 1,000 newspapers emerged in less than 4 months. A huge "communicational noise" was created, many social voices started "*to speak*" simultaneously. New values and terms were promoted by all these social voices trying to influence public opinion since most of the new media were owned or operated by the newly established NGOs. For a short period, "the louder voices in this concert" were more successful in reaching the targeted audience, so everybody learned that it was necessary *to speak with a "strong voice"*. The control and management of the communication system turned out to be the main resource in the post-communist struggle for public attention and political clout as well as having profound repercussions on the emergence and manifestations of ethnic conflicts in Romania.

Most people believe that with the collapse of the communist system in 1989, the media had become strongholds of democracy and cultural pluralism. Looking from a meta-communicational perspective, two aspects were totally neglected during this period of media reorganization:

1) With the emergence of the new organizations and the restructuring of the media, the previous way of thinking was not abolished. The communist past was still present in people's mind and continued to exist in many social rules and legal provisions.

2) The newly emerged concepts and structures were chaotic in the beginning and intransparent to those who were exposed to the sudden multitude of information possibilities. Even those who had promoted these new structural elements of society expressed dissatisfaction with the obvious abundance of information.

The general public did not understand the significance of the new structures and responded with confusion or apathy. Intellectuals, however, praised the opportunity to have access to many channels of information coming from all sources, including the outside world. Missing was some kind of a coherent structure of the media market and a general orientation about the mission and positions of each of the newly developed media products.

This paper addresses the evolution of ethnic tensions in the aftermath of the 1989 breakdown of the communist system in Romania. The main focus will be on the role of the communication system and the actors within that system with respect to ethnic relationships. Based on a social constructivist point of view, I will argue that good will alone will not be sufficient to overcome ethnically motivated tensions. What Romania needs is a new institution dedicated to the task of providing background information to all parties and functioning as mediator in the existing conflicts and those still to come.

2 The Media Structure Before the 1989 Revolution

Figure 1 is an attempt to represent the media landscape in Romania during the communist era. The surface of the society was covered by well established communicational actors who followed precise rules for what to cover and how to cover specific events. So the media institutions ABA MEDIA and IBC generated highly selective information for a clearly defined audience (Level MI). All information input was supposed to support the revered model of the "multilateral developed society" and the "new person", both common goals of the communist policy. These media programs generated by these core institutions were then *duplicated, translated* and *transported* via various mechanisms to local political and social organizations (Level MII). Other media channels were used to convey the messages to social groups such as the youth organization (Level MIII). The goal was total control of the information output and the assurance that only the "good results" of public policy making was reported.

Responses from the society were carefully screened and selectively reproduced using the same hierarchy of media coverage. First the elites were informed, then the political and social groups close to the political elite, and after them the remaining groups. Finally, the information was given to the general public.

It is obvious that such a supervised system of generating politically correct messages created a "silent" and "receptive" community who knew its duty was *to receive, believe and execute* the message. Of course, there were informal communication channels, but, as Fig. 1 shows, these informal channels were disjointed from the official media business. They were either apolitical personal messages or contained clandestine social messages that were not covered by the official media. These secret messages were limited to only a small part of the political and intellectual elite. The population at large was exposed to only the official governmental propaganda. Overall, the system of media control and supervision worked remarkably well and was partially a cause for the adaptive and passive behavior of the majority of people.

180 *Ethnic Conflicts and Civil Society*

Communicational Climate in Romania 1989

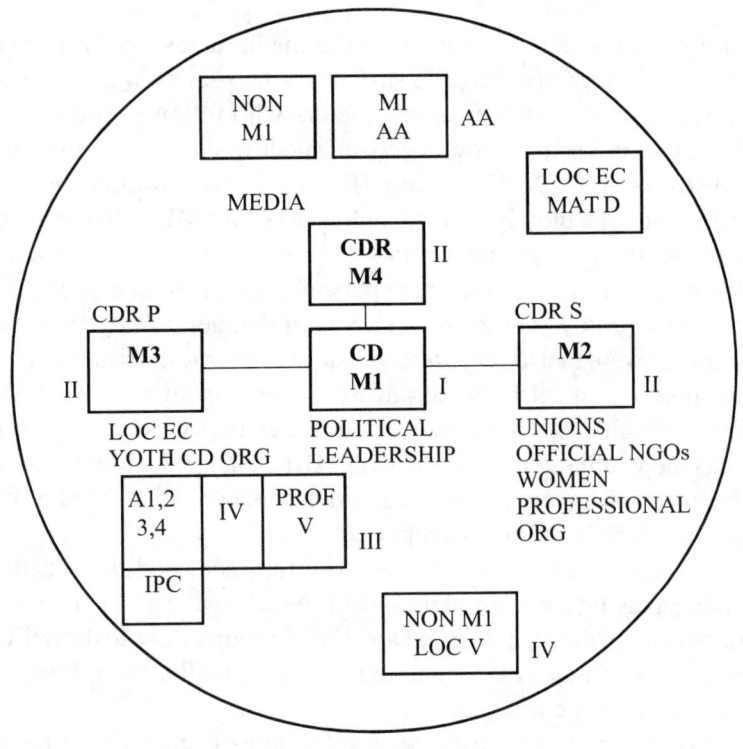

Fig. 1
The scheme of the social communicational instances in a communist society

Legend:
AA	Artistic Activities
CD	Central Discourse
CDR	Reduplicators of the Central Discourse
CDR P	Reduplicators of the Central Discourse Using Technical Professional Discourse
CDR S	Social Reduplicators of the Central Discourse
IV	Individual Values
IPC	Interpersonal Communication
LOC CDR	Local Reduplicators of the Central Discourse
LOC V	Local Values
LOC EC MAT D	Local Economic Material Discourse
M 1,2,3,4	Message 1,2,3,4
NGO	Non Governmental Organization
ORG	Organization
PROF V	Professional Values
YOUTH CDR ORG	Reduplicators of the Central Discourse of the Youth Organizations

3   The 1989 Revolution and its Impacts on the Media System

This system of complacency and unilateral communication experienced a major shock when the communist system collapsed and plural media input entered the Romanian scene. Many "speakers", usually representing specific interests or points of view, became active communicators in the media business. Many languages other than Romanian were then used in reaching out to the different ethnic and social communities. In addition, the influence from the West and a new political way of thinking created a new "language game". New words appeared in the media that were related to the changes in governance and social order, but even more important, new cultural trends were reflected in the media, leading to new phrases and expressions. Sentences used by important people all over the world were repeated by others and new trends were generated. Only those who were able to play the new "language game" were part of the new political or cultural elite, so everybody tried to be literate in the new game. This all led to a new "official" language which represented a mixture of folklore, modern lifestyle, and political jargon. Content was unimportant as long as the rhetoric was correct.

Over a period of approximately two years this new game caught the attention of the intellectual elite before the new language became a common feature of the communicative style of the ordinary citizen.

Figure 2 is an attempt to show the differences between the old and the new situation with respect to public communication and the media. The main change in the media system was pluralism. Parallel to the fact that the elite was trying to stay ahead of the evolving language games, many different actors in society created their own language game in order to address specific target audiences. Among them were the different ethnic groups who were able to receive information in their native language. Very often they were not aware that this information was colored by the interests of the respective publishers since they were still expecting "official" information by the government as they had been used to for all of their lives.

On the stage of the media arena, many actors assumed the role of moderators or mediators. They tried to explain the new situation to the audience and helped to coordinate different media efforts. But these moderators had their own agenda and used their moderation to increase

182 *Ethnic Conflicts and Civil Society*

Communicational Climate in Romania 1990-1993

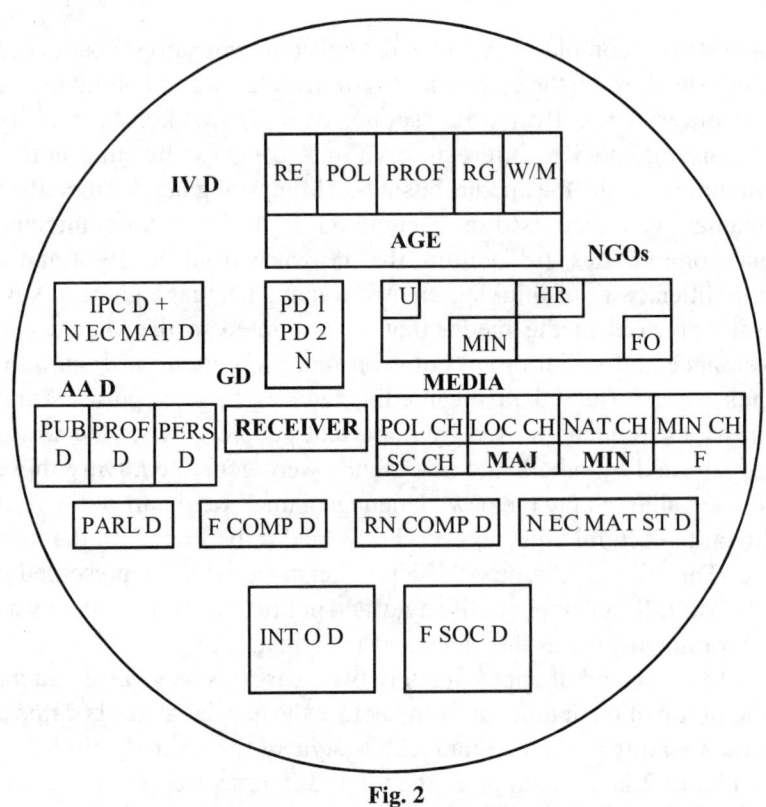

Fig. 2
The scheme of the social voices active in the Romanian society

Legend:
AA D	Artistic Activity Discourse	INT O D	International Organizations Discourse
AGE	Agent		
F	Foreigners	IPC D	Interpersonal Communication Discourse
F COMP D	Foreign Companies' Discourse		
FO	Foreign Organizations	IV D	Individual Values Discourse
F SOC D	Foreign Societies' Discourse	LOC CH	Local Channel
		M	Men
GD	Governmental Discourse	MAJ	Majority
		MIN	Minorities
HR	Human Rights	MIN CH	Minorities' Channel
		N	Other Parties

NAT CH	Nationalist Channel	PROF	Professional
N EC MAT D	New Economic Material Discourse	PROF D	Professional Discourse
N EC MAT ST D	New Economic Material Standard Discourse	PUB D	Public Discourse
		RE	Religious
		REG	Regional
PARL D	Parliamentarian Discourse	RN COMP D	Romanian Companies' Discourse
PD 1	Governmental Parties		
PD 2	Opposition Parties	SC CH	Scandal Channel
PERS D	Personal Discourse	U	Unions
POL	Political	W	Women
POL CH	Political Channel		

their influence and power in the market. Independent media analysts, on the other hand, were either missing or had no voice in this game, so that enlightenment about the new media market came from those with vested interests in the market. This increased the confusion on the side of the consumer and helped to erode the urgently needed trust in a free media system.

In addition to the home-made confusion, citizens were exposed to a large number of foreign products, partially translated for the Romanian market, partially coming from those countries in which the language of some of the many Romanian minorities were spoken and used in official publications. So the communication markets exploded with new information and a plurality of viewpoints that most people had not enough experience to manage. A huge number of shops introduced media products from other countries, which again had the effect that Romanians were exposed to another set of unconventional information, material and cultural standards. Coping with this diversity turned out to be a major challenge for the Romanian public but also provided an opportunity for populists and demagogues to use ethnic identities as resonance for their nationalist or even chauvinist messages. By using their language and their cultural heritage, they were able to insert, covertly or even openly, "hate messages" into the information channels. Through these channels the topic of minorities was "introduced" by minority leaders, parliamentary groups and outside organizations. Often enough this form of ethnic communication turned out to be pure propaganda for supporting the position of ethnic chauvinism.

4 The Media as Facilitators of New Movements

Institutions and political leaders who wanted to address the issue from a humanistic perspective, and resolve or reconcile the evolving ethnic conflicts, had a hard time finding the appropriate terminology that they could use in bringing different ethnic groups together rather than addressing them individually. A specific phrase introduced into the context of one ethnic minority might have been received as a friendly gesture while the same phrase was perceived as a threat by another ethnic minority. This fact could be evaluated as a minor aspect but it proves that the basis for creating a common language platform was not trivial at all and that the old as well as the new language games did not offer much of a choice for reconciling ethnic differences or to restore human relations between members of different ethnic groups. The ethnic languages were well suited to create an identity within each ethnic niche but were not well suited for building bridges to another language or another ethnic group.

Interestingly enough, the new debate about ethnicity made people more aware of ethnic differences than they had been in the past. These differences were amplified in several media products, thus creating a social construction of what each ethnic group was supposed to represent. This even had an impact on professional performance in science, business, and public organizations: old colleagues who worked for years together discovered suddenly one of them belonged to the "majority" and the other to a "minority". So they were more or less forced to negotiate a new way of dealing and communicating with each other. Often the collective memory became reactivated and old historical quarrels were rediscovered. In a qualitative study on ethnic tensions we encountered accusations such as: "We used to have communitarian schools, why don't we have them any more?"; "We used to have publications in our mother tongue"; "We were involved mostly in commerce / or in agriculture / in banking / in building houses"; "We used to have compact communities"; "We used to have our own church". These rather mild accusations were topped by traumatic experiences of overt discrimination: "My father was not promoted because he was a Jew and his boss was a nationalist", or "My teacher punished me only because I was Turkish". These quotes demonstrate that ethnic problems were not resolved during the communist area but only suppressed. Now, being allowed to surface again, these memories had the potential to become powerful agents of violence and revenge. It was absolutely necessary to uncover these suppressed experiences but the media took advantage of these unresolved conflicts and fueled them with further ammunition for hate and repulsion.

5   Motivations for Ethnic Conflict

The dualism of majority and minority had profound impacts on the communicative messages related to ethnic conflicts. The major problem has been ambivalence. On one hand, the message has been *"Look back to your roots"*, on the other hand the message was communicated *"Let's stay together and form a single unity"*. Obviously there is a conflict between the two messages and, although there are potential solutions for overcoming this conflict, most people tended to either ignore the first or the second message. So two subcultures within each ethnic community seemed to evolve: the ethnic fundamentalists and the ethnic integrationists.

These two cultures expressed themselves in different ways: The dominant culture of "We want integration with other minorities and the majority" was expressed in seminars and conferences with the contributions of members representing "the others" (mostly majoritarians), by public debates about majority-minority problems, through bilingual magazines (sometimes tri-lingual like the Jewish magazine called *The Jewish Reality,* which is published in Hebrew, Romanian and English), and through TV and radio programs in Romanian language about celebrations, history, traditions, values, problems of different minorities. The other culture who promoted the "back to the roots" movement conducted seminars about the own culture, history, traditions and personalities. They created more local branches of the ethnic associations, supported publications, books, radio and TV programs in the respective ethnic language, and fostered the development of educational institutions based on one's native language (actually about 80% of the existing minorities in Romania have the opportunity to learn in their native language).

Out of this latter camp came a more radical branch of separatists. These groups can be characterized by the phrase: *"We want to stay away from the majority"*. Such sentiment was implemented by separating Romanian classes from the minority classes and placing them in different buildings, eliminating offers for developing bilingual classes, insisting on unilingual publications and closed sessions only in one's native language, and generating important documents in the native language only. Exchanges were organized with people from those countries from which the various ethnic groups originated or where they formed the majority (for example Hungarians from Romania visiting Hungary). Students were given the opportunity to study in these countries, sending students to learn the mother tongue in the original country, youth camps were organized to bring together students from both countries belonging to the same ethnic group, etc.

The majority of ethnic Romanians played the role of the spectator, at least in the beginning. During the communist regime their history and contributions to the country's development had been romanticized and partially mystified, but there had been no systematic recourse to ethnic supremacy as has been the case in many other countries. However, once the majority was depicted in public as the "oppressor" of ethnic minorities, they also became, at best, confused, and, at worst, emotionally outraged.

As a result of this, the majority was suddenly looking for it's own identity, similar to the many minorities. The majority was driven between the desire to become cosmopolitan players in the world and the romantic notion of revitalizing their Romanian heritage. This new development of ethnic relations can be illustrated by the headlines of the major Romanian newspapers after the collapse of the regime in 1989. The titles of the newspaper refer to:

a) titles commemorating the heroic times between 1840-1918 when Romanians fought for independence and experienced a national conscience revival (articles in the *Danube Star, The People,* and so on);
b) titles containing English words which could have been easily translated. The insertion of English phrases could be interpreted as statements of cosmopolitan attitudes and a desire to take part in the international affairs;
c) titles appealing to a modern lifestyle and Western values similar to the ones that people could find in Western newspapers.

The struggle between the cosmopolitan and the ethnic revival orientation is still visible today. A newly launched newspaper representing the government voice was called *"The Voice of Romania"*, which paraphrases the important nationalist 1848-1859 publication *Karpathians' Voice*.

6 Historical Roots of Nationalism

This trend towards rejuvenating the heroic times of Romanian history has its cultural roots. Romanian history can be interpreted as a permanent struggle for cultural as well as political independence. In the 15th and 16th centuries the language used in the church and in the official documents was Slavonic. Furthermore, Romania was part of the Ottoman empire, in which the development of a national identity was not encouraged. In 1877, when the first step for independence and reunification was accomplished, the nation had the first real opportunity to build a unified national culture.

After the second World War, when the state territory was finally established after many disturbances, the process of building a *new* (communist) *era* and creating the *new* (socialist) *citizen demanded* that the unfinished project of building a unified national culture again come to an end. During the period between 1948-1964 the country was dominated by Russian influence in spite of the privileges and political idiosyncrasies of the Caucescu clan. A real revival of independence and cultural identity did not occur before 1989.

The common desire to use this new opportunity for nation-building and integration provided a welcome opportunity for the representatives of the old regime to exploit public support for nationalism and used it as a powerful label for their own political goals. They created the slogan "We need to re-establish the authentic majoritarian culture" which, of course, presented a serious threat to the minorities. Already mobilized by active populists and sometimes directly encouraged by their ethnic counterparts in neighboring countries, they found additional reasons for pushing a segregationist agenda.

Another factor contributed to the aggravation of the relations between the minorities and the majority. The economic situation worsened over time and placed many people at the edge of poverty or even subsistence. The ones who still had work suffered under small wages, low social status, increased insecurity, and little hope for improvement. So it became more profitable to be a "social person", an activist or a populist. For this reason many people began to found their own organizations: interest groups, citizen initiatives, parties, unions and others. Becoming an ethnic activist turned out to be a profitable and highly respected profession. This new method of generating personal income was not always an asset for the respective organization, let alone for the cause that the organization represented. More and more people competed for leading positions in the respective organizations. One way to succeed was to increase the radical rhetoric. Based on the experience that references to immediate threats and conspiracies are likely to create solidarity with the prospective leader and maximize membership support, some candidates presented the relationship with the majority as a threat to the identity of the respective minority. So friends, colleagues, relatives, and neighbours were demonized as members of the hated majority.

7 Socially Constructed Versions of Ethnicity

How is this development of ethnic conflicts related to the media and the communication system? As stated before, the media amplified the tendency of minorities and the majority to define their own identities as something in opposition to the identity of the others. Elements of this communication strategy have been stressing the values of one ethnic group over the other, reminding each group of its heroic history, depicting the other groups as major obstacles in one's own pursuit to obtain economic stability and a decent standard of living, and most notably, using new language games to distance one's own group from the other. If communication breaks down, violence is likely to be its heir. In this sense, the media have co-created a communicational climate that fosters ethnic tensions and amplifies inter-ethnic conflicts.

In this context we need to define what a minority is. Different from natural ethnic characteristics, minorities based on the theory of symbolic language are social constructions based on attributions by the members of a social system. Groups of persons performing a complex search for identity attribute specific characteristics to either the *cultural construction of what they call majority and the cultural construction of what they call minority,* thus defining ethnic identity. This model doesn't exist in its abstract form; but it helps us to understand what happens when identity is created. The difference of the natural language or natural ethnic diversity lies only in the fact that the attribution process can be substantiated by visible signs. These signs have only symbolic meanings but they are relevant for distinguishing one group from another. Depending on the pressure of the socio-cultural context in which the individual is acting, these attributions of minority and majority are learned and internalized. They form the basic pool of prejudices and stereotypes that help people to become oriented quickly in a complex and confusing world.

8 Coping with Competing Constructions of Ethnicity

The essence of my argument is that creating identity, unity or diversion is a product of communication. There is nothing natural about minorities or majorities. These labels are all social constructions based on historical and cultural attribution processes. To be perceived as a member of one culture or another means to communicate to others the attributed differences between *"I"* and *"them"*. If that is true, communication is also the means to overcome this distinction and correct, if needed, some of the dangerous stereotypes about them and us. There is no simple method to do that and the view that one could deliberately change the use of language is certainly naive. But facing real threats of ethnic violence, we need to focus on communicational means because they are the only means that can touch upon the roots of ethnic violence, while all other punitive methods rely on curing the symptoms. So what can we do to improve communication in this context?

— First, we need to establish mutual communicational conventions of how to address each other and how we can find a common platform for discussing issues without offending each other. This is certainly not a trivial task. Many negotiations fail because each side feels that the language of the other side is inappropriate. It may make sense to invent new "neutral" phrases and expressions in order to create a climate of neutrality and good will.

— Second, we need to teach ourselves and the members of our group to understand the claims and sentiments of the other groups and vice versa. Empathy is a powerful tool for reaching a common agreement. If the others feel that we understand their problems,

they may be more likely to understand our problems. Creating a "common understanding" implies a bilateral effort in translating your values in our language and translating my values in your language. Again we do not mean natural languages when we refer to translation here (those, of course, pose a problem too) but to the diversity in symbolic connotations within the same natural language. Such a process is very difficult and takes time.
- Thirdly, we need to engage in a permanent dialogue that does not threaten the identity of those with whom we communicate. That begins with the use of language and includes respect for each other's habits and customs, religious beliefs, and cultural idiosyncrasies. Once the others realize that we respect their differences, they will be more willing to respect ours. Furthermore, by exploring and respecting mutual differences, commonalities are also revealed and provide the basis for further understanding.

In the present situation in Romania and beyond we must acknowledge the legitimate need to preserve and sustain the authentic values and

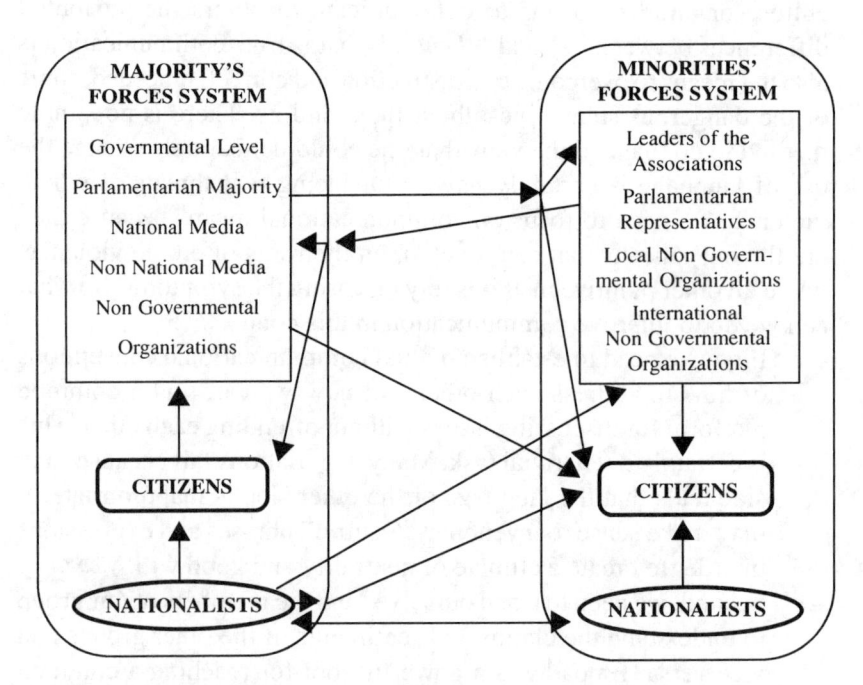

Fig. 3
The scheme of the majority's and minorities' forces system

traditions of majority as well as minority groups. If these values are lost, identity is lost and with it meaning and self-esteem. We need to understand that reestablishing and reassuring self identity (at the individual and at the group level) are essential elements of being an individual and cultural being. These processes are always ambivalent as they carry the virus of ethnic supremacy, chauvinism and segregationism. We have no other choice but to invest all our efforts in reducing the negative impact of ethnicity. We need to learn how to communicate in a multi-cultural society, to uncover the language of negative stereotypes, to address openly the "unpaid bills" in our collective memory (minorities and majority) and to establish rules for continuous communication and trust building. There is a good chance that this investment will pay off in due time. We need to help majority and minority groups to learn to converse in *each-other* languages.

Unfortunately this message has remained widely unacknowledged. On the contrary, private or group interests represented by determined activists and governmental experts keep tensions alive. So a gap emerged between the minority groups and the majority which is further described in Figures 3 and 4:

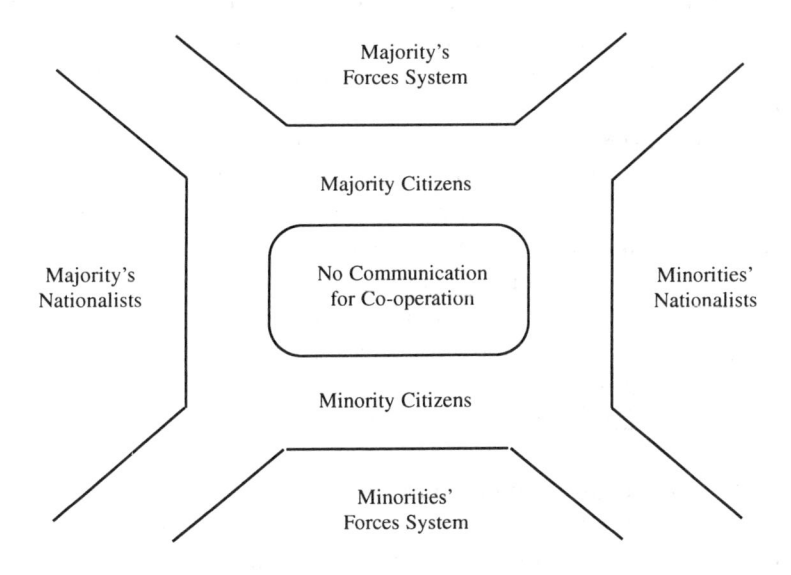

Fig. 4
The scheme of pressures put on the citizens belonging to the majority and to the minorities by the social forces created around the topic interethnic relations

9 A Case Study: Language Games of Different Groups

Our group conducted several studies on the use of language in the communication between and among different ethnic groups. One of the major findings was the observation of language "stress". Most respondents felt overtaxed by the pluralism of languages even if they belonged to their natural mother tongue. In a normal situation, citizens can handle all these "languages" or they can receive assistance in understanding new terms and learning new meanings. In the communication explosion in the aftermath of 1989, the "voices" overlapped and created a multitude of "language games" including new values, new phrases, new cognitions, and new forms of describing social relations. It would have been hard to absorb such a change within one language, but it happened simultaneously in different natural languages, and furthermore in different symbolic languages within one natural language. Confusion was the main response to this sudden outburst of pluralism and new thinking. After the confusion came the quest for simplification and certainty. This need created a welcome opportunity for populist of all kind to take advantage of the situation.

Lacking any mutually agreed upon conventions (except the previous experience of coexisting in mixed communities), the "majority" and "minorities" started to rebuild their own identity after the shock of confusion was overcome.

In this effort both used the media as an important tool for achieving the mentioned goals. In our media analysis we found the following stereotypes repeated over and over again:

Topic 1: Connotations associated with Romania: "old", "famous", "well structured", "culturally rich", "having a beautiful mother country", "loyal citizens";

Topic 2: "Our history and our rights" reflecting on the glorious past of the country";

Topic 3: "Our enemies, our oppressors are the worst people in the world";

Topic 4: "We are strong because we have powerful 'relatives'; it means there are other communities like *us* in the world";

Topic 5: Blaming the others: "Our enemies are X; they pose a major threat to our nation".

This last topic was sometimes repeated even by *non-nationalistic media*, either from a critical perspective, or in the form of quotations from the nationalistic press without comment. It illustrates negative pressures on the majority and the various minorities as a consequence of polarized media coverage.

Several events offered the opportunity to amplify ethnic tensions and blame "minorities" for the climate under which they had been victimized. These opportunities were all violent incidents where the victims were blamed for provoking the violence from which they suffered.

9.1 The Role of Natural Languages

After looking into the constructive mechanisms of symbolic languages and several examples of how symbols have been used to create or aggravate conflict, we can return to the more complex reality of different natural languages. There are laws that regulate the use of official languages in public situations, but these laws have little power to influence informal interaction. If people go shopping, for example, and are addressed in another language than their own they feel alienated and are likely to react aggressively. One would need a *modus vivendi* for an informal, but acceptable, regulation of these situations, but they are not in sight.

Of course, the natural language problem is much more complicated and includes issues of intercultural exchange and cross-cultural communication. On one hand, the native culture needs to be preserved and cherished, on the other hand, economic and social transactions demand fast and efficient communication between people. Multi-lingual education would be an obvious answer to this problem, but with the many different natural languages existing in Romania, the limits of comprehension and learning capabilities of most citizens may be surpassed. As an alternative, one could suggest that everyone regardless of their native tongue has to be able to converse in one common language, normally the language of the majority. This solution is only feasible, however, if it is mutually accepted by all language camps and if the other coexisting natural languages are supported by the dominant culture.

9.2 Modes of Communication Between Natural Language Camps

The following observations are based on four years of monitoring the majority of the Romanian media on the topic: *How does inter-ethnic communication function in the Romanian multicultural society?* The material includes about 5,000 issues of 25 publications serving the needs of the majority as well as minorities. The language used in each of these publications serves different purposes:
- it provides exclusive information to a special minority. The minority language is used to guarantee this exclusiveness; other readers are not welcome;
- it provides information in one of the minority languages meant to be read by the respective minority in conjunction with other minorities or the majority. The language used in these publications (if it is not the majority language) constitutes a barrier for the targeted audience;
- it provides information in the majority language for the majority group only; although meant to be exclusive, anyone who understands the majority language has access to this information;
- it provides information either bilingually or in the majority language (Romanian) so that it can be read by different audiences: the information may still be primarily directed towards one of the minorities;
- it provides information in one minority language and addresses common themes with the same ethnic group of another country; the major goals of these publications is to create a sense of community beyond the national borders.

The right to use one's natural language in special publications may hence serve different purposes. It may be associated with specific strategies either to isolate one ethnic group from all the others, or to create unity with the same ethnic group in another country or to forge ties between different ethnic groups. The language itself is only the instrument for the desired political intention.

It should be noted that most of the publications that we analyzed do not support negative intentions of extreme nationalism or promote hate. In our study we identified roughly 7% of the print media as nationalistic and 2-3% of the media as extremist. Most of them fuel the conflict between Hungarians and Romanians. The Hungarian media (about 12 international external channels using Hungarian language) reach out to 2,000,000 people, often supporting segregationist tendencies and discontent with the Romanian majority. Often the message conveyed is "We need our mother country (Hungary) in order to be really happy".

The Romanian media report the extreme Hungarian *positions* leaving the impression that these extreme positions are shared by the majority of the Hungarians. Images of an aggressive minority are evoked and add tensions to the underlying conflict. These problems do not only refer to Hungarians and Romanians, however. There are also media articles that provoke tensions with respect to the Turks, Armenians, Serbs, Croats, etc.

In essence, our study of the media showed us that the plurality of the media could actually produce as much ethnic isolation as it can serve the goal of inter-ethnic communication. Both objectives are inherently present in most ethnically oriented publications.

10 Conclusions

The issue of mass media and ethnic conflict was the main topic of a conference that took place one year ago in Bucharest. The conference entitled "The Mass-Media role in a multicultural society" was organized by the Council of Europe and European Center for Studies on Ethnic Issues and Social Communication. The conference members echoed several of the main propositions that I have laid out in this paper. Among them are:

1. *"A minority"* can be described as: a group of persons seeking a common identity and by doing so performing special cultural routines that reveal meaning, values, and worldview (constructivist position).
2. To *perform* special cultural routines ascribed to an ethnic origin does not exclude the possibility of individuals learning about or even participating in another set of cultural routines (for instance in mixed marriages). Multiculturality can be performed by a single individual.
3. By performing and repeating these cultural routines, an identity is created and reconstructed with the effect that these routines

form a modality to structure the social system. Individuals learn how to assign desired reactions such as acceptance, admiration, denial or rejection to certain outside stimuli.

4. Learning and reconstructing cultural routines rely predominantly on communication (also on imitation). Many routines are products of direct interactions between, for example, new and old members of an ethnic group.

5. The way that special identities are defined determines the relationship to other identities. If one identity includes claims of superiority or exclusiveness, relationships based on mutual respect are almost impossible to develop.

6. In addition to the direct communication between different ethnic groups, communication occurs on a second level. Individuals, institutions, and other (free-floating) actors use communication channels to convey messages about the inter-ethnic communication itself. These actors prove meta-communicational insights that help members of different communities improve their understanding of their own ethnic culture and critique the interpretations of those who want to exploit ethnic ties for political purposes. Such second level actors can contribute also to an increase in conflict and tensions, if they choose to focus on real or alleged inequities with respect to common resources.

7. Since the second level communication constitutes an important contribution to ethnic cooperation or conflict, new institutions are needed that provide positive information about each ethnic group and facilitate common problem solving.

Last not least, we need to add the international communicational climate and its effect on the national climate. The perceived international climate has a similar effect compared to the second level communicators. Most media publications, even if they are directed to only one minority, are eager to report about the international climate and look for evidence in the international press. Since the international press is very diverse, it is not difficult to find some publication that supports whatever claim a national publication intends to make. It is therefore more important to build a strong second level institutional base inside the country with the mandate to monitor the international press and to convey an impartial impressions of the international climate to all the other domestic media.

Figure 5 illustrates the interactions between the national communicational climate and the international climate. Both climates

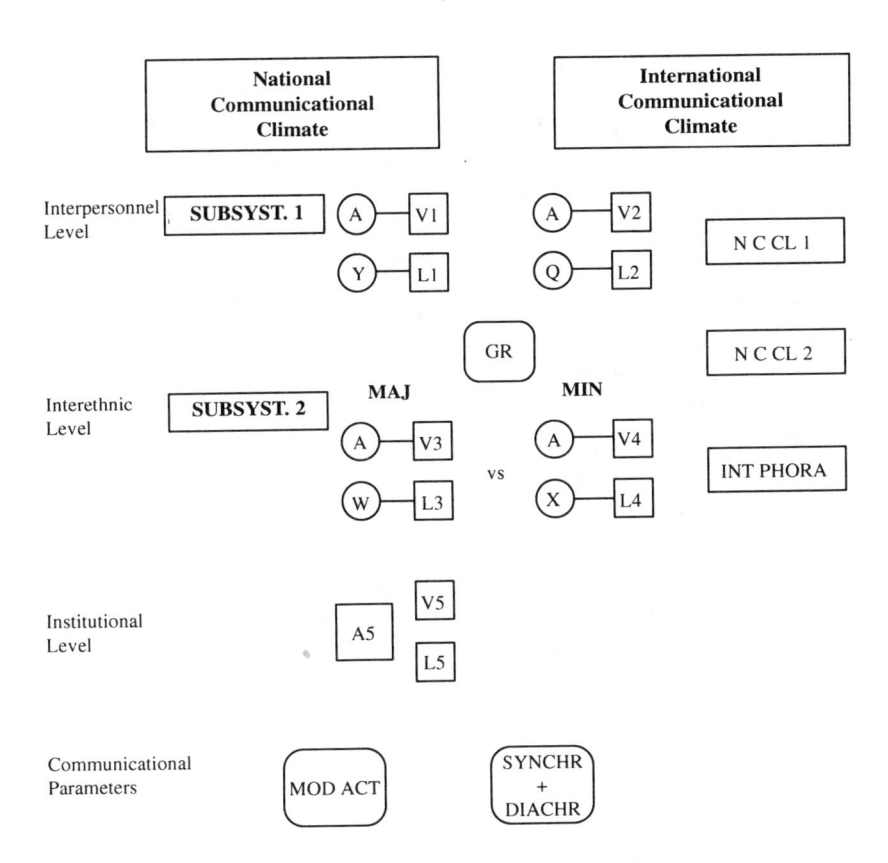

Fig. 5
The schema of the communicational social climate in the framework of the international social communicational climate

Legend:
DIACHR   Diachronic
GR   General Rules
INT PHORA International Phora
L   Language
MAJ   Majority
MIN   Minorities
MOD ACT   Action Model
N C CL 1 New Communicational Climate (bilateral)
N C CL 2 New Communicational Climate (multilateral)
Subsyst. Subsystem
SYNCHR   Synchronic
V   Voice

are characterized by different inventories of rules, routines of communicational activities, and transpiration channels. Our model shows that different sets of rules regulate the communicational process from the subsystem as well as from the system level. Changes in the subsystem level have the potential to induce changes on the system level, i.e., changes in the communication content or form performed by one ethnic group can improve or destroy the existing communication climate in a country. It may even influence the international climate.

In summary, ethnic identities are social constructions based on acts of communication. The content of this communication is not arbitrary in the sense that ethnic identities could be filled by whatever a communicator intends to convey. Identities are evolutionary products of culturally defined routines that link values and cognitions with personal and group actions. The ambiguity and ambivalence of these routines make it possible, however, that populists or other politically motivated persons can selectively amplify those parts of the common construction that emphasizes isolation and aggression. The only way to counteract such attempts is to initiate a second-level communication effort dedicated to enlighten the potential victims of the populists about the mechanisms of selective information and manipulation. This can best be done in a structured dialogue between the members of the respective ethnic groups under the supervision of the second-level communicator.

The lack of internal voices that could serve the role of a second-level communicator and mediator impedes the ongoing process of negotiations between different ethnic groups and communities. In this void, partial communication reinforces tensions rather than helping to resolve them. An institution is needed that, based on a theoretically sound concept and a proven methodology, can serve this desperately needed function.

Our research will continue to focus on the language and message of the media in Romania. This research can help to identify stereotypes and accusations and uncover attempts by populists to exploit ethnic emotions. Furthermore, we hope that we can contribute to a new communication climate in Romania that provides background information to all people about the symbolic nature of communicated messages and to foster second-level communicators who can be trusted by all sides. Hopefully this will all lead to new institutions capable of easing the tensions that have so badly infected our country.

Bibliography

THE ALBANIAN, edited publication by Cultural Union of the Albanians from Romania

ARARAT, bimonthly publication of the Armenians from Romania

BULGARSKA ZORNITA, The Bulgarian Morning Star, publications of the Bulgarian minority from Romania

COLUMNA, periodical of information and culture of the Italian Community

COTEANU, Ion 1984: "Stilistica functionala a limbii româna", The Functional Stylistic of Romanian Language, Editura Academiei

THE DAY – BREAKS, publication of the old believers Russians community from Romania

DUMITRIU-SEULEANU, Carmen 1995: "You lied the people by TV", a study about the credibility of Romanian TV in the ECSEI-SC publication "Demostene"

DUMITRIU-SEULEANU, Carmen 1995: "Radio Romania Speaking", an analysis of discourse performed in news programs by Romanian Radio

DUMITRIU-SEULEANU, Carmen 1995: "Language a Necessary World", an analysis looking to the functions of the language The Courier, publication of the Ukrainian Union from Romania

ELPIS, periodical publications of the Greek Union from Romania

HARGITAJ NEPE, Hargita-People, Târgu-Mureº, daily newspapers of Hungarian community from Romania

THE JEWISH REALITY, publication of the Jewish Community Federation from Romania

NA-A RECI, periodical of the Democratic Union of Serbs and Carashoveniens from Romania

NEPUJSAG, People Newspaper

NOR GHIANK, bilingual monthly publications of the Armenians from Romania

POLONUS, publication of the Polish union from Romania, "Dom Polski"

ROMANIAI MAGYAR SZO, Romanian Hungarian Word

PART IV

CASE STUDIES: DEMOCRATIC EXPERIENCES OF SUCCESSFUL CONFLICT MANAGEMENT

10 Ethnic Coexistence and Cooperation in Switzerland

KURT R. SPILLMANN

The term "ethnic" is difficult to define. What makes the people of different regions of a country feel they belong to a specific "ethnic" group? Is "belonging" determined biologically or culturally? Is it shared language, religion, and history, or similarity in features and physical appearance? Or is it something else still, even more elusive than these usual common denominators which groups generally refer to?

The term "ethnic" is so vague that in the case of Switzerland we had better abstain from using it. All the biological or genetic differences, for example, between the four major cultural (i.e. language) groups of the Swiss population have long ago become diffuse. Switzerland *is* a melting pot. This fact is easily demonstrated by checking Swiss telephone books, where German names fill 50 % of the directories of Geneva or Lausanne. There are groups in Switzerland which distinguish themselves clearly by language, religious denomination, or citizenship in one of the 25 cantons. Yes, cultural differences do exist. But "ethnic" differences?

The Swiss prefer to think of themselves as belonging to several groups at the same time, as having a multilayered identity, or actually more than just one identity. According to circumstance, one or the other of these identities is emphasized. The *Swiss* – or national – identity is displayed vis-à-vis other national identities. But looking at Switzerland from the inside, we realize that there are various lower levels of identification, namely regional, state, communal, language, church, or family identities, too, that overlap more often than exclude each other. But even in the cases of exclusion it is still possible for the various groups to live together peacefully under the larger roof of a Swiss identity.

The peaceful coexistence of these various identities is the most interesting aspect of the Swiss mosaic. The following analysis deals with development of this special feature of Switzerland as well as with the preconditions of keeping it alive and working.

1 Early Switzerland Between Conflict and Cooperation

I should like to start with a review of the historical development that has shaped the situation in Switzerland as it is today.

The nation which we today call Switzerland originated some 700 years ago in a voluntary alliance of three mountain communities. The alliance was formed in order to ward off a common exterior threat. At the same time the founders installed a court of arbitration to resolve conflicts among themselves. The force which pushed the different valleys and districts to cooperation was the political and military threat, mainly from the surrounding kingdoms and larger dominions, as well as the need to replace club-law and blood revenge among themselves with a working legal order.

Achieving common security was central. Military cooperation worked and withstood the test: in 1315 as well as in 1386 and on many other occasions, Swiss armed forces managed to defeat troops of much more eminent rulers (the Habsburgs especially) and so preserved the independence of emerging Switzerland.

Yet in the course of history, severe conflicts between different parts of this developing Switzerland erupted, and that's where our interest starts. How did the Swiss manage to keep member states and various groups together in spite of, time and again, deeply differing interests among them?

Towards the end of the 15th century – after bloody civil wars – the rural communities refused to admit more cities into the Confederation because they feared coming under the control of the cities and losing their independence. Another civil war between the city-states of the Confederation and the rural communities could be averted only with great difficulty. It was the intervention of Niklaus von Flüe, a former politician who had turned mystic and retreated into seclusion, that saved the Confederation. In a new Confederate Pact of 1481 an important basic principle was codified which has retained its validity to this day: The *complete equality* of all cantons (*i.e.*, all component states), urban and rural, was guaranteed. This was the only means by which the Confederation could be prevented from breaking up into different parts.

In the beginning of the 16th century Switzerland had to face a new fundamental conflict: The Reformation split the Confederation into Catholic and Protestant communities. The denominational convictions clashed violently. The conflicting mood of the time expressed itself in many private skirmishes as well as in full-scale civil wars. A first civil war in 1529 ended in a compromise. A second confrontation (two years later) led to the bloody battle at Kappel and the victory of the Catholic cantons. Surprisingly, the victory was not exploited to totally suppress the Reformation. Instead, the Protestant towns that had been defeated were allowed to retain their independence. Thus the same principle as in the political compromise of 1481 was installed in the field of religious tolerance: Catholic and Protestant members of the Swiss Confederacy were trying to accept each other as equals.

These two documents – or rather compromises, exactly 50 years apart – are fundamental to the Swiss model of dealing with political and cultural differences. Both accepted the fact that a larger unity did not necessarily have to be composed of homogeneous parts, but that partners in a greater unity could have different individual interests and values yet still pursue larger common goals as long as they tolerated each other's individual identities and interests.

It must be mentioned, though, that a price had to be paid for keeping the Confederation together with mutually hostile denominational groups within. The price was the impossibility of establishing common goals in foreign relations or of speaking with one voice to foreign kings and nations: The Confederation was unable to pursue any kind of coherent foreign policy. The ensuing passivity or Swiss *neutrality* must be looked at as the result, not so much of a deliberate and rational policy, but as a result of the internal *paralysis* caused by the religious conflict and its specifically Swiss resolution.

This Swiss model of conflict resolution, as developed in the late 15th and early 16th century, asked for acceptance and respect for partners as equals even in the case of diverging opinions, and regardless of size, power, and influence.

The *danger of the Confederation breaking apart* became critical several times. But each time the conviction prevailed that the security of the component states could be better ensured within the larger unit of Switzerland than by breaking up into a multitude of independent small states.

A third form of conflict must be mentioned besides the political and the religious conflict: That is the great social conflict in the 17th century which vented itself in the so-called *Swiss Peasants' War* of 1653 when the exploited and heavily disadvantaged peasants rose against the ruling class in the towns but were badly beaten in a civil war. *In this instance no compromise was sought;* instead the old sovereign rights and privileges of the old families and the townspeople in discrimination against the country dwellers and peasants were restated.

From the start, the Confederation was characterized by *the desire of its component parts for independence*, which caused them to transfer only specific major tasks concerning all to the federal level. In Switzerland this led to the so-called *principle of subsidiarity*, according to which all administrative functions are kept and realized at the lowest possible level and only intercantonal problems and matters that have to be coordinated at the federal level are entrusted to the highest authorities. Even today the administration of Switzerland functions according to this principle, and the three levels – the communities, cantons, and federal government – handle the affairs of state jointly and with as complete a delegation of authority and competence *downwards* as possible.

For a long time there was no federal government or administration at all. Until 1848 there was only the so-called *"Tagsatzung"*, an assembly of delegates from the various member states or cantons. In this assembly, decisions could only be passed *unanimously*, meaning that every canton, even the smallest one, could virtually veto a decision. This reinforced the outward *passivity* and became the cornerstone of the so-called *principle of consensus, i.e., that major decisions could only be made when all different parts were in agreement*. Until 1848 there was no central administration, and the enforcement of common decisions (made at the highest level) was left to each of the component states (the cantons). Even today, the federal government relies in many instances on the cantons to enforce federal laws. Accordingly, the enforcement of federal laws – *e.g.*, in area planning regulation – varies from canton to canton. Within certain limits this is tolerated within the framework of the Swiss conception of state.

In the year 1798 the old Confederation collapsed under the attack of Napoleon's troops. Switzerland was remodeled into a *centrally governed state* after the fashion of France, with a capital, a central government and all the appropriate administrative agencies. But the disinclination of the component states to defer to the central government was so great that civil disorder never subsided. Civil war even erupted, and the experiment in social engineering had to be discontinued after five years (on the order of Napoleon himself). Switzerland returned to federalism (in the Swiss sense, meaning little authority at the top and more authority at the cantonal level). In 1803 Napoleon released – in fact, wrote himself, at least partly – a new constitution for Switzerland which was more conservative in its character and by which the separate states were restored to their independence. Switzerland once more became a confederation of states.

At the end of the Napoleonic Era, in the Paris Treaty of 1814, Switzerland was recognized as a neutral country. In other words, the Great Powers of Europe put into writing that the neutrality of Switzerland lay in their interest. Thus a centuries-old tradition which the Swiss had established of their own free will – namely that they would remain neutral in conflicts between their neighbors – was recognized by an international treaty. And this tradition has undoubtedly ensured Switzerland's survival during the many European wars in neighboring countries during the 19th and the 20th centuries.

In the 19th century, industrialization raised serious new problems for Switzerland. A conflict sprung up between the cities and industrial cantons which embraced economic development and the conservative rural cantons of Inner Switzerland. In order to further economic development, the reform-minded cantons called for a *stronger central leadership* that could guarantee a *more progressive economic policy*. The opposition of the conservative cantons set up an association to protect the vested interests of the Catholic cantons. This led to *the last Swiss civil war in 1847*.

The progressive cantons defeated the conservative cantons. The *Tagsatzung*, now liberal in its majority, decided to write a new constitution with a completely new federal structure, thereby complying with the wishes of the reform-minded cantons. However, the crucial point of the aftermath of this civil war was *that the old principle of the equality of the cantons was upheld*. The autonomy of the defeated conservative cantons remained largely untouched. A federal level of government was created, with an executive and legislative body in which, in accordance with the principle of consensus, the defeated cantons had a part. Not only that, but the legislature took the form of a *two-chamber system*: In one chamber, the so-called *National Council*, the members were elected in proportion to the population of each canton; in the other, the so-called *Council of States*, each canton, irrespective of size, was represented by two deputies.

In this way it was ensured that the small and economically backward mountain cantons could safeguard their rights against the more populous industrialized city cantons. For the new constitution provided that *constitutional amendments* required not only a majority of votes but also the support of *at least half the cantons* in order to be valid.

This rearrangement of Switzerland after the War of the *Sonderbund* created the basis for a conflict-resistant coexistence of the different parts of Switzerland in the modern world.

Let me sum up a few of the most important insights from this foundation of 1847/48 that are still relevant today.

1. The constitution was worked out by all concerned. Even the losing side in the just-ended civil war was involved in the negotiations. In the conscientiously kept minutes of the proceedings all points under dispute were entered, and each one was voted on according to the principle of majority. And this has remained true to this day, so that even the smallest part, the smallest canton, and the smallest group, even every single deputy is given a hearing, and his concern is taken seriously.
2. The winning side, however much it felt justified, resisted the temptation to unilaterally push through its opinions. This leniency (out of respect for the old principle of consensus) made a restoration of the internal peace possible even after a civil war.
3. Disappointed as they were with the Napoleonic experiment, the victors did not erect a central state but chose the form of a confederation with a hierarchy of responsibilities corresponding to the three levels of government, community, canton, and state, delegating every possible function to the communal authorities and calling in the next higher agency only when necessary. In other words, the federal government has authority over the cantonal administrations, and the cantonal administrations again outrank the communal authorities, on the tacit understanding that the federal government does not interfere unnecessarily with the affairs of the cantons, which in turn grant as much autonomy as possible to the communities.
4. Another addition to the constitution was the principle that the Federal Government should settle disputes between cantons,[1]

except in the case of minor disagreements which, in accordance with the tradition of arbitration, the cantons could negotiate between themselves, if necessary in the presence of a federal functionary.[2]

5. Security remained a very important point. The new Confederation was forbidden to maintain a standing army;[3] instead, the old militia tradition was continued; that is to say, every able-bodied eligible male voter had to perform military service. The coordination of these contingency forces lay in the hands of the cantons. During this period it was difficult to lump together the various cantonal contingents with different equipment and training. Only after some rather dangerous experiences during the Franco-Prussian War of 1870-1871 the Confederation was assigned the task of coordinating the armed forces, and in 1875 the Federal Army was formed.

6. The new federal authorities were also charged with safeguarding the rights of the individual. This meant that a citizen could prosecute a claim for his constitutional rights not only at a court in his own canton, but also, if he felt justice had been denied to him, at a higher, federal court. These fundamental rights were only partly spelled out in the Federal Constitution, some of them were considered self-evident.

Among these are:
- the right to life and physical integrity;[4]
- the right to human dignity, freedom, and security;
- right of ownership;[5]
- the right to marry;[6]
- the right to legal protection, equality before the law, and constitutional judges;[7]
- freedom of thought and speech, freedom of expression;[8]
- freedom of creed;[9]
- right of assembly;[10]
- freedom of trade, within the limits of the common welfare;[11]
- right to citizenship;[12]
- freedom of movement;[13]
- the right to vote;[14]
- the right to petition;[15]
- the right to social security, wages, welfare, housing, and health;[16]
- free choice of occupation; and
- the right to education.

Included are also, of course, the civil rights,[17] namely at the federal level:
- the right to elect members of parliament;
- the right to run for office in the National Council,[18] the Council of States, the Federal Council,[19] the Federal Court[20] and other offices;
- the right to vote on obligatory referenda;
- the right to vote on optional referenda;
- the right to vote on popular initiatives;[21]

and at the cantonal level:
- The right to elect officers or run for office in the cantonal parliament and government of a canton, in the cantonal courts, and numerous other offices;
- the right to vote on obligatory referenda for constitutional amendments;
- the right to vote on optional and obligatory referenda;
- the right to vote on popular initiatives;

and at the communal level:
- the right to elect officers and to run for office in the administration; and
- the right to vote on all important matters of the community, optional and obligatory referenda, and popular initiatives

7. Of course, many other details and aspects of the national reform of 1848 could be listed. The important thing is that the local *traditions of autonomy* were integrated, as far as possible, into the larger unit of Switzerland, that every individual and every minority was respected, and that, as much as possible, the principle of consensus was also applied at the federal level, that *collegiality* was made a basic principle. Collegiality means that the government itself is composed of members of *different* parties, *i.e.*, people with different origins, different political affiliations, and different views, who nevertheless *share* responsibility for the affairs of state. In other words, *political power in Switzerland is distributed between representatives of all groups over whom power is exerted*. This principle is still valid today.

Thanks to this constitution, Switzerland shed its negative reputation as a political trouble spot and came to be regarded as one of the most stable countries in Europe, a fact which in turn stimulated economic development.

In World War I, the first deep conflict between the German-speaking majority (the so-called Swiss-Germans) and the French-speaking minority of the Swiss population made itself felt. Because of their traditional ties with German culture, the Swiss-Germans related more intimately to *one* side in the war, while for similar but opposite reasons the French-speaking Swiss felt more closely attached to the other. This led to a political estrangement which could only be overcome when a Swiss-German poet and Nobel Prize laureate, *Carl Spitteler*, gave a widely publicized speech under the title "Our Swiss Position", in which he stated that Switzerland traditionally did *not* take sides in foreign conflicts, since its own interests came first. He cautioned against a break-up of Switzerland, and this speech is said to have contributed to cooling down emotions. The solidarity movements on either side ebbed before a conflict could erupt along the lingual and cultural borders between German- and French-speaking parts.

In the Second World War, too, Switzerland was spared violent internal conflicts, because the memories of World War I were still alive and this time the Swiss position was supremely personified by a French-speaking commander-in-chief, General Henri Guisan. This integrating character saw to it that divided loyalties did not lead to ethnic conflicts between the two language groups.

2 Keeping the Swiss Model Alive and Working

Let us now turn to the present. Before going into the ethnic challenges that have appeared since the end of World War II, several principles of Switzerland's political system which enable it to settle conflicts by non-violent, political means, have to be mentioned.

1. The principle of *subsidiarity* and *federalism*: The Swiss Federation came about through the alliance of smaller units that kept delegating to the next higher level only such tasks as could not be solved at the lower level. Federalism, in the understanding of the Swiss, is a territorial form of separation of powers. The Swiss way to deal with conflicts is characterized not by confrontation between potential conflict groups but by the search for common interests and common viewpoints. The legislature is elected according to the principle of proportional representation which ensures adequate political representation for all minorities. And in

the executive bodies, too, the principle of collegiality – *i.e.*, forming a government from representatives of the most important parties from all sides of the political spectrum – ensures that different parties, different regions, different languages, etc., are represented. To be sure, this makes the leadership less efficient, and quick decisions and decisive leadership are not the strong points of the Swiss system of government. On the other hand, this cumbersome system is fairly successful at conciliating internal tensions.

2. Political parties are independent of region, language, and religious factors of identity. There are no ethnic or language-based parties in Switzerland, and denominational parties refer only in a very general way to the Christian belief. *Political groups are based on political beliefs alone.*

3. Since the constitutional reform of 1848, opportunities for odd associations and interest groups to participate in the political process have steadily increased. Mostly, new trends in Swiss politics originate at the electoral grass-roots. Fundamental rights are anchored in the constitution; introduction of the referendum for constitutional amendments in 1891 consolidated the influence of individuals upon the government, and the mixture of representational and pure democracy results in a *high degree of involvement of individuals and groups of all kinds* in the political process, reducing the potential for dangerous conflicts. But, of course, a system so carefully calibrated to balancing the needs and interests of many groups shies away from major changes, and is therefore in constant danger of losing its adaptational flexibility.

4. An important principle is the *protection of minorities*. An obvious example is the fact that the fourth language in Switzerland, Rhaeto-Romansch, though only spoken by 0.9% of the population, is recognized as a national language, although not as an official language.[22] In parliament and in the armed forces, German, French, and Italian are treated as equals on all levels, although Italian is used less often, due to the smaller number of speakers of that language. But, for instance, the state presidency rotates regularly among members of the Federal Council regardless of their language. It was, *e.g.*, Federal Councilor Flavio Cotti, representing the Italian- speaking minority (of only 7.6% of the Swiss population), who presided over the celebration of Switzerland's 700th birthday in 1991.

5. Another principle is the *two-chamber system*, whereby small cantons with a very small population have as much of a say in the Council of States as the bigger industrial cantons. The so-called "majority of cantons" which is required in federal plebiscites ensures that no decision is adopted which is unacceptable to a majority of cantons.
6. Even if the existing hierarchy (federal law takes precedence over cantonal law, and cantonal law takes precedence over communal law) assures the supremacy of federal law, the cantons and the communities always have the opportunity to enter into agreements with each other concerning matters which are not regulated by federal law or which, by the constitution, are left to cantonal regulation. This makes for a network of intensive cooperation, within which *referenda* by individuals, by interest groups, by communities can function freely.
7. *Arbitration* has existed in Switzerland for 700 years. In case of a conflict (even between unions and industry) the groups involved turn to a court of arbitration which listens to both sides and makes proposals for a settlement. This procedure works to cool the heat of a confrontation, plays for time, and lets the conflicting parties search for a common platform and common points of interest.
8. The *constitutional rights of the citizen can be fought for in court*. This means that they are not just theoretically guaranteed in the constitution. There are administrative courts where the individual citizens can prosecute a claim if they feel unjustly treated by an official. The existence and efficacy of such institutions should give every citizen the feeling of being respected by the State.
9. The fact that *the public and private sector interlock* due to a pervasive *militia system* makes for a *veritable "militia democracy"* in Switzerland. Not even our federal parliamentarians are full-time politicians. All but the members of the executive (in the federal government as well as in most cantonal governments) have another occupation with which they make a living. At the communal level most of the members of the executive and legislature are only part-time politicians who govern their community in their spare time. The same goes for administration of the armed forces where all but the highest officers (the general ranks) have a civilian job as their main occupation. This means that tens of thousands of Swiss citizens who are familiar with the

workings of the political system, are themselves responsible for a small part of it, or are responsible for a small piece of military leadership. This ensures active interest and involvement of an outstandingly large number of Swiss citizens in the well-being of the State.

This *spreading of power* among all groups interested in it, together with the *principle of concordancy, i.e.*, a competition in which all are conscious of striving for the same goals, have made it possible to pursue a common policy despite the existence of widely differing views and a great number of different political parties.

3 How Does the Swiss System Deal with Conflicts? The Case of the Jura

Let us now take a look at the presumably ethnic challenges to the Swiss system. We have already noticed the temporary estrangement between the two main language groups in Switzerland, the German-speaking and the French-speaking populations, during the World War I. Though open conflicts could be avoided during World War II, a serious problem involving the future canton of Jura came to the fore soon after the war had ended. The reason for this was that a section of the French-speaking population received the impression that the principle of equal distribution of power among all ethnic groups had been violated.

At the Vienna Congress in the year 1815, the southern part of the canton of Bern had been severed from the rest and made into a separate canton. To make up for this, the Jura region which had formerly belonged to the prince bishop of Basle was joined to the canton of Bern. Now, 85% of the Jurassic population were largely Protestant German-speakers concentrated in the southern half of the Jura, while the northern half was mainly inhabited by French-speaking Catholics. But until the end of World War II, this circumstance did not cause any open conflicts.

In 1947, Georges Möckli, a Jurassic senior executive officer and member of the cantonal government of Bern, was denied the directorate of the department of public works on grounds that the French language would complicate or obstruct his dealings with Bernese rural communities. In truth, the important department of public works was to be kept under Bernese control, whereas the department of social welfare could be given over to a Jurassic without causing any concern. Of course, this was a slap in the face of all Jurassics and also a severe violation of the Swiss tradition of collegiality and federalist politeness towards minorities. It led to formation of a liberation committee in Moutier which demanded that the Bernese government recognize the Jurassic people and grant them an official flag.

In 1950, these demands were met by way of an amendment to the Bernese constitution. In addition, the Jurassic people were guaranteed two of the nine seats in the Bernese Cantonal Council, and French was recognized as an official language equal to German.

These measures caused a rift in the Moutier committee. Some of its members were satisfied with the way things stood now, while the others vowed to carry on the struggle until cantonal autonomy had been achieved. So one group of Jurassics felt the constitutional amendment at the cantonal level had done justice to the federalist principle, while the more radical group dreamed of equality with and therefore independence from the superordinate canton Bern.

In 1957, the separatists launched an initiative aimed at separating the Jura from Canton Bern. As was to be expected, the inhabitants of Canton Bern rejected the initiative in 1959. An interesting point is that only the northern districts of the Jura voted for the initiative, while the southern districts voted against it.

In spite of a clear majority supporting separation in the three northern districts of the Jura the Bernese government was not prepared to accept this demand. As a result, the independent separatist youth group "Les Béliers" (literally, "the battering-rams") was founded in 1963. And this group kept trying to shake the cantonal government of Bern out of its intransigence by means of various provocations and acts of violence. For instance, in 1964, when the federal minister of defense was to give a speech at a military celebration in the Jura, he was shouted down by the separatists. There were even instances of arson and bombings which caused irritation everywhere in Switzerland.

Since Bern did not budge and (in the opinion of the North Jurassics) disregarded the federalist tradition and the principle of collegiality, the North Jurassics tried to drag the Jurassic conflict onto the international stage. Swiss diplomats abroad had to answer an increasing number of unpleasant questions about the trouble spot Jura and the disrupted internal peace of Switzerland.

In 1967, a newly elected Bernese government proved somewhat more flexible. It formed a 24-member committee and offered to talk with the Jurassic separatists. However, the separatists refused, saying that they did not want to be taken in by the Bernese government.

This is an extremely important point. On one hand, the separatists felt they were not being taken seriously; on the other hand, the Bernese government did not realize that it was *both* trying to take sides *and* judge between the two sides. In a situation like this, the proper thing to do would have been for the federal government to invite both sides to a discussion *between equals*.

In 1968 the Federal Council, together with the Bernese government, formed a "Group of the Four Wise Men", in which four respected politicians studied the Jura problem and suggested solutions to it. The group concluded that the voters of the Jura should decide for themselves about their political future. This was without doubt the right answer. Wrong, however, was that the Federal Council had formed this board together with the Bernese government *without* consulting the Jurassic separatists, who were again not treated as equals.

In 1970 the voting public of Canton Bern approved a constitutional amendment which made it possible for inhabitants of the Jura to decide whether they wanted to be separated from Bern or not. In 1974 the Jurassic districts voted on the question: "Would you like to form a new canton?" 36,802 voted for it, 34,057 against. In 1975, the southern districts of the Jura were asked which canton they wanted to belong to. Finally, in September of that year, polls were conducted among the communities along the new cantonal border. Eight communities changed over from a Bernese district to a Jurassic, one Jurassic community changed over to the Bernese side.

On 24th September 1978, after the constitution for the new canton had been written, the entire population of Switzerland voted on formation of a new canton named Jura and all the constitutional changes this entailed. The bill was passed by 82.3% of the vote and accepted by the majority of the cantons. Even though there are still a number of problems waiting for solutions, by and large the Jura problem has been resolved successfully in a typically Swiss way, demanding lots of time and patience. It is obvious that not all ethnic problems can be resolved that way. If economic or social depravation or exploitation is involved, if value questions are involved, it may be much harder – even impossible – to find a compromise acceptable to both sides of the conflict.

The Swiss approach to ethnic – or rather cultural – conflicts, as to all forms of internal conflict, is based on the principle of *federalist power sharing*. Other nations have chosen the principle of competition and are of the opinion that the best may win. This works fine in a representative democracy where the majority party in the parliament forms the government and pursues its own policy, while the minority party tries to canvass its opinions through opposition and to come into power at the next elections. This system, which can be found in England and the United States, is nevertheless very different from the Swiss system. Federalist power sharing tries to guard the rights of minorities as far as possible and to grant them as large a degree of autonomy as possible. The drawback of this system is a lack of straight forwardness and efficiency. Law-giving processes usually take very long in Switzerland, and the country is probably incapable of a decisive foreign policy, simply because the process of reaching a decision takes so much time! In fact, it requires a very *stable* environment.

On the other hand, the advantage of the federalist system lies in the fact that it intercepts internal tensions at a low level, so that radical changes do not occur, in fact are not even necessary, because all interest groups feel more or less secure within this framework. But for this system to work, it requires what Gottfried Keller, one of Switzerland's foremost poets at the time of the writing of the constitution, called "public spirit" – a conviction that all citizens share certain basic values, opinions, and goals, no matter what their language, their denomination, or their ethnic background. Such a system requires a lot of tolerance and patience and is certainly no easy way out of conflicts. But it has worked well since our last civil war, and the Swiss hope it will continue to do so. This may be one important reason that so many of them still refuse to join the European Union.

This leads me to the final part of my presentation, the "hashed potato trench", so called because hashed potatoes are considered a specialty of the Swiss-German cuisine of the north-eastern part of Switzerland, but not favored by the French-speaking Swiss of the western part. A political system based on public votes is a sort of on-going battle between the winners of a plebiscite – the majority – and its losers, the minority. As long as all the cantons in various configurations keep winning and losing in turns, this creates no problems. However, in a number of key plebiscites regarding Switzerland's participation or non-participation in the process of

European integration the Swiss-German cantons have refused participation while the French-speaking cantons overwhelmingly were in favor of participation.

This has raised the question of whether we are dealing here with an *ethnic* problem – an ethnic problem that might conceivably one day split the Confederation. According to the results of one of our research projects, we could demonstrate that the issue of European integration has not so much opened up trenches between the two main language groups, but between traditionalists and modernists. With some confidence we may assume that in the long run the modernists will win and this issue will not for too long remain a point of contention between the two language groups.

More serious are allegations of economic domination of the French-speaking part of Switzerland by the Swiss-German part, indicated by the fact that 84 of Switzerland's 100 largest firms are headquartered in the German-speaking cantons and only 15 in the French-speaking. The French-speaking Swiss also feel uncomfortable with the mentality of the Swiss-Germans, whereas the latter are notoriously uncomfortable with the French language. However, these are not crucial issues, and once the temporary political differences have lessened, the understanding will once again prevail that cultural differences should be accepted as something natural and that an ongoing debate on cultural issues is an enriching aspect of society.

The important point is *not* to draw borders, because borders tend to create more problems than they solve.

Suggested Further Reading

The standard works on Swiss history in the German language are Beatrix Mesmer's *Geschichte der Schweiz und der Schweizer* (Helbing & Lichtenhahn, Basel, 1986) and the two-volume *Handbuch der Schweizer Geschichte* (Buchverlag Berichthaus, Zurich, 1980). The latter provides in-depth information on the foundation of the Swiss Federation (pp. 161-238), the Reformation (pp. 389-570), the Napoleonic experiment (pp. 785-840), and the constitution of 1848 (pp. 987-1018), among other things. The "only comprehensive history of Switzerland in the English language to appear during the past 50 years" (as the preface claims) is James Murray Luck's 900-page *A History of Switzerland* (SPOSS Inc,

Palo Alto, 1985), of which pp. 37-466 deal with history, and the rest with the present state. A more brief look at the origins and development of Switzerland may be found in chapter 2 of Jonathan Steinberg's *Why Switzerland?* (Cambridge University Press, Cambridge, 1976), written with a sharp sense of what it feels like to be Swiss by one who has himself married into a Swiss family. The third chapter (pp. 53-97) of this book explains the Swiss political system, as well as chapter 11.17 (pp. 717-746) of Luck. Language (including the peculiar position of Swiss-German dialect) is treated in chapter 4 (pp. 98-128).

The intervention of Carl Spitteler during World War I is described in François Vallotton's *Ainsi parlait Carl Spitteler: genèse et réception du "Notre point de vue Suisse" de 1914* (Université de Lausanne, Lausanne, 1991). General Guisan has been biographed by Willi Gautschi (*General Henri Guisan. Die schweizerische Armeeführung im Zweiten Weltkrieg*. Verlag Neue Zürcher Zeitung, Zurich, 1989).

The Swiss Federal Constitution is treated on pp. 297-310 of the book *Modern Switzerland*, edited by J. Murray Luck (SPOSS Inc, Palo Alto, 1978); Swiss federalism is analyzed on pp. 323-338, as well as in the chapter "The evolution of Swiss Federalism. A model for the European Community?" (written by Hansjörg Blöchlinger and René L. Frey) of *European Economy: Reports and Studies* 5: 213-241 (1993). A completely revised edition of *Modern Switzerland* is just being published in German under the title *Blickpunkt Schweiz: 27 Ansichten* (Verlag Neue Zürcher Zeitung, Zurich, 1995), and an American edition from SPOSS Inc. is forthcoming.

Not quite up to date, but the best work on the Jura conflict in the English language, is John R.G. Jenkins' *Jura Separatism in Switzerland* (Clarendon Press, Oxford, 1986). Later developments in the Jura may be followed up in Kurt and Kati Spillmann's essay "The Jura-Problem is not resolved: political and psychological aspects of Switzerland's ethnic conflict", *History of European Ideas* 15 (1-3): 105-111 (1992) and on pp. 145-153 of Andreas Cueni's *Lehrblätz Laufental: Vom schwierigen Weg der direkten Demokratie* (Werd-Verlag, Zurich, 1993).

The most recent and comprehensive descriptions of the Swiss model of ethnic coexistence are Wolf Linder's *Swiss Democracy: Possible Solutions to Conflict in Multicultural Societies* (The Macmillan Press Ltd, Basingstoke, 1994) and Daniel G. Thürer's essay "National Minorities: A Global, European, and Swiss Perspective", *The Fletcher Forum of World Affairs* 19 (1): 53-69 (1995).

Notes

[1] Federal Constitution, Article 14.
[2] FC Art. 14 and Art. 7.
[3] FC Art. 13 §1.
[4] FC Art. 65.
[5] FC Art. 22[ter 71].
[6] FC Art. 54.
[7] FC Art. 4 and Art. 58.
[8] FC Art. 36 and Art. 55.
[9] FC Art. 49f.
[10] FC Art. 56.
[11] FC Art. 31.
[12] FC Art. 44.
[13] FC Art. 45.
[14] FC Art. 43 and Art. 57.
[15] FC Art. 57.
[16] FC Art. 34.
[17] FC Art. 5.
[18] FC Art. 75.
[19] FC Art. 95.
[20] FC Art. 108.
[21] FC Art. 74 §2.
[22] FC Art. 116.

11 Conflict and Integration

The Main Principles of Social Cohesion in the United States

ORTWIN RENN

1 Introduction

When I moved to the town of Worcester, Massachusetts, I started to sample the many ethnic restaurants in the downtown area. Over time I noticed two distinct Lebanese restaurants almost opposite of each other located on one of the downtown streets which had seen better times in the past but still tried to appeal to the few visitors who had found their way into the area. One was run by a Christian Lebanese patron, the other by his Moslem counterpart. Each time that I ate lunch or dinner in either one of the two restaurants, the owner confided to me the most awful stories about the owner of the other restaurant. Not only was I told that the other owner made terrible food, was cheating on his guests, and had a mean and dishonest character, he also was supposed to support terrorist groups back in Lebanon. The Christian owner explained tearfully the misdeeds of the Moslem gangs in Beirut and he was clearly convinced that his Moslem neighbor was transferring money to these gangs. The Moslem restaurant owner made similar claims telling me that many of his relatives had been slaughtered by Christian militia and that this group received assistance from his Christian neighbor. All these accusations were accompanied with hateful outbursts of disgust and anger. After I heard all these stories over and over again, I dared to ask one owner at one of these extended lunch conversations: "If your neighbor is such a bad guy why don't you go out and attack him? After all, he has supported all these people who have been killing your relatives back in Lebanon." The owner looked at me with great astonishment. "You mean, physically attack him? Never! After all, we are both Americans, aren't we?"

This story has left a deep mark in my memories. During my residency as Associate Professor at Clark University in Worcester from 1986 to 1992, I encountered quite a few similar occasions in which people coming from countries struck by Civil War or outbreaks of ethnic violence were able to communicate to their foes without engaging in violent actions or even using aggressive rhetoric. Not that they were less concerned about the problems back home but there was a hidden boundary of constraint that prevented them from getting at each other's throat. This was true for descendants from Protestant and Catholic families of Northern Ireland and even among Jews and Arabs or Serbs and Croats. The existence of such a constraint came as a surprise to me since violence is a rather common experience in American cities. Violent struggles for racial equality or social opportunities have been part of the American history for more than two centuries. Ethnic violence, however, is remarkably low compared to the potential for conflict and hate that characterizes many multi-ethnic populations worldwide.

Can this experience of coexistence of many ethnic groups in the United States be a role model for other countries which fight endless battles along ethnic lines and suffer from violent clashes between these groups? Is there anything to learn from the US social system for the emerging new nations in Eastern and Central Europe and their attempt to create a peaceful society based on civil values and rights?

In the following paragraphs I will try to sketch out some responses to these questions. Most of these responses are drawn from *personal experience* and reflect the observations of a European visitor to and temporary resident of the United States. My interpretations of these experiences cannot claim intersubjective validity. As much as I tried to be a critical and self-conscientious observer of the US society, personal values and preferences have certainly shaped my view of ethnic coexistence in the US and influenced my selection of what I deemed important and revealing. Furthermore, any analysis of the US society will yield a complex, often inconsistent and ambiguous picture. As the President of the American Sociological Society (ASA) recently remarked in his official address to the 1997 ASA Annual Congress in Toronto, ambivalence is the main characteristic of modern societies, in particular the American society.[1] For each trend that one can observe there will be a countertrend or even several of them. For the sake of presenting a clear and unequivocal argument, I have simplified this complexity and reduced my analysis to five central principles of ethnic coexistence in the United States. Although these principles clearly reflect subjective impressions, I have also consulted the more analytically oriented literature on the subject of social integration and conflict resolution in order to avoid a purely subjective and impressionistic characterization.[2]

2   Tocqueville Revisited

The most famous European observer of the American society was Alexis of Tocqueville who wrote a precise and profound analysis of the political and social system during his visit to the United States in the middle of the 19th century.[3] Although Tocqueville witnessed the deep racial division in the late 19th century American society, he was also impressed by the strong integrative forces that made America the melting pot for many European and, less effectively, Asian immigrants. He was aware that the idea of a melting pot served more as a myth for new immigrants than emerged as a reality.[4] But compared to Europe with its long history of wars between different nations, religions, and social classes, the American society had evolved into a multi-cultural entity that, according to his observations, could be characterized by a few all-encompassing and binding principles for the society as a whole, though leaving sufficient room and space for each individual and social group to design their own lifestyle. Social conflict was present everywhere but it did not jeopardize the foundations of the American political system. Tocqueville was fascinated by the "community values" shared by the people in one neighborhood and the diversity of values among neighborhoods. Most astounding for him was the observation that the political system proved robust in spite of the diversity of the people that it served.

From the days of Tocqueville's visit to the second world war and even thereafter, the social system in the US has been based on several integrative principles as well as routinized social mechanisms. Four principles stand out as forming the specific cultural glue from which integration and peaceful coexistence emerged over time.[5] These four principles are:
– belief in a meritocratic reward system;
– pragmatism in response to pluralism of values;
– checks and balances in power relationships; and

– religious vision.

These four principles are the building blocks for the central value of American patriotism which can be placed in the center of a square that is marked by the four corners symbolizing the above mentioned four principles. Before describing these principles in more detail, it is necessary to be aware of some of the special historical circumstances that characterize the evolution of the US society.

3   The Immigration Society

The majority of US Americans are either descendants from immigrants or immigrants themselves. There are two notable exceptions, however: the native Indians and the African Americans. When the first European settlers arrived, the land was already occupied by the native Indians. Their culture and lifestyles, however, exerted only a marginal influence on the social and cultural identity of the new evolving nation. Most native Indians were prosecuted, expelled or forced to move to remote reservations. Except for the early period of the colonization by white settlers, where a cultural exchange took place at least in modest forms, the immigrants' culture showed hardly any interest in adopting or even exploring Indian habits or lifestyles. Native Indians were socially and politically marginalized and forced to adaptation or isolation. As a result, the new culture in the United States was and largely still is a culture of immigrants. Until today native Indians have neither the power nor the strength to reclaim their right of ownership or to induce much of their culture into the American Way of Life.[6] Folklore art and environmental values may be the only cultural niches in which native Indians have exerted any influence on the mainstream culture. Violent clashed were common in the 18th and 19th century but, due to the great imbalance in power distribution and in access to weapons and forces, violent opposition died over time. Native Indians were and to a large extent still are socially and culturally marginalized.

The second exception refers to the African Americans who had been shipped to America against their will. Serving as slaves on the southern farms, they were treated as second class human beings (or worse) and formed their own communities linking traditional African, Christian, and American lifestyle elements. Violent conflicts were rare as long as the white majority had all the means to oppress any insurgence and to construct legitimations for sustaining the feudal structure. This article is not the place to review the history of African Americans and their contributions to building the American nation.[7] The main point I would like to make is that African Americans were largely excluded from playing a significant role in the evolution of the European dominated American culture and self-image. Similar to the native Indians, their influence on culture was restricted to areas of art, music, and folklore. In the course of time, however, other elements relating to religious practice, social organization, and innovative lifestyle factors found entrance into the mainstream white culture. In spite of these few integrative pathways, most African Americans lived and still live today in neighborhoods of their own (often city ghettos) with only limited exchange of ideas or communication with the dominant white culture. In addition, their access to the resources available to the white majority is seriously restricted. Many white Americans experience the lifeworld of the African Americans only through TV (the image depicted there is often distorted by romanticising, "exoticising" or ignoring elements of this complex sub-culture within the dominant culture). Those middle class African Americans who have the resources to leave the traditional neighborhoods and move into the class dominated neighborhoods (based on income) tend to adopt the values and lifestyles of their new neighbors, thus strengthening the elements of the European based value system.[8]

The path towards integration and political emancipation was often accompanied by harsh conflicts and occasional violent clashes between the African Americans and representatives of the white majority. The continuous struggle for political influence and economic equality met with resistance from most representatives of the white immigrant society. In particular, newly arrived immigrants who were eager to enter the job market and start a social career regarded the descendants of the former slaves as an unwelcome competition for economic positions and social resources.[9] The African American communities responded by organizing political opposition groups, mass mobilization, and mostly non-violent protest. This constant struggle for political recognition has been regularly intersected by violent riots in times when the development towards equality was stalled or when expectations for improvement exceeded perceived political opportunities for change.

The special history of native Indians and African Americans could be taken as a case study in itself for how an overwhelmingly immigrant society deals with those members whose ancestors were forced to live along with or separate from the majority in social positions inferior to the positions of the majority. The present status of ethnic conflicts in Central and Eastern Europe, however, has more resemblance to the situation of the different ethnic groups within the European dominated stream of immigrants to the United States. Hence, I will focus on the integrative mechanisms and institutions that have facilitated ethnic cooperation among European immigrants. I will also not cover the interesting history of Asian Americans, in particular those coming from China and Japan,[10] but focus on ethnic cooperation and conflict among the predominantly European immigrants.

4   The Immigrants' Culture: The Vision of Equal Opportunities

As explained in the previous section, the American culture has been mainly shaped by the various cultures of European immigrants and to a lesser degree by African Americans, native Indians, and Asian immigrants. Within that dominant immigrants' culture, there was no special group or internal faction that could claim a right or privilege to be the legitimate heir to the land and its resources. In contrast to some of the recent conflicts such as in Cosovo or in the West Bank of the Jordan river, no group has been able to make an argument that they owned the land before the immigrants arrived. All European immigrants were hence equals in the eyes of history. Such a starting point provides a sound foundation for a meritocratic and individualistic social structure.

Everyone who had entered America through New York or San Francisco could expect a rather similar social career.[11] The first generation of immigrants usually settled close to their former countrymen and -women who had come one or two generations earlier and had built homes in ethnic neighborhoods of the cities or in ethnically dominated villages. The newly arrived immigrants struggled with the language, kept many of their national and ethnic habits, and were partially dependent on the help of their neighbors. They tried to get work as unskilled labourers or farm workers and made sure that their children attended school and learned a professional skill. The second generation was normally bilingual, aspired for better paid jobs and became somewhat more mobile, although most of them remained in their original neighborhoods. The third generation was normally successful in climbing the social career ladder. They were highly motivated to succeed in a meritocratic system, they were supported by their parents who embraced the American value system and were not as emotionally divided between the two cultures as were their grandparents. They cultivated energy and zest in order to compete against the "rest of the world". Members of the third generation often moved away from the ethnic neighborhoods and founded or joined class-oriented neighborhoods. The rich preferred to live next to the rich, and the richer next to the richer. The ones who did not make it remained in the old neighborhoods. Since the residents with higher incomes moved away from the ethnic enclaves, only the poor stayed there. These neighborhoods attracted other poor people from different ethnic backgrounds or new immigrants. The cleavage of ethnic bounds was slowly exchanged for the cleavages of income and class.

5   The Four Principles of Social Cohesion

Meritocracy

In addition to the similarity in social careers over the three-generational path, the American social structure is characterized by several strong bonds.[12] The first and most important principle is the common belief in a meritocratic system, i.e., the conviction that anyone with the right abilities and talents can get any position in the society regardless of ethnic background, religion or social class. It should be emphasized that this integrative principle is based on belief and not necessarily reality. American history is full of examples of discrimination and undue privileges. At the same time, however, hardly any country that I know has placed so much emphasis on legal and social actions against discrimination and abuse of power. Providing equal opportunities to all US citizens lies at the heart of the Constitution and fair play is the common principle that unites almost all factions of the society.[13]

The hardships of immigration were much easier to tolerate if there was an expectation that the new society would provide a fair share of its vast resources to those who deserve it. Many of the new immigrants were aware of the fact that they themselves would not be able to collect the fruits of their hard work. The aspiration towards deferred gratification patterns has two important consequences. First, most of the immigrants provided all their personal strength, abilities and resources to contribute to the economic well-being of the society and its economy. In conjunction with a predominantly Protestant and puritan culture, this effort led to the building of a strong capitalist expansion. Second, the hope that the following generations would harvest the fruits of one's own work served as a tranquilizer for enduring social inequality and hardship. As long as everyone believed that their children or grandchildren would have an equal opportunity to reach higher positions in their social and economic career than was possible for the immigrants themselves, ethnic conflicts were less pronounced. This was the case despite the fact that specific ethnic groups were usually over-represented either on the top or on the bottom of the social stratification scale during the various immigration waves. The belief in a meritocratic system that would level out these overt differences was one of the major social mechanisms to avoid violent opposition towards oppression and injustice experienced by the first and sometimes second generation of immigrants.

Pluralism of Values and Pragmatic Response to Diversity

A second important principle is the pursuit of pragmatism in response to diversity and cultural pluralism. The early American settlers showed little tolerance to anyone who wanted to live together with them in their communities.[14] These settlers had fled religious prosecution in Europe but had no reluctance setting up their own rather suppressive religious order once they had established their own settlements. Anyone who wanted to be part of their community was forced to share all their values and lifestyle regulations. Some contemporary communitarians idealize these early communities; which did provide meaning, identity, a sense of belonging, and solidarity. But the price was high: social control was ubiquitous and normal life was regulated to the last detail. In spite of this pervasive control within the community, the members of each community were rather indifferent about other communities and their social system. Having gone through the experience of prosecution, the early immigrants were probably empathetic with respect to the ordeal of other prosecuted communities with different values and religious beliefs. In addition, the land appeared so expansive in space that it was unlikely that one community would disturb the activities of another community. Whatever the reason, most communities did not show much inclination to become missionaries of their own style. Preachers who traveled from community to community did not compromise on the central positions of Christian belief but had little problem with adjusting their message according to the audience (even praising slavery in the South and condemning it in the North). This rather pragmatic attitude should not be mistaken for active tolerance. Hardly ever did one subculture show any interest or much appreciation for another subculture, they merely coexisted in spite of the possibility of one subculture being physically able to dominate another.

This pragmatism is still a strong national feature of US citizens. Any visitor of the United States can find communities which live in totally isolated worlds of their own such as the Amish people or some Hippie communities. As long as they do not conflict with the basic legal regulations of the country nobody is bothering them nor do others try to alter their lifestyle. (Television, of course, is the most severe challenge to these groups.) Conflicts arise when certain groups trespass the line of legality. Prominent examples are the struggle over the Mormon practice of polygamy, the reluctance of Amish people to introduce hygienic practices in animal husbandry, and the more recent attempts of right wing isolationists to build communities that are divorced from the national political system. But the pragmatism extends far beyond the coexistence of different and sometimes bizarre subcultures, it has evolved into a guarantee for the right of each individual to be the ultimate authority for his or her lifestyle. Civil rights have been the sacred cows of American politics. Free speech includes the right to be nasty, obscene (but not on public TV), fascist, or communist - as long as the civil rights of others are not violated.

Another little anecdote may illustrate this point. At one time during a visit in a suburb of Detroit, I met a recently retired soldier who was truly a white supremacist. As much as I tried to argue with him, he was absolutely convinced that people of colour were less intelligent, lazy, mostly criminals, dependent on welfare and a burden to society. He had forbidden anyone of his family to have contacts with people of colour and he was supporting a small movement which wanted to collect financial resources and political support for sending "them" back to Africa. It was useless to present arguments or appeal to his values - nothing could change his convictions. Several days after I made his acquaintance, I accompanied him to the local bank. In front of the bank a beggar was asking for money. "Look at him", my companion told me, "that is what I mean: Can't he work like anyone else? He wants to live on my money, Don't you even dare to give him anything!" He looked at him with disgust and entered the bank. When we both left the bank again, we saw two white young men approach the beggar and start to attack him. Before I even could ask for help, my companion, who obviously had not forgotten his military skills, grabbed the two men, shook them heavily, and helped the old beggar stand on his feet. When my companion noticed a glance of astonishment and surprise on my face, he replied. "Don't think that you convinced me of anything. But in this country all Americans have certain rights and nobody has the right to violate them".

This anecdote shows both the deep feeling of intolerance and bigotry and, at the same time, the deep conviction that civil rights are a national treasure that one needs to defend, even if these rights protect people that one dislikes or hates. The question, of course, remains why this belief in civil liberties dominates over the strong feeling of righteousness and moral superiority, which are both prolific in the US society and may be derived at least partially from the puritan heritage of the past. Some sociologists refer to exchange theory and explain the preoccupation of US citizens with civil rights by eluding to the common experience of symmetry in social relations. If you do not act on me, I will not act on you. This symmetry was originally a principle governing the relations between communities rather than individuals. When ethnic neighborhoods were established and slowly transformed into neighborhoods of class and income, these entities became the focal points of exchange processes. Some had specialized in specific trades or skills and depended on the support of others. Later, when individuals started to move from community to community, the need to get along with each other transcended this pragmatic attitude into an individual right.[15]

Other analysts refer to the tradition of the Enlightenment, which had a strong influence on the founders of the American political system.[16] Also plausible is a link to the dominating belief in meritocracy. If all are supposed to have equal opportunities to succeed in economic or political careers, basic individual rights are the necessary conditions for a fair system of competition.

US history includes many instances in which civil liberties were highly endangered, for example during the McCarthy area in the early

1950s. Many critical analysts of the US society also point out that powerful people refer to Civil Rights all the time but do not practice them.[17] Special groups in the American society such as Hispanics and people of colour have gone through severe periods of overt discrimination and still suffer more subtle forms of discrimination today. All of this is certainly true but, compared to European history, the American society has excelled in terms of democratic stability, social cohesion, and a record of at least trying to honor Civil Rights of all individuals. A fraction of this astonishing stability is certainly caused by American pragmatism which does not give space to collective subdomination under one ideology or any kind of "politicalisms", be it communism or fascism. The Germanic trademark of being consistent with one's own belief system and convictions, even if it means to betray common sense or basic human values, is alien for most Americans. Ronald Reagan, who certainly was more ideological in his views than most other presidents, made secret deals with the archenemy Iran in order to free American citizens. He obviously violated all publicly announced statements that he would never do business with the Ayatollahs who he framed as the devils. He in fact communicated with the devil "just" because a few American lives were at stake.

Checks and Balances in Power Relationships

The excellent record of political stability and peaceful coexistence (apart from the Civil War) is partially rooted in American pragmatism, but is also a product of a strong feeling of distrust in any kind of (human) authority and a true belief in the value of pluralism.[18] This distrust in authority is the third general characteristic of American political culture. No other political system has been so articulate about checks and balances within the political system as the Unites States. Congress controls the presidency, the supreme court controls both the legislative and the executive branch of Government and vice versa. Checks and balances can be found almost everywhere within the political structure - from the local up to the national level. But the feeling of distrust goes deeper than this. Public life in the US is dominated by an adversarial style of argumentation over truth, politics, and the "good" life.[19] Hardly any scientist can claim to have compelling evidence for the truth without encountering another scientist who challenges the original claims. Be it art, fashion, lifestyle, or moral values - one thing is always true about them in the US: they are or will be controversial.

Again one might be tempted to relate this feeling of distrust to the overarching principle of pragmatism. But I believe this distrust has additional roots. It might have been developed from the original experience of political authority in Europe which caused many people to leave their homelands and settle in America. But it was further developed over the evolution of the American society. To live in small, independent communities that imposed their own social rules on their members implied a distinct distaste for centralized governments and centralized rules stretching beyond the absolutely necessary federal mandates. American politics has been constantly oscillating between centralization and decentralization (for example the permanent quarrels about the federal bank in the 18th and 19th century). Any movement towards more centralized power immediately triggered a counter-movement towards more decentralization and less federal authority.

In addition, American society was always divided into urban and rural fractions.[20] The urbanites perceived themselves as the civilized, technologically advanced, culturally brilliant elite while the rural residents perceived themselves as the natural, fortune hunting, simple minded but clever, and morally superior citizens - in short: the true Americans. These two traditions are still prevalent in US society long after the pioneers have settled down and the new frontiers in the West have been cultivated. In analogy to the checks and balances in the political system, urban intellectualism and rural common sense keep each other in a delicate balance. As much as science and cultural excellence are revered national icons, plain common sense is still regarded as a national virtue and not, as in many European countries, as a sign of an intellectual deficiency. Intellectuals may be celebrated when they make breath-taking discoveries but they are usually ignored if they make suggestions concerning politics or moral standards. The whole judicial system is thoroughly based on laypeople who serve as jurors in trials. All these examples demonstrate the tendency of American society to create or promote counterweights when the general tendency moves towards placing too much emphasis on one side of the scale. It may take a few years before the balancing forces begin to act, but history so far has always come up with a counter-movement once a movement became too powerful. Pareto's analysis of elite and counter-elite keeping a society from moving too far to the right or to the left was meant to capture the newly developing democracies of Europe but, in a much deeper sense, the structure of the US society matches this description better than any other social system that I am aware of.[21] Any claim for truth, political correctness, cultural excellence, or true life style provokes counterclaims. The trivial statement that truth is found in the middle is an integral part of the American political and social culture.

There is one exception to this rule which brings me to the fourth main characteristic of the American social system. This is religion. Societies need some overarching values on which they can base their daily life, including the management of diversity.[22] Postmodern thinkers may be convinced that pluralism and tolerance in themselves are sufficient agents for producing social and political stability. I have my doubts about this. Unlike the postmodernists, I would claim that a reference point for orientation or moral guidance is not only essential for social cohesion, it also includes the notion of something eternal, holy, or universal in order to become effective. Values may be internalized in the process of socialization without any explicit reference to reason or revelation. Traditions may serve as substitutes for religious dogmas. The more a society develops plural lifestyles, embraces many different, partially contradictory systems of worldviews, and offers a wide diversity of cultural values systems, the more it relies on a set of central beliefs and guiding principles in order to guarantee social cohesion and integration. This function in the United States is partly met by the belief in meritocracy and the veneration of Civil Rights. In addition, religion and teleological vision provides this integrative guidance for a "good" life.

Religious Vision and the Sense of Mission

Compared to European nations, even Mediterranean societies, religion plays a major role in the life of most Americans. Churches in Europe have become partly social players in politics, partly agents of providing responses to individuals looking for meaning or tradition. The role of churches in the United States includes these two objectives, but goes far beyond. Most Americans expect not only meaning but also personal orientation and moral guidance when joining religious denominations.[23]

In addition, they use churches as a platform for practicing charity and social responsibility.

Religious practice has been a dominant feature of the early settlers and has continued to mark community life until the middle of the 19th century. The inner-community order was largely driven by religious beliefs and practices. When ethnic cleavages weakened over time and class relations became more formal, people relied even more on the services of churches for finding orientation and comfort. The mixing of ethnic groups and the new social clusters of class-oriented neighborhoods promoted a confusing proliferation of different churches and denominations. Rather than having one type of religious organization serving a particular ethnic group in the neighborhood, modern Americans are exposed to a large choice of churches and religious organizations from which they can freely choose. Many people change their denominations if they are dissatisfied with the religious practice of their traditional church or if they move into another area. This has caused some European observers to conclude that it is not the metaphysical part of religious life that attracts people to join churches but its social function of providing contacts, relationships, intimacy, and emotional support. Church life has taken the place of the vanishing ethnic linkages. It has been my observation, however, that people may change denominations and do not care much about special dogmas or religious traditions, but they do expect clear moral and social guidance from their churches regardless of which ones they may decide to join.

As one would expect from the pragmatist attitude of most Americans, the teachings by the different religious organizations can be very consistent, strict and even oppressive within each denomination, but the messages differ substantially between these organizations. Fundamentalist, naturalist, liberal, conservative, and esoteric churches compete with each other. In spite of this plurality, there are common grounds of almost all churches: they emphasize community values, social responsibility, family stability, and certain moral codes. Most of the churches are Christian and thus comparable with each other. But even Moslem or Buddhist traditions in the United States demonstrate similar patterns when it comes to basic values and responsibilities. In addition to guidance for everyday life, churches provide metaphysical explanation and meaning for one's own life.

The Focal Point: Political and Cultural Patriotism

So most Americans can balance their life in a symbolic space embraced by four corners: meritocracy as a promise for social and economic career; pragmatism in political and cultural affairs; pluralism of lifestyles through balancing truth claims and authority; and emotional and spiritual guidance through religion. Each of these corners constitute their own world. Being in the meritocratic system the only things that count are money and success. Social status is almost entirely dependent on wealth. Educational level and professional prestige, usually seen as equally important elements of status in Europe, play only a minor role in the United States. Pragmatism calls for coexistence of lifestyles and worldviews but is in opposition to welfare systems or patriarchal political authority. Equal opportunity is cherished but state assistance is rejected. The adversarial system provides diversity in science, culture, and regulatory politics. Checks and balances are crucial instruments for preventing new monarchs in politics as well as in other social or cultural domains. Lastly, religion is the remaining space in which the losers of the meritocratic system, the confused pluralists, the frustrated truth preachers and the distressed career hunter may find emotional support and peace. All four corners constitute essential prerequisites for social stability and ethnic cooperation. If one is missing or threatened, violence may become more prevalent.

The four corners marking the major principles of ethnic and social cohesion constitute a dynamic movement towards building a new identity as American citizens.[24] It is interesting to observe that Americans normally refer to the country of their ethnic roots when someone inside the United States asks them where they come from. They immediately identify themselves as Americans when they are asked the same question abroad. Having experienced the powerful forces of the four principles in action, they have internalized them as an integral part of what it means to be an American. This feeling includes a sense of personal and cultural identity, political commitment, and national pride. It is reinforced by a multitude of symbolic actions; including: special ceremonies when displaying the national flag, the daily recitals of the pledge of allegiance in most public schools, and the veneration of the national anthem. Most importantly, political and cultural patriotism serves as a constant reinforcement of the four principles, even in the absence of institutional control. The interpenetration of institutional structure supporting and sustaining the practice behind the four principles, the symbolic reinforcement of these principles in public and private life and the transmission of these principles via primary and secondary socialization is probably the main reason for the astonishing stability of the political system in the United States over the last three centuries and the relative absence of violent clashes between ethnic groups or social classes.

6 The Mechanisms of Social Cohesion: The Role of Language

The four main principles of American culture and its culminating point of patriotism are contingent on some rather mundane conditions that are often taken for granted but may lead to cultural erosion when missing. The most important lubricant for the functioning of the social system is the common language.[25] Within the three generation cycle it was mandatory that the immigrants became fluent in English. Neither meritocracy nor pragmatism make much sense if communication is limited. Except for few segregationist communities, there had been a consensus among all Americans that the language in the United States is English and that you can only take part in the meritocratic career game if you accept the rules of competition. One of these rules prescribes the command of the national language.

It is worth mentioning that the American language is more than a means of communication. For a European traveler it is always amusing to discover the multitude of euphemisms that characterize the use of the English language in everyday situations. If you are asked "How are you?", nobody expects an honest answer. The phrase has lost its original meaning and serves as a mere greeting ritual. Nobody ever needs to go to the toilet but only frequents the bathroom or washroom. Our children had a laugh when they heard that other children of the neighborhood took the dog out to the bathroom, which meant the next tree. One could quote thousands of examples in which fairly unfriendly, indecent or reprimanding messages are hidden in a euphemistic language coat. Such a language game, as modern linguists would call it, serves a distinct cultural function. If you don't know the taboos and sensitivities of other people or communities, you tend to be more cautious with your own phrases.

Any time you ask an American how he or she liked her last travel to any other country (particularly if that country is the home country of the person who asks the question) you will certainly experience an outburst of superlatives such as marvelous, splendid, gorgeous, wonderful, exciting and so on. Only if you insist on more information then all the bad experiences will be revealed. It is important for most Americans to establish a friendly and positive atmosphere when they start a conversation. Far from being superficial, as many European critics have characterized this behavior, Americans make use of euphemistic language because it allows interaction without offense but also without further commitment. You don't owe anyone anything by remaining overly polite but you can still test whether it is worth while investing more time or resources in this relationship.

Being fluent in the language is therefore a condition for, as well as a reinforcement of the structural characteristics of the social fabric in US society. In recent times, however, this requirement has been undermined by a new wave of immigrants who do not follow the routine path of the three generational routine of social integration. This deviation from the old pattern has several reasons.[26] First, the common experience of the American people as being descendants of immigrants fades away with each generation living in the US. At all times the ones who had immigrated first felt superior to those who came later, but over time the assimilation process made the new immigrants part of the old establishment. This integration process took time and was not accomplished without experiencing conflicts and rejection but there was a common expectation among the old and the new immigrants that one wave of immigration after another would be absorbed by the country without major turmoil or an attack on the main principles of social cohesion. With new waves of immigrants from Latin America, Africa and Asia, however, traditional Americans feel more and more threatened and fear cultural innovations that they are not willing to accept.[27]

It is interesting to note that in the South of the United States the original immigrants from Mexico call themselves Spaniards (although they did not come from Spain), whereas the new immigrants from Mexico are called Hispanics. The labeling of new immigrants with special phrases points to a new distinction among American citizens. They like to be classified in accordance with their years of residence in the United States rather than by ethnicity, class or religion.

The second reason is that the new immigrants, in particular the Hispanics, settle in the vicinity of their own countrymen and -women as all the other ethnic groups have done before, but due to their sheer number and internal business opportunities, they are not bound to learn English in order to take part in the meritocratic system. Within an Hispanic neighborhood the opportunities for business success may be limited and constrained but there are enough resources available to make a decent living, at least for many. Third, the children of the new immigrants are less motivated to become bilingual. They do not see the need for this extra work as they can get along with Spanish as the main language. Thus, the traditional generational transition from one's native mother tongue to the American language is not occurring, or is at least delayed. Fourth, many modern values and lifestyles are in opposition to the traditional forms of integration which lasted up to three generations. This is particularly true for the "old-fashioned" value of deferred gratification. The new immigrants demand to be part of the social system from the beginning and want to have an equal share of the resources. Being more aware of their political power, they push for reforms that may lead to earlier rewards for them and their immediate offspring.

This reluctance of many new immigrants to learn the language has further alienated the relationships between the old and the new immigration culture. Some States force children of immigrants to learn English, while others try bilingual language training, or offer even classes in Spanish instead of English. The battle is still ongoing and there is no consensus in sight. The danger that new immigrants will build segregated, self-contained communities of their own has been on the agenda of the political debate for the last two decades.

7 Some Recent Challenges to Social Integration in the US-Society

The language challenge is only the tip of the iceberg of several recent developments that may have an impact on the future development of social integration. The meritocratic system has been revived and revitalized under the Reagan administration but it also shows its ugly sides. The belief that everyone can make it if one is willing to do hard work has been seriously challenged by the large number of homeless families, by the erosion of the traditional blue collar worker communities, and the waves of lean management and production reforms that were felt among executives as well as middle class citizens.[28] Although the US economy succeeded in providing good employment opportunities after the recession in the late 1980s, the lower middle class is sliding towards poverty and the lower classes are often left in economic despair. The well-meant equal opportunity policies and anti-discrimination laws have partially divided the country into those who feel that these goals are still not met and those who feel that these policies have gone too far. Both camps have erected a language game of politically correct terms (and thinking) which poses another challenge to the otherwise pragmatic attitude towards political differences.

The adversarial system has partially resulted in political paralysis because whatever claim is being voiced will be contested by someone. Consensus is out of reach when dealing with numerous political and social problems. In contrast to the extending pluralism in science, culture, and politics, many people retreat to religious values and join fundamental church organizations. The representatives of these organizations have trespassed another invisible line between politics and religion and have become active participants in the political arena. Several sociologists have diagnosed an "unholy" division line between the conservative religious right and the liberal religious left. Both camps exploit the integrative force of religion for their own political purposes.[29] Similar arguments can be made for religious leaders of the African American communities and other ethnically defined denominations. The strength of religious belief of providing meaning and solidarity is partially sacrificed on the altar of political power and economic greed.

The new tensions between old and new immigrants, the weakening of the traditional means of integration, and new economic and social developments have left their mark on the American scenery. Political groups such as the far right have started to use terrorist attacks to promote their objectives. Terrorism from inside is a rather new phenomenon in the US. The absence of terrorism was always a signal that pragmatism and pluralism worked hand in hand in preventing terrorism or other forms of clandestine violence. By providing space for all kinds of political and cultural groups and, at the same time, creating constraints on the means to articulate their political messages, incentives for joining terrorist organizations were low. Again the exception to this has been racial violence and secret organizations (such as the Ku Klux Klan). At this point it is not clear whether we are witnessing the evolution of a new politically motivated manifestation of violent conflicts between different political fractions or a transitional irritation without major consequences for the political and social fabric of US society.

The recent trial against O.J. Simpson is a lucid indicator for the delicate balance between the races. As soon as the defense team was able to attribute racist motives to the L.A. police activities leading to the arrest of O.J. Simpson, the overwhelming evidence against him played hardly any role. Instead, the underlying cultural conviction that all people should have equal opportunities regardless of race dominated the trial and finally led to the acquittal. The verdict left America divided in two camps. A wide majority of white people were convinced that Simpson was guilty, whereas people of color felt he was innocent. The case has been a prominent example for the mutual colonization of one principle over another. The balance between the four principles is certainly in jeopardy.

In spite of these alarming trends, I do not see any immediate danger of American society falling into rival fractions or even reviving ethnic conflicts. Like similar episodes in US history, the present situation has also witnessed counter forces that are already at work. President Clinton has announced a new education initiative that includes a program for children of new immigrants to learn English (even if they attend bilingual schools). Against extensive pluralism and individualism a new or revitalized movement of communitarianism has swept over the country.[30] The religious right and the fundamentalist movements have gained power in several regions but have provoked joint efforts by scientists and liberal politicians to create countermeasures. The system of checks and balances seems to work effectively and the attitude of pragmatism is so deeply rooted in the American soul that disintegration is unlikely to occur. One should only remember the shock waves of the late 1960s which brought racially motivated riots, protest against the Vietnam war, and rebellion against the traditional values of religion and patriotism. This attack on the American social fabric was at least as powerful as the ones that America is struggling with today. The result, however, has been that the open society was able and still is able to absorb such shock waves. Each wave changes society to some degree but it does not endanger its foundations.

8 Lessons for Other Countries for Coping with Ethnic Conflict

At this point I can come back to my original question. Can the United States be a role model for other nations that face ethnic conflicts or experience symptoms of disintegration? The main focus of this book is on the area of the former Yugoslavia. What can the Serbs, the Croats, the Albanians, what can the Catholics, Orthodox, or the Moslems learn from American history?

As pointed out before, the United States is a country of immigrants. It is much easier to set up a system of mutual respect and cooperation if nobody has a claim to be the legitimate owner of the land. The present situation in Yugoslavia is characterized by competing claims about the right to be at a specific place and to expel those who have arrived later. No serious historian will give any credibility to such claims. History is full of migrations and changing ethnic composition. This point is always important to make, but it does have little impact on the actual situation since people's behavior relies upon perceptions, not historical evidence. As long as one or the other ethnic groups insists on being the natural heir to the land, it will be difficult to cultivate a climate of equal opportunities.

The combination of pragmatism and pluralism is certainly an effective cure against ethnic nationalism and social violence. These two principles cannot be prescribed like medicine, however. They have evolved over time in the United States and have been deeply inscribed into the American psyche. In addition, they depend on a tradition of peaceful coexistence over longer periods of time. If too many old bills are still open it is difficult to remain pragmatic. But the two principles may serve as guiding posts for the resurrection of the new States within the former Yugoslavia. Similar to the small communities that created order and identity in the United States in the pioneering days without bothering to become involved in the affairs of other communities, the communities in the former Yugoslavia could try to pursue a similar path in the aftermath of the civil war. Rather than forcing integration among different ethnic and religious groups within one community, which certainly would constitute the most desirable outcome if it were feasible, the countries should concentrate their forces to create stability, order, and civil behavior within the existing ethnic or religious communities. The focus on the existing communities should include a clear understanding of pragmatic interactions with other communities with different ethnic or religious compositions. The idea would be to prepare people for a civil society within the community in which they live today and in which the bonds of ethnicity and religion are strong incentives to act as responsible citizens. Once this transition into a civil culture has been accomplished, a gradual exchange of ideas and people between the different communities may evolve. The alternative of forcing people to live together in an atmosphere of hate and revenge may only aggravate the feeling of betrayal and build up the level of tensions until the untamed forces seize the opportunity to strive back.

The meritocratic system in the United States has been another major agent for easing ethnic conflicts and facilitating social relations. It is based on capitalist economic structures and a weak redistribution principle. It lacks elements of social justice but promises equal opportunities for all those who try. Again such a system has evolved over time and cannot be placed on top of another country. Another factor need to be taken into account here: The strong conflicts that gave rise to the civil war in Bosnia were partially attributable to a division between urban and rural populations. Whereas in the United States capitalism was an ally for both urbanites and rural people as the land offered many opportunities for the rural adventurers as well as for urban industrialists, the people in Bosnia were in a different economic situation when socialism collapsed. Due to the globalization of economic forces and lack of competitiveness of the local agriculture, the rural population turned out to be the main loser of modernization. The cities, in particular Sarajevo, profited from the new openness to the world, although traditional elites were disempowered and replaced by a new class of business executives and cultural innovators. The capitalist movement turned the existing social structure upside down. As the traditional elite of the cities joined forces with the rural displaced population, they were able to exploit ethnic tensions as an instrument to regain power and influence. As much as a meritocratic system may be an engine for ethnic plurality and coexistence, it may also create or promote social disintegration, which in turn mobilizes ethnic resentments and conflicts.

The lesson to learn from this experience is that the introduction of capitalism and a free market economy needs to be accompanied with politics of social and regional justice. This is easier said than done.

All previously communist countries struggle with this challenge. In addition, the European and American branch of capitalist behavior has been strongly influenced by puritan ethics which made sure that the accumulation of capital was used for reinvestment rather than consumption and that surplus profits were partially redistributed through private channels such as charities or foundations. In countries that miss this puritan tradition, capitalist behavior consists often of clever bargaining, cheating on others, and demonstrative consumption. If religious and cultural institutions have neither the power nor the resources to influence the moral behavior of its members, they become only dresscoats for legitimizing unethical conduct. Murderers and rapists like to appear on national TV as pious attenders (not sinners) of religious services. This appearance perverts the potential of religious beliefs for setting moral standards. Having the Mafia as a role model will certainly ruin any nation's morale. Establishing free market systems is not sufficient in order to boost the economy and improve the standard of living for the majority of the people. What is needed is a framework of economic checks and balances that assure accumulation of productive capital, security of personal savings, a fair and progressive tax system, and the cultivation of human capital, i.e., knowledge, skills, education, and training. In addition, some policies of efficient redistribution are probably necessary to balance inequities among regions and social classes.

Turning to the last principle of integration in the US, the force of organized religion, it has become obvious that religious affiliations do not appear to be the solution to ethnic conflicts, but rather one of the causes of civil war or social unrest. Northern Ireland is another telling example in addition to Bosnia or Croatia. This view, however, obscures the cause-effect-relationship. The fact that somebody is Catholic or Orthodox does not cause any social conflict; just as being a Jew, a Croat or a Serb is not a reason for becoming victimized in ethnic conflict. Ethnic conflicts arise when representatives of one group attribute specific characteristics or rights to their own groups and other characteristics and obligations to competing groups. Ethnicity is often used as a scapegoat and a means to distinguish one group from another group. If, for example, the human eye were unable to distinguish between black and white, racial conflicts between the two would hardly be possible. As long as one group can be identified by some distinctive feature or behavioral pattern, these differences can be exploited by associating them with symbolic attributes or prejudices. That is the reason why political or social conflicts often turn into ethnic conflicts. Religious affiliations are not as obvious as ethnic differences but they are still rather effective in labeling groups. In addition, religion does provide rationalization for discrimination since the reference to divine revelations stipulates ultimate truth claims. Fueling conflicts between religious groups is a rather successful strategy, although most religious dogmas provide little evidence for justifying violent behavior.

The American religious practice may present an interesting alternative to the European standard of powerful religious churches that often act in conjunction with political parties or institutions. Separation of religion and politics is the first step on a route to prevent exploitation of religious needs. A second step is the process of decentralization in accordance with political subsidiarity. All religious practices that can be governed on a local level should be located on this level. The people's needs for spiritual direction and moral orientation can also be served best when it is done on the parish or community level. Local and regional autonomy does not necessarily conflict with the need for a central authority in terms of dogma or unified interpretations of religious documents. It is important that the needs of the local communities and its members are supported and met within the local setting. Spiritual needs are existential for humans and if they are not met by religion they will be met by political or cultural ideologies.

The process of providing guidance within the respective religious faith would certainly be much more effective if two developments could be initiated. First, the representatives of the different churches should get together and design a set of universal religious values and moral norms that they feel are collectively binding regardless of religious denomination. Some theologians of the Christian churches and the Islamic faith have already started to work on a system of world ethics to be adopted by all religious denominations and beyond. It is much harder for politicians or populist demagogues to exploit religious feelings if the leaders of the religious organizations have agreed in advance on major principles of non-violent conflict resolution and respect for civil rights. In addition, the churches should be able to set up a crisis prevention process for those cases in which violent conflicts are likely to occur. Without doubt, the religious leaders in Yugoslavia have been rather reluctant, to say the least, in promoting peaceful means of conflict resolution.

Second religious practice could be an important corrective to any meritocratic system. The American balance of exerting individualist behavior in the economic sector and aspiring to egalitarian values in one's religious practice has created a strong tie between selfish capitalist behavior and socially responsible actions of each individual. Such a personal balance does not eradicate the need for collective corrections for social justice. But it provides a strong counter force to the emergence of clear losers and winners in the global capitalist markets and corrects the image of the ruthless and irresponsible business leader. If people are convinced that immorality pays and that values and moral norms are only obstacles to personal success and career, they will not only try to walk the allegedly successful path to wealth and influence but they will also be susceptible to all kinds of demagogues who promise social justice and convey nothing but hatred and jealousy. I am aware that nobody can arrange for such a personal coupling of economic performance and socially responsible actions. However, religious organizations worldwide could make this task a priority in their own work. They might offer opportunities for those who would like to take their responsibility seriously and provide a platform for those who, for whatever reason, have difficulties succeeding in a meritocratic system.

Last not least, the crisis of ethnic violence is also a crisis of the nation state. The American system has only succeeded because the various principles jointly forged a strong tie of patriotism and, along with it, a feeling of a common mission towards its own destiny as well as the outside world. This conviction of belonging to a nation that is worth the effort to serve has been the engine of the American struggle to cope with inner conflicts and ethnic tensions. In the former Yugoslavian republics, however, the bond of being one nation has been continuously weakened. Nationalism or even chauvinism are certainly not the correct answers to overcome today's problems. They have made lives miserable for millions of people throughout the history of nation-states. But a sense of patriotism helps to overcome ethnic conflicts within one nation and to find commonalities beyond class, gender or religion. Globalization of the economy and the creation of communities within the global village, which defy national boundaries, make it increasingly harder to establish ties among members of heterogeneous nation states. This process can not be reversed. One of the main challenges of the future will be to make communities and regions powerful enough to direct their own affairs and provide sufficient coordination and guidance through supra-national agreements that help each region to find and define its own destiny.

The successful management of ethnic conflicts will not so much depend on the willingness of international organizations to send in troops (although this will also be necessary on occasion) but on the ability and readiness of these organizations to provide economic and political incentives for troubled regions as a means to balance economic development and social justice and to regain cultural identity within a global consensus on socially responsible behavior. In particular, they need to support the building of institutions and cultural infrastructure devoted to the building of a Civil Society.

Notes

1. N. Smelser, Presidential Address: *Rational Action and Its Limitations*. Annual Meeting of the American Sociological Association. Manuscript (Toronto: August 1997).

2. My own analysis has benefited from the following major sources:

   A. Aguirre and J.H. Turner, *American Ethnicity. The Dynamics and Consequences of Discrimination*. Second Edition (Mc Graw Hill: Boston 1998);

   R.D. Alba (ed), *Ethnicity and Race in the U.S.A. Toward the 21. Century* (Routledge: New York 1985);

   M. Carnoy, *Faded Dreams. The Politics and Economics of Race in America* (Cambridge University Press: Cambridge 1994);

   M. Marger, *Race and Ethnic Relations in America: American and Global Perspectives* (Wadsworth: Belmont 1991);

   P.I. Rose, *They and We: Racial and Ethnic Relations in the United States*. Fifth Edition (Mac Graw Hill: Boston 1997).

3. A. de Tocqueville, De la Democratie en Amerique. In: Oeuvres, Papiers et correpondances. Edition definitive publiee sous la direction de J.-P.Mayer, tome I. (Gallimard: Paris 1951), Vol. 1.

4. Dispelling the myth of multiculturalism has been the focus of the book by: P. Brimelow, *Alien Nation. Common Sense about America's Immigration Disaster* (Harper Perennial: New York 1996).

5. Evidence for the four principles have been found in several sources, most pronounced in: R. Daniels, *Coming to America: A History of Immigration and Ethnicity in American Life* (Harper: New York 1991) and S. Lebbertson and M.C. Waters, *From Many Strands: Racial and Ethnic Groups in Contemporary America* (Russell Sage: New York 1988).

6. Compare Aguirre and Turner, 1998, pp. 115-126.

7. See the classic review in: J. Turner, R. Singleton and D. Musick, *Oppression: A Sociohistory of Black-White Relations in America* (Nelson-Hall: Chicago 1984).

8. R. Blauner, *Black Lives, White Lives: Three Decades of Race Relations in America* (University of California Press. Berkeley 1989).

9. S. Olzak, *The Dynamics of Ethnic Competition and Conflict* (Stanford University Press: Stanford 1992).

10. See the review of Asian Immigrants to the United States in: R. Takaki, *Strangers from a Different Shore: A History of Asian Americans* (Little and Brown: Boston 1989).

11. L. Dinnerstein and D. M. Reimers, *Ethnic Americans: A History of Immigration*. Third Edition. (Harper and Row: New York 1988).

12. See references of footnote 5.

[13] E. Shils, The Virtues of Civil Society, *Government and Opposition,* Vol. 26. No. 2 (Winter 1991), pp. 3-20.

[14] Compare Aguirre and Turner, 1998, p. 50. For a historical review see: D. Zaret, *The Heavenly Contract: Ideology and Organization in Pre-revolutionary Puritanism* (University of Chicago Press: Chicago 1984).

[15] A.B. Seligman, *The Problem of Trust* (Princeton University Press: Princeton 1997), pp. 144-150.

[16] M. Lacob, The Enlightenment Redefined: The Formation of Modern Civil Society, *Social Research,* Vol. 59 (1992), pp. 475-495.

[17] For example: M.D. Pohlmann, *Black Politics in Conservative America* (Longmanns: New York 1990).

[18] G. Kateb: *The Inner Ocean: Individualism and Democratic Culture* (Cornell University Press: Ithaca 1992). See also: R.L. Hanson, *The Democratic Imagination in America: Conversations with Our Past* (Princeton University Press: Princeton 1985).

[19] Renn, O., Style of Using Scientific Expertise: A Comparative Framework, *Science and Public Policy,* Vol. 22 (June 1995), pp. 147-156.

[20] Earle and G. Cvetkovich, *Social Trust. Towards a Cosmopolitan Society* (Praeger: Westport 1995).

[21] V. Pareto, *Sociological Writings.* Selected and Introduced by S.E. Finer (Praeger: New York 1966).

[22] A.B. Seligman, *Innerwordly Individualism: Charismatic Community and Its Institutionalization* (Transaction Press: New Brunswick 1994).

[23] J.D. Hunter, *Culture Wars* (Basic Books: New York 1992).

[24] P. Salins, *Assimilation. American Style* (Basic Books: New York 1996); see also: R. Freedman, *Immigrant Kids* (Puffin Books: New York 1995).

[25] D.A. Hollinger, *Postethnic America* (Basic Books: New York 1995).

[26] T. Morganthau, America: Still a Melting Pot? *Newsweek,* August 9, 1993, pp. 16-22; see also: P. Brimelow, 1996.

[27] D. Vigil, *From Indians to Chicanos: the Dynamics of Mexican American Culture.* Second Edition (Waveland Press: Prospect Heights 1997).

[28] B. Ehrenreich, *Fear of Falling. The Inner Life of the Middle Class* (Harper: New York 1990); or see also: M. Kaus, *The End of Equality* (New Republic: New York 1993).

[29] J.D. Hunter, 1992.

[30] A. Etzioni, *The Spirit of Community. Rights and Responsibilities and the Communitarian Agenda* (Crown: New York 1993) or A. Etzioni, *The New Golden Rule* (Basic Books: New York 1998).

PART V

SYNOPSIS

12 Ethnic Cooperation and Coexistence

International Mediation, International Governance, and Civil Society for Ethnically Plural States

ANDREAS KLINKE AND ORTWIN RENN

This synopsis explores the possibilities and limits of ethnic conflict mediation, the structural prerequisites of ethnic cooperation in the international system by international governance, and, finally, the necessary political and societal conditions on the national level and the subnational level of communities for a lasting and peaceful polyethnic coexistence in a Civil Society. Before these subjects are discussed, the common insights of the plenary session at the end of the workshop are presented in the first section and a summary of the main arguments and theses of the papers in this volume is provided in the second section of this synopsis.

1 Outcome of the Plenary Discussion

Given the scope and the limitations of the workshop, the final discussion was focused on three questions:
- Does ethnicity lie at the heart of the present conflicts?
- What are the potential routes for building a Civil Society?
- How can the international community help to accomplish the goal of building Civil Societies in nations troubled by ethnic conflicts and violence?

With respect to the first question, all participants agreed that ethnicity is not a clear objective concept but a social or cultural attribute that is not necessarily associated with only negative impacts or connotations.

Ethnicity can be a powerful agent for creating and sustaining identity and emotional security. At the same time, however, it implies the potential to assign collective blame to an ethnic group and to facilitate projection of one's own problems and deficiencies onto others. It legitimizes violence and immoral behavior. In particular, in times of confusion over moral orientation and social values, the experience of economic hardship and inequality with respect to economic and social resources, ethnic bonds tend to become more pronounced since they provide the only remaining support for social stability and continuity. The main dilemma, however, is that the positive and the negative sides of ethnicity are inseparable from each other. One cannot mobilize only the positive aspects without risking the promotion of the negative impacts. Ethnicity is hence characterized by intrinsic ambivalence.

The experiences in Switzerland and the United States, the only two cultures that were presented as potential role models during the workshop, demonstrate that powerful institutions are necessary to sustain the delicate balance between the benefits and the shadows of ethnicity. This task requires permanent institutional effort and continuous political attention. As long as ethnic groups identify themselves as distinct social entities, ethnic conflicts can never be "resolved". Social and cultural institutions are instrumental, however, in designing and implementing peaceful and constructive means and processes for coping with ethnic tensions.

With respect to the second question, most participants agreed that the path towards a Civil Society is likely to fail under the circumstances in former Yugoslavia. The economic situation is desperate, the war has destroyed almost all trust in the remaining political as well as social institutions, emotions are still out of control, and the political elite who are responsible for much of the ethnic violence is still holding power. Alternative institutions that could offer guidance and emotional support are not in sight. Territorial claims are far from being resolved and the tacit peace agreements rely on reinforcement by foreign troops. Under these circumstances, so the common accord, one cannot justify an optimistic outlook for the future. The group discussions did not stop here, however. In spite of all the difficulties, all participants agreed that the next steps should be:
– to restore the economic base on a regional level as a means to provide economic security to the residents and to create employment opportunities to divert public attention from taking

revenge so that they can start reconstructing their own livelihood. In addition, employment was seen as a crucial path to bring the young and confused soldiers back into normal life and to restore normal relationships with "business partners" from other communities and even different ethnic groups.
- to transform the debate on ethnic conflict into an open debate about the causes and reasons for the violent outbreak of the conflict. Several participants attributed the conflict to the schism between rural traditionalists and urban cosmopolitans, others believed that the conflict was fueled by the old communist elite to remain in power, and others mentioned the historical evolution of unresolved conflicts over land and resources. Many additional factors that might have aggravated the conflict were mentioned during the discussion. The main suggestion, however, was to initiate a public discourse in all parts of former Yugoslavia which would explore the real reasons for the outbreak of violence. Most participants were reluctant to provide more than speculative answers to this question, but they insisted that such a discourse was needed to overcome the superficial explanations given to the people during the civil war.
- to bring those people who have committed crimes to justice. Although this suggestion was approved by all participants, there were many different opinions of what this should mean in practice. On the one hand the argument was made that only the warlords should be taken to court since they are accountable for the atrocities while the common soldiers acted more or less as puppets of their leaders' ambitions. On the other hand it was argued that people would not stop seeking revenge and would not develop any confidence and trust in political institutions if the criminal acts of all individuals involved were not taken to court.
- to increase local and regional autonomy and start building institutions on the local level. Although all participants were well aware of the danger of decentralized control over institution building, they envisioned no alternative other than restoring power on the local level. Many participants shared the experience that even during the worst times of the war some communities with an ethnically mixed population were able to sustain control and civil order. A top-down-approach was not regarded as effective since it would be sabotaged by local interests. Only when the local

communities were to take their fate in their own hands, would there be at least a chance of improvement. Those local communities that have been resisting ethnic violence should form the core group of a new movement towards decentralized civil governance.

- to initiate public education and communication programs that help people to cope with the new situation and to gain confidence in governing themselves. The values of collectivism, paternalism, and traditionalism are still pervasive within each ethnic group. The idea is to promote an appreciation for individual rights, democratic processes, and social responsibility without sacrificing cultural independence and autonomy. The role models of the United States, as well as Switzerland, provide interesting and promising suggestions for organizing such a process. But there will be no possibility to transfer either of the two systems into the troubled areas of former Yugoslavia. Each country and each region must find its own appropriate way.

- to sustain international supervision and control throughout the time required for the necessary process of institution building. The workshop took place before the Dayton peace accord but the participants already envisioned a brokered solution during the deliberations. They were in disagreement, however, over the conditions leading to stability or instability of a brokered peace treaty. Some participants believed that a peaceful solution would only be possible by splitting Bosnia into three parts, others insisted on the territorial integrity of Bosnia in its former boundaries. There was, however, unanimous support for external intervention and for a continuous role of the international community in supervising and controlling the development towards a more peaceful future.

The last question on the expected role of the international community triggered feelings of disappointment and anger. All participants complained about the lack of commitment by the international community, in particular the European countries. They agreed that the international community had failed in stopping aggression and following up on their verbal promises or threats. If intervention had come earlier, so many participants argued, it would have prevented much of the disaster and improved the chances for healing the wounds. At this point in time, they were skeptical that the international community could do much more than monitoring and controlling the labile peace process and provide economic and institutional assistance to the various regions. All participants felt that exchanging ideas and people, helping communities to draft new legislation, and offering assistance for institution building would be appropriate and welcome contributions from the international community. Many expressed more confidence in non-governmental organizations' ability to become the brokers for such assistance than in governmental agencies or international organizations.

Several of the suggestions presented during the final discussions have found their entrance into the papers of the individual contributors, as these were completed after the workshop. The following sections will first summarize the written papers, highlight the main messages of each paper, and then focus on three major issues: mediation, governance and civil society.

2 Summary of the Papers

This section focuses on the theoretical framework describing patterns of behavior of ethnic groups within states and the relationship between the state and its ethnic minorities. Based on the country reports in this volume, we attempt to sum up briefly and fragmentarily the situation of some states in Eastern Europe, as well as the model of multi-ethnic coexistence in Switzerland.[1] The summary will be supplemented by further literature concerning issues of ethnic behavior.

Ethnic groups or minorities who politically demand more autonomy within the nation-state or pursue separatist endeavors cause autonomy movements which represent a gradual disintegration. In accordance with Pfetsch (1994: 208), seven behavioral patterns of ethnic minorities towards the respective state can be summarized:

(i) isolation as a widespread strategy of protection, especially by small groups;
(ii) adjustment with renunciation of own identity;
(iii) communalism[2] which should be understood as self-assertion on the local level;
(iv) autonomy which can extend from cultural to economic and political rights;
(v) remigration to mother countries;
(vi) separatism as separating from the present state and creating a sovereign state; and

(vii) irredentism as striving for unification with the state in which their own nationality forms the majority.

Just as relevant is the behavior of the political authority, or in other words, the relation between the groups striving for sovereignty and the political power. Again Pfetsch (1994: 209) comes up with five behavioral patterns of political authorities in states which will be adopted concerning the case studies and the theoretical approaches: (i) suppression and oppression; (ii) appeasement, i.e., maneuvering with concessions but without realization; (iii) granting of limited rights for an indefinite or a limited period; (iv) guarantee of complete autonomy; and (v) release from the state.

The former and newly created countries in Eastern Europe and the Commonwealth of Independent States (CIS) were coined for decades by communist state systems in which a centralistic structure of dictatorship forced collective property, collective administration in economy, and a seemingly peaceful ethnic cohesion of different ethnic groups and minorities. This ethnic cohesion under constraint was fundamentally challenged by the decline of the communist system and the subsequent transition to democracy. These states and their people do not have any commonly developed democratic tradition of personal responsibility in a polyethnic society. They lacked the process of individual socialization of democratic values and norms for a civic culture in a well-balanced political system where passiveness, traditionalism, and the relationship to parochial values were compensated by political activity, involvement, commitment, and rationality. The clash of centralistic authorities left behind a situation of uncertainty and insecurity regarding the political system, the economic survivability, the social structure, and above all, the different ethnic groups and their previous cohesion. A situation of anarchy has developed among the ethnic groups in which mutual distrust has prevailed and all the ethnic groups have felt aggrieved and threatened by each other. The consequence was that ethnic groups have claimed their independence and the territorial split from the former nation-state. In order to obtain territorial autonomy or to force their power interests against others, ethnic groups and communities believed that their prospects in a military conflict would be better than in peaceful negotiation processes for common cooperation and coexistence. Especially ethnic actors in former Yugoslavia and in the Caucasian republics have calculated enforcing their interests and relative power in war more positively than in nonviolent conflict settlement. If, thinking back to the hypotheses of peace and conflict studies in the introduction, it can be observed first that the power interests of these ethnic actors are indivisible in this conflict situation at that time; and secondly, that the conflict subject concerns the controversial values of territory, border, security, and spheres of influence. Therefore, a violent conflict or war is more probable than a peaceful conflict management or even cooperation.

In the case of Yugoslavia the disintegration was strongly influenced by groups who have identified the re-emerging ethnic identities of the others as offensive threats. These ethnic groups and their newly created republics were not equally powerful in terms of people and economic resources. They have different access to military equipment, different support from external allies, and incompatible claims to the same territory. Aggravating the situation, fanatic advocates of ethnic identity appeared and fueled the animosity which accelerated the violent conflict management. In this situation of security dilemma, the incentives of the ethnic actors for a preventive war were high (comp. Posen 1993: 35pp.).

In the case of Ukraine and Russia the potential for a military conflict between the two was relatively slight. The respective ethnic cohesion was not viewed as an offensive threat in their mutual perception, they even had a comparatively benign perception of the other's identity. Patterns of conflict settlement have contributed to the peaceful transnational relation and to reducing the probability of a violent conflict management. Posen (1993: 38) noted that "(a) principal stabilizing factor here is the presence of former Soviet nuclear forces in both Russia and Ukraine, which provides each republic with a powerful deterrent".

The case of Switzerland demonstrates that concordance democracy can ensure a peaceful coexistence of different ethnic groups and minorities, where all have legal access to power and relatively autonomous rights in a federal structure by which they are enabled to develop unimpaired the peculiarity of their ethnic and cultural identity. This peacefully polyethnic coexistence grew with the history of the nation and the development towards democracy. Individually, the people have internalized the underlying values of a peaceful and equal polyethnic society. The process of individual socialization and nationalization helps to ensure adjustment of every single person in an ethnic community which is naturally integrated in a Civil Society of different ethnic communities. Three institutional mechanisms guarantee

the political integration of different ethnic groups and cultural minorities (Heckmann 1992: 218):
(i) a strongly institutionalized balancing of interests in the form of hearings ("Vernehmlassungsverfahren");
(ii) federalism as a principle which organizes cooperation without destroying peculiarities; and
(iii) a high legitimacy of the political system.

In this connection federalism is the most important institution for the protection of ethnic minorities. Minority protection is integrated into the constitution of the system so that federalism does not explicitly seem a principle of minority protection (Kimminich 1985: 164). In Switzerland the term 'nation' will not be understood as ethnic community but as a community of common institutions, history, and interests (Heckmann 1992: 218). Different ethnic groups are constitutive and their affiliation is basically determined. A contract more or less exists between different ethnic groups.

3   International Mediation of Ethnic Conflicts

Beside long-term and lasting peace structures of international governance in the international system, which can not only generate "negative" peace but also further stable and just structures of "positive" peace in international relations, the demand exists for immediate and effective mediation and settlement of potentially violent conflicts escalating to armed conflicts or wars within and among nations. According to Bercovitch (1992: 7) mediation in international relations can comprehensively be defined as *"a process of conflict management, related to but distinct from the parties' own efforts, where the disputing parties or their representatives seek the assistance, or accept an offer of help, from an individual, group, state or organization to change, affect or influence their perceptions or behavior, without resorting to physical force or invoking the authority of the law."*

This can mean a peaceful outside intervention of a third party by an arbitrator or a mediator.[3] The mediation can be provided by a representative of a third nation or an international organization who is not directly involved as a disputant and who is recognized as a neutral mediator by all conflict opponents.[4] In this sense international mediation can be understood as a real alternative for successful and peaceful conflict management in international relations as opposed to expensive and armed conflict dealing. "In the present international environment, where the sophistication and destructive capability of weapons could make conflict so costly, where there is no adherence to a generally-accepted set of rules nor a central authority that can regulate patterns of international behavior, and where, in addition, power is diffused among many units that jealously guard their sovereignty, mediation offers an effective way of dealing with differences between antagonistic states" (Bercovitch 1991: 3). If mediation should be practicable and successful, the opponents must not pursue their own self-interests in the sense of a zero sum game so that the damage or loss of the others are their own benefit or advantage. On the contrary they must volunteer to strive for an amicable solution. Thus, the decisive fundament of mediation is marked by the voluntary participation, consensus, if necessary, accepting an autonomous decision-making, and mutual gains (comp., e.g., Bercovitch 1991: 4). Only these elements can enable a satisfactory outcome for all disputants. Without voluntary willingness of the conflict adversaries to reach a consensual solution, international mediation is not feasible because every commitment of states to peacefully settle their disputes clashes with the principle of sovereignty which is determined in chapter one article 2.1 and with the non-interference in domestic affairs of states in article 2.7 of the UN charter (comp. Czempiel 1994: 139pp.). With internal conflicts of states like civil wars, the chances of outsiders, e.g., international organizations, to intervene in favor of settling conflicts peacefully are thus naturally fewer. Civil wars belong to the category of domestic affairs. The fact of a civil war can be ascertained only then when military force has already been used. A peaceful settlement cannot take place from outside, but only by the disputing parties themselves. In agreement with the conflict parties, a peacekeeping force can induce a ceasefire and an outside mediation can help to manage the conflict. So internal peace can be restored, but the conflict per se cannot peacefully be settled. Such a conflict must always become manifestly armed before it will be a problem of the international community (Czempiel 1994: 152).

The range of using mediation to settle international conflicts has stretched from conflicts about sovereignty, over wars of independence of colonies, to disputes over the use of natural resources. "In a majority of the wars fought since 1945 involving at least 100 fatalities, the disputing parties accepted the intervention of a mediator" (Susskind/

Babbitt 1992: 30). Nevertheless, successful mediation efforts are still rather rare in international relations, although a few relevant international conflicts were peacefully settled by outside interference of international mediators.[5]

According to quantitative surveys from Bercovitch and Regan (1997), 981 conflicts worldwide were approached by means of mediation since World War II. Success or failure was measured by three categories: ceasefire, partial settlement, and full settlement. In 38.5 % of the cases the mediation process achieved a success in the kind of a ceasefire agreement, partial or full settlement of mediation. In nearly 20 % of the cases the disputes were at least partially settled. Only 5 % of the conflicts were completely settled by mediation.

The vice general secretary of the UN Cordovez mediated between the Soviet Union and Afghanistan with the result that the Soviet retreat was reached since 1982. The regional Organization of African Unity (OAU) mediated in the case of the Libya-Chad-conflict (Amoo/Zartman 1992).

"The most notable examples are Washington's long-running efforts to promote Arab-Israeli agreements and to find a solution to the Cyprus problem, both of which began only after land has been taken and was being held by force" (Walker 1993: 103). A conspicuous and very promising example is the – so far successful – mediation and settlement of the conflict in the Middle East between Israel on one side, and Egypt, Jordan, and the PLO on the other side. According to the four conflict management forms of conflict theory in the introduction, a phase of unregulated conflict management with several wars until 1975 changing by the international mediation of USA into a phase of regulated conflict management and even conflict termination can be observed. First of all, Israel made peace with Egypt and in the 1990s with the PLO and Jordan. The decades long conflict between these antagonists can be considered to be terminated because patterns of behavior were institutionalized in a peace treaty and norms and rules were commonly agreed upon which regulate the disputed borders and territories. The peace in the Middle East is mainly indebted to the American outside intervention for their successful mediation (comp. Mandell/Tomlin (1991).

At the end of September 1995, the US Assistant Minister of State, David Holbrooke, and the EC arbitrator, Arnt Bildt, brokered an agreement between Bosnia, Croatia and Rest-Yugoslavia on basic principles for the republic Bosnia-Hercegovinia (NZZ 1995). The US-

American President Clinton was instrumentally negotiating the decisive peace treaty of Dayton, Ohio, between Croatians, Serbs and Bosnians. In the difficult case of Bosnia-Hercegovinia, the question arises whether the agreement of Dayton in November 1995 – which was achieved by international mediation under the chairmanship of the US President Clinton between the Croatian President Tudjman, the Serbian President Milosevic, and the Bosnian President Izetbegovic – has the quality of a durable peace treaty or whether it is more than a ceasefire agreement. The success of the international mediation and of the peace treaty cannot be assessed at this moment in time. At least the unregulated conflict management of war has changed into regulated conflict management, but still the conflict is not nearly terminated. At the moment the incompatible positions of the ethnic actors continue but the antagonists have commonly agreed upon rules and norms for their cooperation in a Bosnia-Croatian federation and a Serbian republic.

Third party interference of mediation in internal affairs of states concerns the issue of nation-state sovereignty. The modern term 'state' assumes sovereignty outwardly, and internally, the hierarchical priority of state power over the intra-social forces and, at the same time, non-hierarchical forms of horizontal self-coordination (comp. Scharpf 1991: 612). "For the most of the post-war era, few questioned the prevailing consensus that international borders were sacrosanct and that the way governments behaved at home was essentially their own concern" (Walker 1993: 102). International mediations dealing with ethnic tensions implying secessionist demands within a state concern the least cooperation-conducive values of territorial sovereignty and borders.[6] Here, the probability of a violent conflict management is very high, the antagonists tend to enforce their interests by force of arms. In such cases a successful mediation towards a peaceful conflict management and settlement with mutual satisfaction will be very difficult. The conflict settlement often lasts only temporarily because the violent conflict potential can escalate and break out over and over again; as we have seen in the case of Bosnia-Hercegovinia after the peace agreement of Dayton and other ceasefire agreements before.

In accordance with Walker (1993: 106pp.), institutional structures in Europe which are intended for monitoring democratic behavior and for mediating conflicts can be realized, if necessary, and desired within and among the participating members.[7]

... Europeans are trying to create a regional system to oversee how governments behave at home regarding minority and other human rights issues. Their efforts include the following: a variety of procedures designed to apply pressure on states to comply with the norms of behaviour subscribed to by all European states, Canada and the United States in the CSCE; using the desire of Central and East European states for membership in the Council of Europe and the EC as a source of influence over their domestic laws and practices; and efforts by both the Council of Europe and the CSCE to broaden acceptance of judicial review or at least some form of third-party involvement in all disputes about compliance with minority and other human rights agreements. (Walker 1993: 106)

Such relations among states, which are marked by norms, rules, and principles of international organizations, international regimes or regional integration, have an impact on the behavior of the states so that the anarchic structure of the international system will be reduced and the peaceful cooperative structures of international governance increases.

4 International Governance Reducing Ethnic Conflicts

International governance means setting up institutionalized and sustainable cooperation structures among nation-states, i.e., institutions for collective problem and conflict management and settlement in which states would voluntarily cooperate according to predetermined norms, rules, principles and decision-making procedures. Thus, international governance represents internationally institutionalized patterns of behavior and action of states which is based on the possibility of free consensus and thus the renunciation of force among the participants (Rittberger 1989: 183pp.). The states voluntarily submit to collective decision-making, they regulate their behavior and act according to collectively defined rules. The normative institutionalization of cooperation implies the willingness of participating actors to put back the option of self-help and abandon the use of force. On account of the self-chosen agreements, the states restrict and regulate the anarchy in the international system. This horizontal self-coordination and self-organization among nations emphasizes the "progressive" interest of knowledge; analyzing how states govern themselves and so tame or even overcome the anarchical structure of the international system.

> However, institutionalized cooperation between states for the collective handling of problems or conflicts turns our attention away from the model of "international anarchy" to one of "international governance", i.e. to how states manage collectively to rule themselves without setting up "international (supranational) government". (Rittberger/Efinger/Mendler 1988: 3)

In this sense, international governance civilizes the relations between the states so that the "realistic" assumption of invincible anarchic structures in the international system can be substituted by the idea of *"regulated anarchy"*.[8] This alternative view of international society refers to horizontal self-regulation of international actors which is just in a situation of status nascendi.

The institutionalization of cooperation without constraint in the form of international governance is functionally equivalent to, in Weber's words, legal systems with the legitimate monopoly of force within states or to a higher, sanctioning authority on the international level (comp., e.g., Zürn 1987: 31; Rittberger 1989: 189). On the international level three institutional forms of international governance can be recognized: regional integration, international organizations, and international regimes.[9] International organizations as well as international regimes are institutions in the sense of including stable patterns of behavior on account of role ascription and rules.[10] International regimes are marked by a set of principles, norms, rules, and decision-making procedures which sustainably regulate the behavior of international actors in an issue area and which get the mutual expectations of actors to tally (Krasner 1983: 2). Whereas formal organizations are able to be corporate actors, the norm orientated and stabilized behavioral patterns of international regimes do not possess any actor's quality. In reality both international organizations and international regimes are quite often bound up with each other. So states frequently agree to establish international regimes in conferences which are arranged by international organizations. Definitely, international regimes can adopt regime generating functions. On the level of decision-making procedures, international regimes comprise activities which were safeguarded by specialized organizations. In this sense international organizations place important information at all participants' disposal, they control the rule compliance and monitor the behavior, and they suggest modifications to improve the rules aimed at achieving regime goals.[11] Regimes ensure the informal transparency in issue areas and increase the information by costs which are less for participants than for outsiders. They avoid sub-optimal results and reduce the transaction costs (comp. Keohane 1984: 85pp.; Rittberger 1990: 47). Beyond the renunciation of use of military force per definition, international regimes can produce qualitatively broader implications for peace structures reaching beyond the expected allocation of values in the issue area. Insecurity and uncertainty will be decreased and confidence can be built among participating international actors to continuos willingness for cooperation and to converging expectations by the contracting parties regarding the compliance with rules (comp. Wolf 1991: 45). Three consequences and impacts of international regimes can be identified (Breitmeier/Wolf 1993: 341pp.).

Firstly, in the issue area of the regime the problem solving subsumes just and sustainable conflict regulation. "We may measure 'justice' by the amount to which the procedures of conflict regulation and the value distribution within the issue area are regarded as fair by the participating actors" (Breitmeier/Wolf 1993: 342).

Secondly, regimes can change the context by democratizing domestic structures. "In the *domestic* realm, regimes may change actors' interests and preferences, or affect perceptions about other actors" (Breitmeier/Wolf 1993: 343). The mechanisms of regimes may encourage learning of democratic behavior by participating actors.

Thirdly, regimes can change the context by civilizing the international system. The civilization of international relations may occur by spill-over effects that reach beyond the issue area. "(R)egimes may 'civilize' relations among actors in the sense of fostering further co-operation by establishing epistemic communities and by contributing to confidence-building" (Breitmeier/Wolf 1993: 342).

The spreading of human rights and democracy[12] in the world are decisive elements for the protection of ethnic groups and minorities within states. Enforcing human rights policy is pursued on two levels in the contemporary international system.[13] On the one hand, a number of international organizations, especially the United Nations globally and the Conference on Security and Cooperation in Europe (CSCE), are the upholders of human rights policy. On the other side, states attempt to enforce over and over again goals of human rights in their national foreign affairs (comp. Delbrück 1984: 314). Universal human rights protection has been developed within the foundation of United Nations in 1945. The charter of the UN contains in article 1.3 and 55c the competence of the organization inducing international cooperation in order to encourage and to secure respect for human rights and civil rights for all indiscriminate of race, sex, language or religion. All participating states commit themselves to cooperating to this end (art. 56). With these regulations the dealing with human rights was removed from the domestic affairs of states. Since then, UN authority for questions and issues of human rights exists as a safeguard. A further definition of international human rights was carried out with the "International Bill of Rights". The "International Bill of Rights" subsumes the general declaration of human rights in 1948 and the pacts passed in 1966 and coming into force in 1976 about economic, social, cultural, civil, and political rights which were ratified by 103 states. In addition, the authority of the UN was extended by agreements which either contribute to combat massive violations of human rights or contribute to the protection against discrimination of groups.[14] For example, the agreement of genocide in 1948, the agreement of racial discrimination in 1966, and the agreement of apartheid in 1973 should specially be mentioned with regard to ethnic groups and minorities.

Global processes of democratization and legal acceptance of norms of human rights in Europe began in the middle of the 1970s. In Latin America such processes did not begin to develop until the mid 1980s and were not widespread at that time. In Africa, noticeable movements did not begin until the mid 1980s; but only since the 1990s the wave of democratization has truly begun. Since the beginning of the 1990s the situation has distinctly improved in Eastern Europe and in the Soviet Union. In 1990, elections were hold in thirteen of the fifteen republics of the Soviet Union, just as in Poland, Hungary, Czechoslovakia, etc. The elections were not as free as in the West but in the Soviet Union, e.g., a multi-party system of parties had started (comp. Czempiel 1991: 88pp.).

Nevertheless, the world system still consists of a number of states with governments which were not democratic-constitutionally legitimized by a majority. Additionally, it was taken into account that Western-style democracies have been the result of a long period of social process of experiences and maturity and can not simply be transferred to other situations with different historical social forces (comp. Tetzlaff 1993). The struggle for values and fundamental human rights which should be recognized by everyone is a promising indication that, on the international level, the nations seem to need a common idea. This common idea is a concept of human rights in which all participating cultures and states can find their own experiences and norms. Despite difficulties of realizing this idea there are beginnings for the argument of a tolerant, pluralistic, and multi-religious world society in which heterogeneous cultural communities can peacefully coexist side by side (Tetzlaff 1994: 297pp.).

One of the least predictable regime consequences of the CSCE were the inspirations for human rights and civil rights in Eastern Europe in the 1980s. The Western demand at the beginning of the CSCE-negotiations for a human rights regime in the whole of Europe was only admitted into the CSCE-final act by "issue-linkages"[15] with other policy areas. Ropers and Schlotter (1989: 331) observed that an evolution of the declaring human rights could be seen to emerge towards the beginnings of an action determining regime. As a result of the official spreading of the final act in Eastern Europe and the Soviet Union, as well as the high value of prestige, the CSCE-rules had an effect as a strong confirmation of human rights. So the continuing CSCE-conferences have ensured until then an unknown, norm-specified monitoring of human rights. Since 1985 all CSCE-members have agreed that debate on human rights issues do not constitute an interference in domestic affairs.[16]

Just within the framework of the CSCE – or now the Organization for Security and Cooperation in Europe (OSCE) – the protection of minorities has been able to evolve into an effective international regime.[17] In the world of the OSCE-states, ethnic minorities often live in border areas as well as in regions which were sometimes the subject of territorial displacements in European history. These border areas fell under other state authority in which the distribution of power should be changed by calculated politics of resettlement, e.g., in the Baltic Nations (comp. Meyer 1994: 109). With the mitigation of the East-West conflict the CSCE focused its attention more on the issues of minorities. In the course of the Vienna conferences of 1986-1989 about the "human dimension of the CSCE" much detail was devoted to minority questions. At the beginning of the 1990s a number of norms for minority protection were developed and were consensually anchored (comp. Auswärtiges Amt 1993: chap. IV). The Copenhagen final document of 1990 has emphasized that human rights are not only effective for members of national minorities, but also that they can practice and enjoy their rights individually or in the community with other members of their group. Members of national minorities might not be put at a disadvantage from practicing or not practicing of one of these rights. Additionally, the right was granted to participate effectively in public affairs and at the same time help in the protection and in the promotion of the identity of such minorities.[18] The Copenhagen final document explicitly contains the link between the respect for human rights and civil rights, creating pluralistic democracies in all European states, and the building up of an entirely European peace order (Schlotter et al. 1994: 20pp.). The procedures for minority protection consist of several executive bodies and mechanisms side by side. The most important authority is the High Commissioner for national minorities, which represents an instrument for conflict prevention as soon as possible. He ensures early warning and early measures with the prospect of tensions concerning issues of national minorities which involve the potential of a conflict having a negative effect on peace, stability, and relations among participating states. A further procedure is the mechanism of the human dimension dealing with the delegating and mission of impartial experts and correspondents who are supposed to facilitate the solution of a problem of the human dimension, to consult, and to mediate in conflict situations (comp. Bartsch 1995: 206pp.; Meyer 1992: 19pp.). Other procedures are missions with the object of politically preventing conflicts and managing crisis. There is also the procedure of peaceful dispute settlement and conferences controlling whether participating states keep the minority protection norms and implement them adequately.

With the end of the East-West conflict, and in the course of reorganization and transformation in Eastern Europe, the CSCE lost its traditional function and a number of new exercises have emerged; primarily supporting the transition from former communist states toward democracy and rule of law, and preventing and managing political crisis. In order to be able to manage the new issues better the regime has transformed into the regional Organization for Security and Cooperation in Europe with complex institutional structure consisting of some political decision committees, specialized executive bodies, and procedural mechanisms. The question of minority protection has become one of the most important issue areas. In 1992, an "office for democratic institutions and human rights" was established to cope with issues related to holding elections, implementation of commitments in the field of the human dimensions, and facilitating cooperation, organization and supplying information for building democratic institutions (comp. Bartsch 1995: 189pp.).

International regimes can guarantee the institutional framework for international governance in which states voluntarily institutionalize norms and rules for their mutual behavior regulating and settling conflicts. So the international actors do not only achieve a peaceful and regulated conflict management, but also conflict termination and possibly even conflict resolution where the irreconcilability of different goals concerning the allocation of values may be abolished. In this sense, regime formation in the framework of the CSCE has been able to accomplish a relevant contribution for overcoming the East-West conflict, for setting up democracies in Eastern Europe. Although not definite, it is possible that the particular regimes of human rights and minority protection have been able to lay the foundations for nonviolent management of ethnic conflicts in some cases after the collapse of the Soviet Empire like, e.g., in the Baltics and in Ukraine.

An important question of the regime formation in the CSCE process is the transferability of the successful institutionalization as a model for regional peace strategies in other areas of the world.[19] Although, the CSCE have failed somewhat in their capacity to act towards the crises and wars due to the fragmentation of Yugoslavia and the Soviet Union, there are some proposals for initiatives and conferences according to the CSCE model. These initiatives have not yet progressed as far as the CSCE process. With it, the CSCE process should not simply be copied, but the function as a model should rather lie in the "discursive design" – which can be transferred – in order to develop specifically regional peace strategies (Schlotter et al. 1994: 106). Just the "discursive design" makes possible the gradual extension of the package of commitments, and so achieving at least a conflict attenuating impact in times of crises. Answering the question: how structures and procedures of the CSCE can be transferred to other areas in the world?, Schlotter et al. (1994: 100) have identified the following aspects which were relevant for the CSCE success in analyzing the respective area: (i) the willingness to renounce the use of military force by conflict management; (ii) the existence of relevant actors able to carry out a function of initiatives or able to forge links; (iii) the possibility of either limiting a region with regard to security politics or assembling all involved conflict actors; and (iv) a distribution of interests by the actors which admits a complementary compensation among them.

5 Ethnic Coexistence Within a Civil Society

From the highest level of the international system the view comes back to the national level of states, the subnational level of federal states, and the lowest political level of communities where ethnic cooperation is politically and socially relevant to peaceful coexistence in a Civil Society. The assertion of communal identities by ethnic minorities or groups essentially concerns internal autonomy or demands for secession and establishment of new states.[20] This section will deal with the prerequisites for the internal autonomy of ethnic groups within polyethnic societies and the particular perspective on ethnic cooperation and coexistence on the communal level. In this perspective the idea of communitarianism[21] becomes the focus, i.e., the relationship between individual and community or society in the sense of Civil Society.

Before discussing the idea of communitarianism as a social basis of peaceful polyethnic coexistence on the communal level the (con)federal structures within states should be considered. Concordance or consociational democracy like the model of Switzerland can only be partially transferred for a transitional phase of newly created states towards (con)federal democracies, like the models of the USA and Canada, which can guarantee internal autonomy and power sharing for ethnic groups and minorities.

In a wide sense, the federal principle means that societally and politically autonomous entities have a unification in mind which has been shaped for specific common purposes and in which the member states still maintain a wide degree of their original autonomy. The modern perspective of federal government was strongly coined by the United States of America. The fundament of the American federation is the constitution comprising the initial document of 1787 and numerous amendments. This constitution represents rules and regulations which settles a unification of states. The constitution establishes a union of states which are organized in a manner so that power and authority are distributed between a central government, which is independent from the governments of the states in certain affairs, and the governments of the states which are independent from the central government in certain affairs. Thus, the central government, as well as the states, immediately have an effect on the people. The competencies and responsibilities between the central government and the states are not always obvious in certain affairs. The constitution occasionally is ambiguous, contradictory, and imprecise. Even if the constitution is sometimes uncertain, it is clear that a government is not subordinated to any other government in the United States when acting within the framework of its authority. According to the underlying rights, the power and control are distributed between a central power and regional powers which are not subordinated to each other, but equal. The states exercise the highest authority within their areas and they are not subordinated corporations in the legal sense. The structure of organization, on which the American union is based, is the separation of powers between different equal governments.[22]

Beside the complexity of the American bicameral system there exists the internal autonomy of the states so that federalism comprises three levels of governing: the national level, the level of the state, and the local level of the community. These three levels and their linkages are largely reflected in the American political party system. Many members of the House of Representatives and the Senate worked in administrative bodies on the level of the states or on the communal level. An important factor is the decentralization and the federalization of the political parties in America. Within the political party system the candidates for a seat in Congress and the already elected members in Congress are mostly left to their own devices. The members of Congress coming from the same state achieve a high degree of political correspondence because, in an abstract sense, they were socialized in the same state. Many delegations of states from different political parties meet in the House of Representatives and some of them explicitly strive for political correspondence. If looking at elections, American politics take place on the communal and individualistic level. Interests and groups of interests have access to politics and politicians on all territorial levels. The groups of interests of the states and of the communities have a tendency to concentrate upon politics and politicians on the level of state and on the communal level.[23]

The relationship between territoriality and national identity is due to relevant importance for the structure of the federal system, including the ethnic, cultural, linguistic, and religious structures which can reach from the homogeneity of nation-states (e.g., Austria and Germany) to differentiating multinational societies. In the United States, the ethnic, cultural, racial, linguistic, and denominational differences are not territorially determined and national identities are not defined by cultural distinctions. The minorities are subject to the pressure of adaptation, which is high. The competencies of the states in the field of culture and education only compensate it in parts (Schultze 1983: 97pp.). There exists a wrong ideology of the melting-pot and constraints of subordination under the American Way of Life for ethnic, denominational, and linguistic minorities. The USA is a society which is not only composed by migrants having different ethnic and cultural descent, but also a common, i.e. American identity. So America is not a multicultural society, but a society with a pluralism of cultur (Tibi 1996: 28).

In the framework of political culture, the objective dimensions of the political system can be associated with the subjective dimension of society. Generally, political culture describes the subjective dimension of the societal fundaments in political systems. This contains the whole of all politically relevant and individual characteristics of personality, latent predispositions in attitudes and values for political acting, also in their symbolic marking, and concrete political behavior (Berg-Schlosser 1989: 746pp.). In their more precise application of political culture, Almond and Verba (1972: 473) concluded that the United States has a democratic political culture which fosters democratic stability by a pattern of political attitudes, which they call "civic culture". "(A) successful democracy requires that citizens be involved and active in politics, informed about politics, and influential" (Almond/Verba 1972: 474). In the American Society they had observed a relatively high percentage of active citizens in the affairs of the community. But the political culture also comprises passive citizens who are non-voters, poorly informed, and politically apathetic. Therefore, a civic culture contains apparently contradictory political attitudes so that democratic political systems are mixtures of contradictions which requires a blending of apparent contradictions called "balanced disparities".

> On the one hand, a democratic government must govern; it must have power and leadership and make decisions. On the other hand, it must be responsible to its citizens. (...) The maintenance of a proper balance between governmental power and governmental responsiveness represents one of the most important and difficult tasks of a democracy. (Almond/Verba 1972: 476)

The civic culture is transmitted by a complex process of political socialization which takes place in a number of social institutions like the family, peer groups, school, workplace, and the political system on the different levels, particularly, on the communal level (Almond/Verba 1972: 498). Their empirical research had shown that the Americans – more than other societies – are group orientated, which was already recognized by Alexis de Toqueville more than one hundred years before (comp. Ornstein 1988: 291).

Dealing with political culture and the view on the communal level leads inevitably to the contemporary debate on communitarianism.[24] The idea of communitarianism assumes an individual who is a part of the community and constitutes himself just by the connection with this community. At the same time, the social nature of people only makes possible the rational and moral structure of community. Thus, a priority of the individual over the community cannot be maintained because the individual is not thought of as independent from society.[25] This constitutes a view of human beings in society as responsible individuals being active in communities within an active society; i.e., citizens actively and periodically participate in political formation of opinion and will, for example, in political parties and associations. And so active citizens can perceive functions of control to constitutional institutions of legislative and executive power. In his classical work "The Active Society" (1968), the communitarian Amitai Etzioni defined three main elements for the active orientation of actors:

> a self-conscious and knowing actor, one or more goals he is committed to realize, and access to levers (or power) that allow resetting of the social code. (We repeat that the active self as a rule is not an individual, since one man is generally unable to transform collectivities, but a combination of persons who jointly activate their social grouping and thus alter their collective life and their individual selves.) (Etzioni 1968: 4pp.)

New social options arise because mankind is more and more able to transform social bonds rather than accommodating to, or only protesting. The postmodern society is characterized by a continuous increase of power about instruments available, an exponential growth of knowledge, and the ability of mankind to control instruments and knowledge. If a society will be more responsive to its members, then, at the same time, it gets closer to its societally idealistic values. Between societal ideals and societal reality of established interests, status constellations, and power politics exists an unbridgeable gap because there never exists a society which would not stay behind its values. Nevertheless, just the activation of a society and the rise of sensitivity to requirements of its members makes possible a more complete realization of societal values (Etzioni 1968: 5pp.). In this context, community will be defined as a societal unity which has available autocratic integrative mechanisms, i.e., the maintenance of its boundaries, its internal structure, and its political organization are guaranteed by its own processes and not by external units, supra-units, or sub-units. So, the defined communities are political communities and not cultural, religious, etc. There are three kinds of integrative processes. "It has sufficient coercive power to countervail the coercive power of any member unit or coalition of them; it has a decision-making center that is able to affect significantly the allocation of assets throughout the community; and it is the dominant focus of political loyalty for the large majority of politically active citizens" (Etzioni 1968: 554). The availability of the means of violence makes a distinction between a political community and other communities. "This control protects the community from the arbitrary interference of member-units, makes the community the ultimate arbitrator among the members, serves to counter secessionist pressures, and makes the political community the focus of the defense against external units" (Etzioni 1968: 554).

Beyond the active orientation of individuals the communitarians demand a new morality in society because clearly outlined and collectively accepted values able to provide societal orientations for individual and common behavior and actions have been largely lost. Regarding the United States, Etzioni (1993: 25) suggested therefore that "(w)e do require a set of social virtues, some basic settled values, that we as a community endorse and actively affirm". This moral orientation is to be an affair of community. Certainly, the highest instance of morality is the individual conscience, but man receives the first moral standards from the community in which he is born. The process of socialization conveys the social values which were developed by the community. A new moral orientation consequently means the shoring up of morality in the community so that it leads to a civil society in which everybody is each other's keeper (Etzioni 1993: 30pp.). The relevant social institutions which can strengthen moral values as instances of socialization are the communitarian family and the communitarian school (Etzioni 1993: chap. 2 and 3). In addition, the communitarian idea proposes the rebuilding of community institutions on the local level, i.e., citizens should support communal institutions by actively participating and, in a wider sense, political participation. On the national level, the cultural common interest should not be seen as a melting-pot with a homogeneous identity where immigrants or foreign citizens give up their cultural legacy and their ethnic origin or identity, but as an ethnic and cultural pluralism in the unity. In view of the American society, Etzioni suggested a concept of multiculturalism which comprises an overarching community and various legitimated subcultures. The plurality of ethnic or cultural identities and groups cannot replace the implications of an overarching community.

> Without a firm sense of one supra-community, there is considerable danger that the constituent communities will turn on one another. Indeed, *the more one favors strengthening communities, ..., the more one must concern oneself with ensuring that they see themselves as parts of a more encompassing whole*, rather than as fully independent and antagonistic. (Etzioni 1993: 155)

The idea of pluralism does not mean a boundless and societally unwholesome diversity in society by which all groups attempt to get what they can get and not take much care of issues of the community. The "pluralism-within-unity" necessitates that groups voluntarily restrict their competition, if common interests are threatened or violated (Etzioni 1993: 217).

The association of particular moral qualities in a society with the particular political system of a liberal democracy is expressed in the term of civil society that is already mentioned above. Civil manners of behavior as a characteristic mark of civil society makes the difference between a well-ordered democracy and a more anarchically structured political system.

> This idea of civil society has three main components. The first is part of society comprising a complex of autonomous institutions – economic, religious, intellectual and political – distinguishable from the family, the clan, the locality and the state. The second is part of society possessing a particular complex of relationships between itself and the state and a distinctive set of institutions which safeguard the separation of state and civil society and maintain effective ties between them. The third is a widespread pattern of refined or civil manners. (Shils 1991: 4)

Shils realized the core of a civil society lies in the mutual recognition and respect of the moral dignity of antagonists in social life (comp. also Kotzé/Du Toit 1995: 28). "Civility ... considers others as fellow-citizens of equal dignity in their rights and obligations as members of civil society; it means regarding other persons, including one's adversaries, as members of the same society, even though they belong to different parties or to different religious communities or to different ethnic groups" (Shils 1991: 12pp.). In such a civil society the civil manners of individual and collective behavior and actions penetrate all political institutions and levels as well as all societal fields and daily life. So, to a peaceful working of the institutions of civil society will be contributed and in conflict situations opponents become less irreconcilable so that conflict terminations and conflict resolutions are more probable. That could mean that civil manners can have an effect on types of conflict so that dissensual conflicts with little prospect of cooperation-conduciveness decrease and consensual conflicts with high cooperation-conduciveness increase. Regarding the relationship between the political system of the state and the societal structure of a civil society, Shils (1991: 4) noted:

> The state lays down laws which set the outermost boundaries of the autonomy of the diverse spheres and sectors of civil society; so, civil society from its side lays down limits on the actions of the state. Civil society and the state are bound together by the constitution and by traditions which stress the obligations of each to the other as well as their rights vis-à-vis each other. The rights of individuals and collectivities with respect to each other are provided by the constitutions and the laws and traditions.

The concept of civil society postulates a pluralism of partially autonomous spheres and autonomous institutions of economy, religion, culture, ethnicity, intellectual activity, and political activity. In civil society, like the USA, ethnic groups or minorities live in autonomous spheres and have legal access to powers which are ensured by laws and by constitution. Civil society takes a particular kind of state with limited powers for granted. These powers enact laws which protect the different autonomous spheres. "The laws of such a society are, among other things, intended to hold conflict in check by compelling adherence to agreements, and by inflicting sanctions on actions which criminally damage other persons" (Shils 1991: 15). Both the state and the citizens are bound by law and constitution. Citizens of ethnic groups and ethnic groups as a whole are protected from arbitrary and unjust decisions of high political authorities, the police, the military, and the prevailing majority. The cases of Yugoslavia and the Caucasian republics have shown that the lack of civil manners and so a civil society do not only lead to disorder and secessionist efforts, but also to anarchy and internal wars.

> Without such a civility, a pluralistic society can degenerate into a war of each against all. Civility works like a governor of civil society. It limits the intensity of conflict. It reduces the distance between conflicting demands: it is a curb on centrifugal tendencies. (Shils 1991: 15)

One may conclude from the exposition above that the transferability of the idea of civil society to newly created states is by no means comparable with the transferability of political structures like the model of a federation, although both urgently link up if a well-ordered democracy with ethnic coexistence is considered. The transference of a political system of a federation might be a relatively simple task, if the political and societal groups accept it and voluntarily agree on a common constitution by contract. That can be partially seen in the case of Bosnia-Hercegovinia where a federal structure was agreed upon as a political system. However, a newly created state cannot simply impose the model of civil society on itself because, certainly, the fundament of civil society will be laid in the framework of laws and the constitution, but civility and civil manners have to be individually internalized as basically societal values and to be learnt as collective interests in a process of socialization by social institutions. This process cannot be accomplished in a relatively short period, for a long time is required for learning civility and civil manners and for the mutual confidence necessary to foster coexistence in a polyethnic society. Looking at the collapse of the communist systems and the demise of a utopian socialist role model, there is hardly any alternative left for countries struggling with building identity and civility at the same time. The path is difficult but worth pursuing.

Notes

[1] The summary of the American model is neglected in this chapter because the American Civil Society receives more attention in the final chapter.

[2] In this sense communalism means a behavior which is orientated by ethnic, religious, and/or cultural phenomena. In this context the term relates to conflicts between ethnically, religiously, and culturally determined groups in society. See Nohlen (1989: 434).

[3] Comp. Bercovitch (1991: 3) who differed between two categories of third party forms of conflict management. "They have little in common, apart from the fact that both involve an outsider entering a conflict and helping the parties with their management efforts. We have legalistic-normative procedures (e.g. adjudication and arbitration) that rely on the parties to abide by explicit ruling or judgment handed down by a third party. And we have voluntary procedures (e.g. mediation, conciliation, etc.) that involve various forms of assistance and facilitation, short of judicial or coercive steps, designed to help the parties reach an acceptable outcome."

[4] Kriesberg (1991: 19) made a distinction between mediating services. "The services may be provided by a person, group, or organization playing the role of a mediator, or by a quasi-mediator, a social entity not so designated, who may even be a member of one of the adversaries."

[5] The relevant literature seems to disagree on the question of whether there are still few successful international mediations or if there are already numerous successful mediations. On one side, Walker (1993: 102) has suggested that "(s)uccessful mediation efforts are scarcer still", on the other side, Czempiel (1994: 147) has suggested that many successful mediations can be enumerated. The decisive point might be that the success of a mediation may be assessed differently, and that by a number of mediations the success may be seen relatively.

[6] Comp. the hypotheses of the conflict issue typology in the introduction.

[7] Comp. also Schlotter, Ropers and Meyer (1994: 85pp.) for a detailed description of transnational mediation mechanisms in the framework of the CSCE.

[8] See Rittberger and Zürn (1990: 53pp.). "The term 'regulated anarchy' is borrowed from the ethnosociological literature on pre-state or segmented societies. It refers to the existence of acephalous societies, that is, societies without a central public agency which is capable of enforcing its normative control with publicly approved (physical) sanctions. A segmented society is composed of groups which enjoy equal or similar status and which are similarly differentiated in their internal structures. Segmented societies are held together through spontaneous coordination, a mechanism which is functionally equivalent to the one installed by a central authority for organizing collective action. (...) Regulated anarchy, as a system of rule in segmented societies, presents itself as a powerful analogy for the study of international relations, in general (...)."

[9] The representatives of the functionalistic school expect a peaceful conflict regulation between states primarily as a result of the impact of regional integration. In contrast to functionalism, in regime theory 'integration' is not a central objective

and multilateral behavior of international actors does not indicate denationalization (Wolf 1991: 17).

[10] See also footnote 10 in the introduction for the more precise distinction between international organization and international regime.

[11] See Zürn (1994: 26pp.) for the definition of international organizations and international regimes as institutions and their linking up with each other.

[12] Comp. Schwartländer (1981) for detailed and expert treatises on the connection between human rights and democracy.

[13] Comp. Delbrück (1993) for the problem of universalizing and enforcing human rights protection.

[14] Comp. Dicke (1993: 270pp.) for the development of human rights in the UN.

[15] In a wider sense, "issue-linkage" can be understood, according to Axelrod and Keohane (1985: 239), as "... attempts to gain additional bargaining leverage by making one's own behavior on a given issue contingent on other's action toward other issues. Issue-linkage may be employed by powerful states seeking to use resources from one issue area to affect the behavior of others elsewhere; or it may be employed by outsiders, attempting to break into what could otherwise be a closed game. Linkage can be beneficial to both sides in a negotiation, and can facilitate agreements that might not otherwise be possible."

[16] See Ropers and Schlotter (1989: 331pp.) for the development and the respect for human rights in the CSCE-context.

[17] As has been mentioned above, an international regime consists of norms, rules, principles, and decision-making procedures which have to become effective, and so define a regime as such. In this sense, Bartsch (1995: 137) has identified the following elements for an effective regime of minority protection: The agreement of minority protection norms, the creating of minority protection procedures, the implementation of minority protection norms, and the implementation of minority protection procedures. Schlotter et al. (1994: 77pp.) have also noticed that the process of the CSCE concerning minority protection since 1990 is equivalent to regime formation which is developed further at present as endeavors of the UN or on the level of the Council of Europe.

[18] See the document of the meeting concerning the human dimension of the CSCE in Copenhagen from June the 29th, 1990 in Auswärtiges Amt (1991: pp. 35-57). Comp. also Meyer (1994: 112) and Bartsch (1995: 197pp.).

[19] See Schlotter et al. (1994: 95pp.). Comp. also Schlotter (1994) who discussed the CSCE in the tension between universalism and regionalism, and its integration into the system of the UN.

[20] Comp. Gurr and Harff (1994: 118pp.) who dealt with communal identities and the formation of new states.

[21] Since the 1980s in American political philosophy a controversy exists between the so-called libertarians and the so-called communitarians. The core of the debate concerns the normative fundamentals of societal and political institutions, political ethics, and the relationship between individual and state.

[22] Comp. Wheare (1959: 3pp.) for the federal structure of the United States. Comp. also Frenkel (1984: 92pp.).

[23] See Ripley (1988: 166pp.) for the linking between the national level, the level of the states, and the communal level.

[24] At this point the debate on communitarianism will not be gone into, but merely the elements will be taken up which are relevant for ethnic cooperation and coexistence in a society.

[25] See Druwe (1993: 179pp.). Comp. also the introductions of Avineri and De-Shalit (1992) or Honneth (1993) for the term and his definition. And see the whole editorial book for the debate about it.

Bibliography

ALMOND, Gabriel A. / VERBA, Sidney 1972: The Civic Culture. Political Attitudes and Democracy in Five Nations, Princeton

AMOO, Samuel G. / ZARTMAN, I. William 1992: Mediation by Regional Organizations: The Organization for African Unity (OAU) in Chad, in: Bercovitch, Jacob / Rubin, Jeffrey Z. (eds.) 1992: Mediation in International Relations. Multiple Approaches to Conflict Management, New York, pp. 131-148

AUSWÄRTIGES AMT (ed.) 1991: Sicherheit und Zusammenarbeit in Europa. Dokumentation zum KSZE-Prozeß 1990/91, Bonn

AUSWÄRTIGES AMT (ed.) 1993: 20 Jahre KSZE 1973-1993. Eine Dokumentation, Bonn

AVINERI, Shlomo / DE-SHALIT, Avner 1992: Introduction, in: Avineri, Shlomo / De-Shalit, Avner (eds.) 1992: Communitarianism and Individualism, Oxford, pp. 1-11

AXELROD, Robert / KEOHANE, Robert O. 1985: Achieving Cooperation under Anarchy: Strategies and Institutions, in: World Politics, Vol. 38, No. 1, pp. 226-254

BARTSCH, Sebastian 1995: Minderheitenschutz in der internationalen Politik. Völkerbund und KSZE/OSZE in neuer Perspektive, Opladen

BERCOVITCH, Jacob 1991: International Mediation, in: Journal of Peace Research, Vol. 28, No. 1, pp. 3-6

BERCOVITCH, Jacob 1992: The Structure and Diversity of Mediation in International Relations, in: Bercovitch, Jacob / Rubin, Jeffrey Z. (eds.) 1992: Mediation in International Relations. Multiple Approaches to Conflict Management, New York, pp. 1-29

BERCOVITCH, Jacob / REGAN, Patrick M. 1997: Managing Risks in International Relations: The Mediation of Enduring Rivalries, in: Schneider, Gerald / Weitsman, Patricia A. (eds.) 1997: Enforcing Cooperation. Risky States and the Intergovernmental Management of Conflict, London/New York, pp. 185-201

BERCOVITCH, Jacob / RUBIN, Jeffrey Z. (eds.) 1992: Mediation in International Relations. Multiple Approaches to Conflict Management, New York

BERG-SCHLOSSER, Dirk 1992: Politische Kultur, in: Nohlen, Dieter / Schultze, Rainer-Olaf (eds.) 1989: Politikwissenschaft. Theorien, Methoden, Begriffe. Pipers Wörterbuch zur Politik (edited by Dieter Nohlen), Vol. 1, München, pp. 746-751

BREITMEIER, Helmut / WOLF, Klaus Dieter 1993: Analysing Regime Consequences. Conceptual Outlines and Environmental Explorations, in: Rittberger, Volker (ed.) 1993: Regime Theory and International Relations, Oxford, pp. 339-360

CZEMPIEL, Ernst-Otto 1991: Weltpolitik im Umbruch. Das internationale System nach dem Ende des Ost-West-Konflikts, München

CZEMPIEL, Ernst-Otto 1994: Die Reform der UNO. Möglichkeiten und Mißverständnisse, München

DELBRÜCK, Jost 1984: Menschenrechtspolitik, in: Boeckh, Andreas (ed.) 1984: Internationale Beziehungen. Theorien, Organisationen, Konflikte. Pipers Wörterbuch zur Politik (edited by Dieter Nohlen), Vol. 5, München, pp. 313-315

DELBRÜCK, Jost 1993: Die Universalisierung des Menschenrechtsschutzes: Aspekte der Begründung und Durchsetzbarkeit, in: Zunker, Albrecht (ed.) 1993: Weltordnung oder Chaos? Beiträge zur internationalen Politik, Baden-Baden, pp. 551-566

DICKE, Klaus 1993: Menschenrechte, in: Woyke, Wichard (ed.) 1993: Handwörterbuch Internationale Politik, Opladen, pp. 269-276

DRUWE, Ulrich 1993: Politische Theorie, München

ETZIONI, Amitai 1968: The Active Society. A Theory of of Societal and Political Processes, London/New York

ETZIONI, Amitai 1993: The Spirit of Community. Rights, Responsibilities, and the Communitarian Agenda, New York

FRENKEL, Max 1984: Föderalismus und Bundesstaat. Band I: Föderalismus. System, Recht und Probleme des Bundesstaates im Spannungsfeld von Demokratie und Föderalismus, Bern

GURR, Ted Robert / HARFF, Barbara 1994: Ethnic Conflict in World Politics, Boulder/San Francisco/Oxford

HECKMANN, Friedrich 1992: Ethnische Minderheiten, Volk und Nation. Soziologie interethnischer Beziehungen, Stuttgart

HONNETH, Axel 1993: Einleitung, in: Honneth, Axel (ed.) 1993: Kommunitarismus. Eine Debatte über die moralischen Grundlagen moderner Gesellschaften, Frankfurt a.M., pp. 7-17

KEOHANE, Robert O. 1984: After Hegemony. Cooperation and Discord in the World Political Economy, Princeton

KIMMINICH, Otto 1985: Rechtsprobleme der polyethnischen Staatsorganisation, Mainz/München

KOTZÉ, Hennie / DU TOIT, Pierre 1995: The State, Civil society, and Democratic Transition in South Africa. A Survey of Elite Attitudes, in: The Journal of Conflict Resolution, Vol. 39, No. 1, pp. 27-48

KRASNER, Stephen D. 1983: Structural causes and regime consequences: regimes as intervening variables, in: Krasner, Stephen D. (ed.) 1983: International Regimes, Ithaca/London

KRIESBERG, Louis 1991: Formal and Quasi-Mediators in International Disputes: An Exploratory Analysis, in: Journal of Peace Research, Vol. 28, No. 1, pp. 19-27

MANDELL, Brian S. / TOMLIN, Brian W. 1991: Mediation in the Development of Norms to Manage Conflict: Kissinger in the Middle East, in: Journal of Peace Research, Vol. 28, No. 1, pp. 43-55

MEYER, Berthold 1992: Erst die Spitze eines Eisbergs. KSZE-Konfliktmanagement und nationale Minderheiten, HSFK-Report 8/1992, Frankfurt a.M.

MEYER, Berthold 1994: Überfordern Minderheitenkonflikte die "neue" KSZE?, in: Meyer, Berthold / Moltmann, Bernhard (eds.) 1994: Konfliktsteuerung durch Vereinte Nationen und KSZE, Frankfurt a.M., pp. 108-124

MEYER, Berthold / MOLTMANN, Bernhard (eds.) 1994: Konfliktsteuerung durch Vereinte Nationen und KSZE, Frankfurt a.M.

NOHLEN, Dieter 1989: Kommunalismus, in: Nohlen, Dieter (ed.) 1989: Pipers Wörterbuch zur Politik (Politikwissenschaft. Theorien – Methoden – Begriffe; edited by Dieter Nohlen and Rainer-Olaf Schultze), Vol. 1, München, p. 434

NZZ from 28th September 1995

ORNSTEIN, Norman J. 1988: Interessenvertretung auf dem Kapitol, in: Thaysen, Uwe / Davidson, Roger H. / Livingston, Robert G. (eds.) 1988: US-Kongreß und Deutscher Bundestag. Bestandsaufnahmen im Vergleich, Opladen, pp. 281-299

PFETSCH, Frank R. 1994: Internationale Politik, Stuttgart

POSEN, Barry R. 1993: The Security Dilemma and Ethnic Conflict, in: Survival, Vol. 35, No. 1, pp. 27-47

RIPLEY, Randall B. 1988: Kongreß und Einzelstaaten: Zentralisierter Interessenausgleich, in: Thaysen, Uwe / Davidson, Roger H. / Livingston, Robert G. (eds.) 1988: US-Kongreß und Deutscher Bundestag. Bestandsaufnahmen im Vergleich, Opladen, pp. 156-174

RITTBERGER, Volker 1989: Frieden durch Assoziation und Integration? Anmerkungen zum Stand der Forschung über internationale Organisationen und Regime, in: Moltmann, Bernhard / Senghaas-Knobloch, Eva (eds.) 1989: Konflikte in der Weltgesellschaft und Friedensstrategien, Baden-Baden, pp. 183-205

RITTBERGER, Volker / EFINGER, Manfred / MENDLER, Martin 1988: Confidence- and Security-Building Measures (CSBM): An Evolving East-West Security Regime?, Tübinger Arbeitspapiere zur Internationalen Politik und Friedensforschung, No. 8, Tübingen

RITTBERGER, Volker / ZÜRN, Michael 1990: Towards regulated anarchy in East-West relations: causes and consequences of East-West regimes, in: Rittberger, Volker (ed.) 1990: International Regimes in East-West Politics, London, pp. 9-63

ROPERS, Norbert / SCHLOTTER, Peter 1989: Regimeanalyse und KSZE-Prozeß, in: Kohler-Koch, Beate (ed.) 1989: Regime in den internationalen Beziehungen, Baden-Baden, pp. 315-342

SCHARPF, Fritz W. 1991: Die Handlungsfähigkeit des Staates am Ende des zwanzigsten Jahrhunderts, in: Politische Vierteljahresschrift, Vol. 32, No. 4, pp. 621-634

SCHLOTTER, Peter 1994: Zwischen Universalismus und Regionalismus: Die KSZE im System der Vereinten Nationen, in: Meyer, Berthold / Moltmann, Bernhard (eds.) 1994: Konfliktsteuerung durch Vereinte Nationen und KSZE, Frankfurt a.M., pp. 96-107

SCHLOTTER, Peter / ROPERS, Norbert / MEYERS, Berthold 1994: Die neue KSZE. Zukunftsperspektiven einer regionalen Friedensstrategie, Opladen

SCHULTZE, Rainer-Olaf 1983: Föderalismus, in: Schmidt, Manfred G. (ed.) 1983: Westliche Industriegesellschaften. Pipers Wörterbuch zur Politik (edited by Dieter Nohlen), Vol. 2, München, pp. 93-106

SCHWARTLÄNDER, Johannes (ed.) 1981: Menschenrechte und Demokratie, Kehl

SHILS, Edward 1991: The Virtue of Civil Society, in: Government and Opposition, No. 26, pp. 3-20

SUSSKIND, Lawrence / BABBITT, Eileen 1992: Overcoming the Obstacles to Effective Mediation of International Disputes, in: Bercovitch, Jacob / Rubin, Jeffrey Z. (eds.) 1992: Mediation in International Relations. Multiple Approaches to Conflict Management, New York, pp. 30-51

TETZLAFF, Rainer 1993: Demokratie und Entwicklung als universell gültige Normen? Chancen und Risiken der Demokratisierung in der außereuropäischen Welt nach dem Ende des Ost-West-Konflikts, in: Böhret, Carl / Wewer, Göttrik (eds.) 1993: Regieren im 21. Jahrhundert. Zwischen Globalisierung und Regionalisierung, Opladen, pp. 79-108

TETZLAFF, Rainer 1994: Demokratie und Menschenrechte als regulative Ideen zum Überleben in der Weltgesellschaft?, in: Hein, Wolfgang (ed.) 1994: Umbruch in der Weltgesellschaft. Auf dem Wege zu einer "Neuen Weltordnung"?, Hamburg, pp. 279-304

THAYSEN, Uwe / DAVIDSON, Roger H. / LIVINGSTON, Robert G. (eds.) 1988: US-Kongreß und Deutscher Bundestag. Bestandsaufnahmen im Vergleich, Opladen

TIBI, Bassam 1996: Multikultureller Werte-Relativismus und Werte-Verlust, in: Aus Politik und Zeitgeschichte, B 52-53/96, pp. 27-36

WALKER, Jenonne 1993: International Mediation of Ethnic Conflicts, in: Survival, Vol. 35, No. 1, pp. 102-117

WHEARE, K.C. 1959: Föderative Regierung, München

WOLF, Klaus Dieter 1991: Internationale Regime zur Verteilung globaler Ressourcen. Eine vergleichende Analyse der Grundlagen ihrer Entstehung am Beispiel der Regelung des Zugangs zur wirtschaftlichen Nutzung des Meeresbodens, des geostationären Orbits, der Antarktis und zu Wissenschaft und Technologie, Baden-Baden

ZÜRN, Michael 1987: Gerechte internationale Regime. Bedingungen und Restriktionen der Entstehung nicht-hegemonialer internationaler Regime untersucht am Beispiel der Weltkommunikationsordnung, Frankfurt a.M.

ZÜRN, Michael 1994: Theorien internationaler Institutionen, in: Meyer, Berthold / Moltmann, Bernhard (eds.) 1994: Konfliktsteuerung durch Vereinte Nationen und KSZE, Frankfurt a.M., pp. 21-41